Alex Soifer from USC Shoah Foundation, Holocaust – Jewish Survivor Interviews. Courtesy of the University of Southern California. Filmed 10 July 1996 in Montevideo, Uruguay.

Krinki in Ruins
(Krynki, Poland)

Translation of
Krinik in khurbn: memuarn

Author: A. Soifer

Originally Published in Montevideo 1948

A Publication of JewishGen, INC
Edmond J. Safra Plaza, 36 Battery Place, New York, NY 10280
646.494.5972 | info@JewishGen.org | www.jewishgen.org

Krinki in Ruins (Krynki, Poland)
Translation of *Krinik in khurbn: memuarn*

Author of the Yiddish Book: A. Soifer
Translated by: Beate Schützmann-Krebs
Extraction of the English translation: Donni Magid
Layout and Name Indexing: Jonathan Wind
Reproduction of Photographs: Sondra Ettlinger
Cover Design: Nina Schwartz

Printed in the United States of America by Lightning Source, Inc.

Library of Congress Control Number (LCCN): 2022935153

ISBN: 978-1-954176-48-5 (hard cover: 230 pages, alk. paper)

About JewishGen.org

JewishGen, an affiliate of the Museum of Jewish Heritage - A Living Memorial to the Holocaust, serves as the global home for Jewish genealogy.

Featuring unparalleled access to 30+ million records, it offers unique search tools, along with opportunities for researchers to connect with others who share similar interests. Award winning resources such as the Family Finder, Discussion Groups, and ViewMate, are relied upon by thousands each day.

In addition, JewishGen's extensive informational, educational and historical offerings, such as the Jewish Communities Database, Yizkor Book translations, InfoFiles, Family Tree of the Jewish People, and KehilaLinks, provide critical insights, first-hand accounts, and context about Jewish communal and familial life throughout the world.

Offered as a free resource, JewishGen.org has facilitated thousands of family connections and success stories, and is currently engaged in an intensive expansion effort that will bring many more records, tools, and resources to its collections.

Please visit https://www.jewishgen.org/ to learn more.

Executive Director: Avraham Groll

About the JewishGen Yizkor Book Project

Yizkor Books (Memorial Books) were traditionally written to memorialize the names of departed family and martyrs during holiday services in the synagogue (a practice that still exists in many synagogues today).

Over the centuries, as a result of countless persecutions and horrific atrocities committed against the Jews, Yizkor Books (Sefer Zikaron in Hebrew) were expanded to include more historical information, such as biographical sketches of famous personalities and descriptions of daily town life.

Following the Holocaust, the idea of remembrance and learning took on an urgent and crucial importance. Survivors of the Holocaust sought out other surviving residents of their former towns to memorialize and document the names and way of life of those who were ruthlessly murdered by the Nazis. These remembrances were documented in Yizkor Books, hundreds of which were published in the first decades after the Holocaust.

Most of these books were published privately, or through landsmanshaftn (social organizations comprised of members originating from the same European town or region) that still existed, and were often distributed free of charge. Sadly, the languages used to document these crucial histories and links to our past, Yiddish and Hebrew, are no longer commonly understood by a significant percentage of Jews today. As a result, JewishGen has undertaken the sacred responsibility of translating these books into English so that the culture and way of life of these communities will be preserved and transmitted to future generations.

In 1986, a group of farsighted JewishGenners started a project to pool their efforts together in groups based upon their ancestors from each town and donate money to get the Yizkor books of their ancestral towns translated into English. As the translated material became available, it was made accessible for free at www.JewishGen.org/Yizkor. Hardcover copies can be purchased by visiting https://www.jewishgen.org/Yizkor/ybip.html (see below).

It is our hope that the translation of these books into English (and other languages) will assist the countless Jewish family researchers who are so desperately seeking to forge a connection with their heritage.

Director of JewishGen Yizkor Book Project: Lance Ackerfeld

About the JewishGen Press

JewishGen Press (formerly the Yizkor Books-in-Print Project) is the publishing division of JewishGen.org, and provides a venue for the publication of non-fiction books pertaining to Jewish genealogy, history, culture, and heritage.

In addition to the Yizkor Book category, publications in the Other Non-Fiction category include Shoah memoirs and research, genealogical research, collections of genealogical and historical materials, biographies, diaries and letters, studies of Jewish experience and cultural life in the past, academic theses, and other books of interest to the Jewish community.

Please visit https://www.jewishgen.org/Yizkor/ybip.html to learn more.

Director of JewishGen Press: Joel Alpert
Managing Editor - Jessica Feinstein
Publications Manager - Susan Rosin

Notes to the Reader

The images in the original book were reproduced from photographs from the time of the first edition. These reproductions were already of poor quality, being pre-war and at least 30 or more years old. As a result the images in the book are not very good and the best achievable.

A reader can view the original scans of the book on the websites listed below.

The original book can be seen online at the Yiddish Book Center website:

https://www.yiddishbookcenter.org/collections/yizkor-books/yzk-nybc313836/soyfer-a-krinik-in-hurbn-memoarn

or
at the New York Public Library Digital Collections website:

https://digitalcollections.nypl.org/items/418a5ad0-9a18-0134-f1d6-00505686a51c

To obtain a list of Shoah victims from Krynki (Krynki, Poland) the reader should access the Yad Vashem web site listed below; one can also search for specific family names using family name option. These lists are continually updated by Yad Vashem, so it is worthwhile to periodically search these lists.

There is more valuable information (including the Pages of Testimony, etc.) available on this website: https://yvng.yadvashem.org/

A list of all books available from JewishGen Press along with prices is available at: https://www.jewishgen.org/Yizkor/ybip.html

Credits and Captions for Book Cover

Front cover:

Top:
Hassids of Slonim Synagogue, July 2009. Photo by Leszek Kozlowski, https://creativecommons.org/licenses/by/2.0. Hosted by Flickr.com. Cropped. This synagogue, destroyed by the Nazis in 1941, has long been used as a warehouse.

Bottom:
Krynki Jews marched to work by Nazis, 1942. Courtesy of the Communal Cultural Center in Krynki.

Back cover:

Top:
Kavkaz Synagogue windows, Krynki, 2012. Courtesy of Phillip Simons. This 19th century synagogue, destroyed in 1941, has been used as a cinema, later a sports and culture center. In 2020 the provincial board awarded funds to renovate it. The Kavkaz (Caucasus) district and synagogue were named after the Caucasus mountains, where the sheep, goat, ibex and other skins came from, that were used by Krynki's several tanneries.

Bottom:
"New" Jewish Cemetery, 2011. Courtesy of Ruth Scott.
Background photo: *Deep multi-level nimbostratus cloud* by Simon A. Eugster, Creative Commons Attribution-Share Alike 3.0 Unported license. Hosted by Wikimedia.org.

Krynki lives.

May the translation of this book not only help to keep alive the memory of the old, lost Shtetl Krynki; but may this work contribute to the preservation of the Jewish cultural heritage of this town and, in the course of growing understanding and reconciliation, bring it to life again.

The author, who was born in Krynki, tells us how he experienced "Krynki, a town of work, sorrow and struggle" in his youth, and how the dark cloud of World War II descends upon the town with all its increasingly terrifying horrors.

Miraculously, the author survives the Auschwitz concentration camp, where he actively participates in the prisoners' resistance plans. Driven by the unconditional will to give posterity a testimony about perhaps the most terrible crime of mankind, the author survives the ordeal of other concentration camps and finally the death march!

His work gives a voice to all those who can no longer speak to us.

Let us remember them, their stolen lives and their endless suffering during the Shoa.

Never again!

Beate Schützmann-Krebs
Berlin
May 2022

GeoPolitical Information

Krynki, Poland is located at 53°16' N 23°47' E and 136 miles ENE of Warszawa

	Town	District	Province	Country
Before WWI (c. 1900):	Krynki	Grodno	Grodno	Russian Empire
Between the wars (c. 1930):	Krynki	Grodno	Białystok	Poland
After WWII (c. 1950):	Krynki			Poland
Today (c. 2000):	Krynki			Poland

Alternate Names for the Town:

Krynki [Pol, Rus], Krinek [Yid], Krienek, Krinki, Krinok

Nearby Jewish Communities:

Odelsk, Belarus 9 miles N
Kolonia Izaaka, Belarus 9 miles N
Vyalikaya Byerastavitsa, Belarus 11 miles ESE
Gródek 12 miles SSW
Indura, Belarus 13 miles NNE
Sokółka 16 miles NW
Michałowo 18 miles SSW
Jałówka 18 miles SSE
Kuźnica 18 miles NNW
Supraśl 18 miles W
Svislach, Belarus 21 miles SE
Mstibovo, Belarus 22 miles ESE
Lunna, Belarus 24 miles ENE

Wasilków 24 miles WSW
Sidra 25 miles NW
Zabłudów 25 miles SW
Volpa, Belarus 25 miles ENE
Ros, Belarus 26 miles E
Golobudy, Belarus 26 miles SE
Janów Sokolski 27 miles WNW
Narew 27 miles SSW
Nowy Dwór 27 miles NNW
Białystok 28 miles WSW
Vawkavysk, Belarus 29 miles ESE
Hrodna, Belarus 29 miles N
Skidel, Belarus 29 miles NE
Narewka 30 miles S

Jewish Population: 3,542 (in 1900)

LITHUANIA

BALTIC SEA

RUSSIA

Vilnius

POLAND

GERMANY

Krynki

BELARUS

Berlin

Poznan

Warsaw

Lodz

Prague

UKRAINE

CZECH REPUBLIC

Krakow

SLOVAKIA

Munich

AUSTRIA

250 miles

250 Km 500 Km

POLAND – CURRENT BORDERS

Map of Poland with **Krynki** indicated

Original Book Cover

א. סויפער

קריניק אין חורבן
(מעמואַרן)

פרייז: $ 3.00 אמעריקער

אַרויסגעגעבן דורך די קריניקער הילפס־קאָמיטעט
פון אורוגוויי און אַרגענטינע
מאָנטעווידעאָ
1 9 4 8

TABLE OF CONTENTS

	Foreword	6
	Krinik in Khurbn	18
Chapter One		19
Chapter Two	The Russians Are Coming	35
Chapter Three	Life under Russian Power	39
Chapter Four	War between Germany and Russia	42
Chapter Five	On the Way	49
Chapter Six	In Captivity	67
Chapter Seven	The Escape	71
Chapter Eight	In the Woods	73
Chapter Nine	Back in the Ghetto	94
Chapter Ten	The Liquidation of the Ghetto	100
Chapter Eleven	The Factory Camp	103
Chapter Twelve	The Last Way	108
Chapter Thirteen	Death—Life	111
Chapter Fourteen	Birkenau	113
	Yizkor - Memorial Notices	188
	Name Index	211

The author with friends and family in the late 1960's. Photo courtesy of Israel Diament

From left to right:

Alex Sofer, Rokhele Sofer, Sheinke Liberman, Rebecca Zakheim Gerber, Srul (Simon) Gerber, Yankochone Liberman (Sheinke's husband), Fanny Zakheim, Jaime Liberman's wife, Jaime Liberman, Hershel Zakheim

During his life, various spellings were used for the author's name, which is derived from the Hebrew סופר. Moreover, depending on the transcription system, the pronunciation of the name varied. Therefore, his name is written in the book in different versions.

Beate Schützmann-Krebs

Krinki in Ruins
(Krynki, Poland)

53°16' / 23°47'

Translation of:
Krinik in khurbn: memuarn

By: A. Soifer

Published in Montevideo 1948

Acknowledgments

Translator:

Beate Schützmann-Krebs

Our sincere appreciation to Beate Schützmann-Krebs,
for permission to put this material on the JewishGen web site.

Her original project may be viewed at:

https://www.jewishbialystok.pl/Krynki-przet%C5%82umaczone!-Prac%C4%99-wykona%C5%82a--
Beate-Sch%C3%BCtzmannKrebs,5353,8331

We wish to thank Donni Magid for his meticulous extraction of the English
translations to facilitate the preparation of the following web pages.

We also wish to thank Sondra Ettlinger for extracting the pictures
from the original book which enabled the addition of them to this translation.

This is a translation from: *Krinik in khurbn: memuarn*;
Krinki in Ruins, ed. Alex Sofer, Montevideo 1948

א סופיעם

קרינק אין חורבן

מאנטעווידעא

1 9 4 8

A. Soyfer — three months after liberation in camp clothes

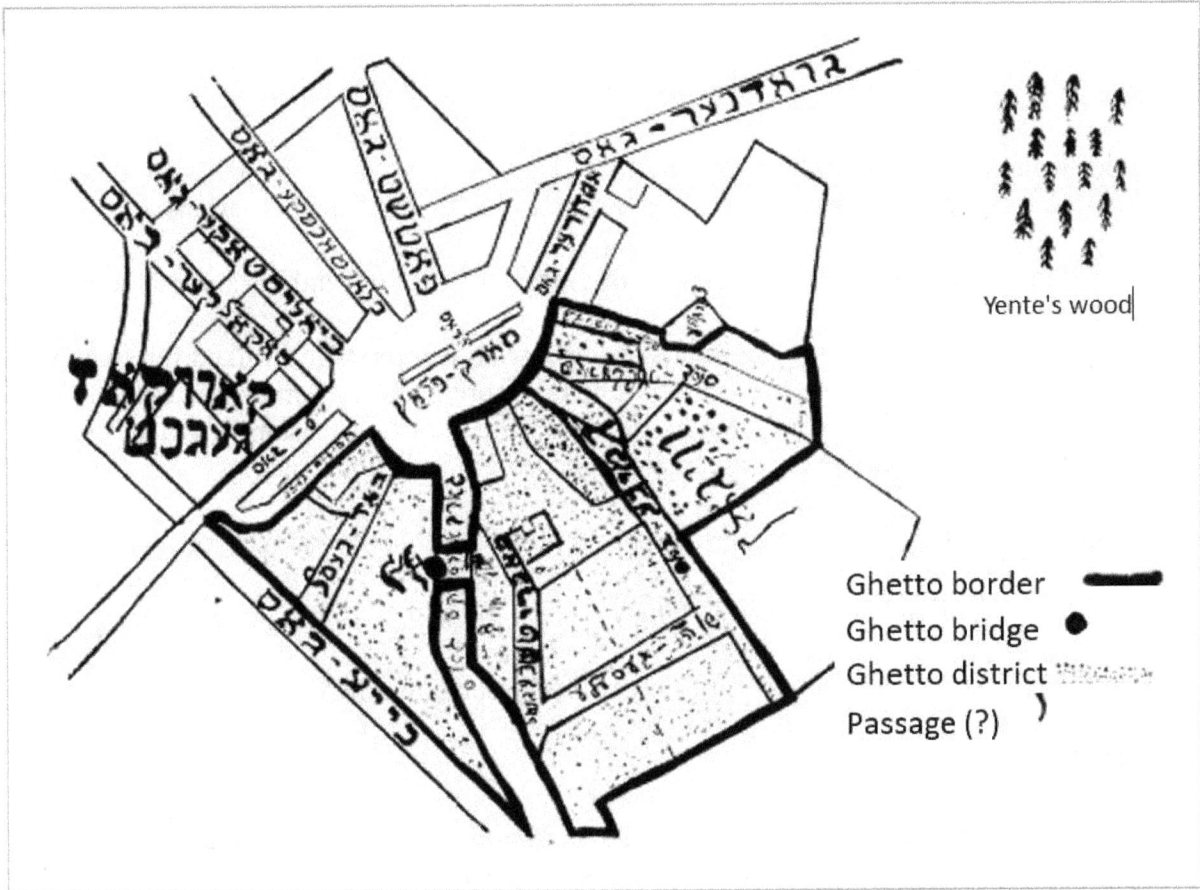

Yente's wood

Ghetto border —
Ghetto bridge ●
Ghetto district ░░░░
Passage (?))

The original city map

[Page 8]

Foreword

The Krynki Relief and Compatriots Associations of Uruguay and Argentina dedicate this book to the memory of our dear and proud Jews of Krynki who were killed by the Nazi barbarians.

The Paving stones of Krinker streets remind us of the footsteps of our fathers and mothers, of

those who were closest to us. They remind us of our Jewish workers who walked for years with pride and security, with poems and songs, dreaming of a better, more beautiful tomorrow. Our Jewish Krynki was the first city to send its heroic youth into battle, they were the first partisans of Poland! Over forests, fields and over the whole country echoed the praises of the heroism of our martyrs.

May this book serve as an eternal memorial to our thousands of unknown martyrs.

The Committee of the Krinker Relief in Uruguay

The Committee of the Krinker Relief and Compatriots Association in Argentina

[Page 9]

All the images of my shtetele Krynki are rising again before my inner eye. In a valley between very flat mountains, in the flint layer of Poland, near Bialystok, lies my hometown.

About ten thousand human lives are cocooned in its bosom, of which 80 percent were Jews.

The round market in the middle is the center of the shtetl. Two rows of stores — the source of income for Jewish small traders — are divided by the so-called "brom" [gate], which unites both sides of the market. Here, in the market, people bought and sold during the day and walked about during the evenings until night time. There were no limits for almost endless "hakofes" [circumambulations], until the couples used to get tired and march off through the "Shishlevetser" street [the street to Swisłocz]. Then, after passing the "bolnitses" [the hospital with its complex of buildings) remaining on the highway, some of them would often walk up to the "Shyemanitse" [Siemianówka]. Others use to make their rounds in the "Kashtanen-Aleye" [Chestnut avenue], passing Lublinke's yard, towards Yente's forest. This was only a small grove, but it still connected each resident with so many threads spun by his bygone days: they were no longer there, gone in infinity, leaving an empty echo in the soul.

In recent years, the grove had been cleared little by little, with the consequence that the Jews walked a little further to the the Shalker Forest, although the way was arduous. However, on their day of rest, the Sabbath, Jews would need the green pine forest, a clear sky overhead and the chirping of birds in the air. On the high, sandy mountain, groups of young people used to bath their limbs in sun rays, and there was joy, interwoven with hope.

In the summer evenings of the Sabbath, the young people and the parents with their children, would return home. People met for "shaleshudes",[1] "shtshav-borshtsh" [sorrel-beet-soup] and cold "ladishkes" [earthenware jugs with milk] covered on the top with cream. They were simple meals and yet so tasty … holy evenings, which we valued far too little at that time! In the evenings after work, the Krinkers would cluster around the verandas in the market.

[Page 10]

Once, Mair Cheikels got very angry because people used to sit on the veranda and not inside, in his tavern. He took black pitch and spread it on the popular seat. But the gang wiped it off with their suits and continued to sit there.

If you go further, you would come to Yosele Mastovlonski's veranda, on the corner of Bialystok Street. This is the porch where large gatherings are held, especially the May Day celebrations. All May Day marches of all parties started from here. The veranda was used as a tribune for the speakers who talked to the people. After that, "the shtetl" used to really seethe, it discussed and commented on the speeches and for a long, long time this remained the number one topic of the day's conversation.

Winter Shabbat in the shtetl was different. Very early in the morning, shouting gentiles would come to heat the stoves. They boiled water for the "bunkes" [a kind of narrow-necked pitcher] so that they could be served with the first glass of tea, along with a piece of braided Sabbath chala (white bread] as a snack. It is getting warm in the parlor. The fathers have gone away to pray. Soon, the "tsholent" [slow-cooked Sabbath stew] will be brought from the bakery. The food of the Sabbath has a thousand flavors.[2]The family gets together, they drink tea and talk about the daily worries of the week. And no type of problem was ever missing. Family ties were very strong. One endeavored to help the other, at least with advice. And there was never a lack of advice...

Sabbath nights in winter! Why, oh why have you left me forever? You, the glorious, shimmering evenings, when the sleds, manned by youngsters, chased quickly over the shiny snow. The tinkling of bells mingled with the girls' laughter, and how fast the horses galloped! Boys used to throw snowballs into the sledges, but nobody minded... no, things are even merrier, and laughter echoes even louder through the frosty air.

[Page 11]

All this was on the Sabbath holiday. On weekdays, life tended to flow very slowly and was interwoven with sorrow and worry. In general, the population was very poor. Everyone toiled hard for a living. There was a great class difference among the Jews. Great factory owners lived in luxury and enjoyed all the good things. But the rest had to toil very hard in their daily lives. Especially the women had a hard time. The water was usually far from the house. And the wells used to be frozen in winter with a layer of ice one meter thick. The holy mothers of our people were exceedingly efficient when they had to draw dozens of buckets of water for washing or later for the preparations for Passover. One struggled, but without ever complaining about it to the Almighty. Everyone worked in his or her field and hoped for a better tomorrow.

Gabarske [tannery) street stretched from the market to Pohulanke [-street]; next was the great shul [Synagogue][3] with the shul's yard, where we played "nyemtshik , tshizshik"[4] after learning, and the girls hopped around on one leg in between.

It often happened that rascals tried to throw a little stone to hit one of the countless windows of the shul.

Later, they used to get very frightened, when we exchanged those stories that in the night deceased people were haunting the shul, saying psalms and punishing every bad child.

Hundreds of legends entwined around the shul, and the brats actually balked at going into its "polish" [ante-chamber] to do some naughty things, because the "tore-bret" [table for washing corpses] was located there. The great Bes-Hamedresh [3] and (Yente's) "Khaye-Odem"[5] Bes-Hamedresh surrounded the shul's yard. Once, when people stood on the shul's roof (of course, when it was built) they could see how it smoked from all over the city of Pohulanke! The same as in Lodz! Big, tall chimneys with a circumference of 30 meters smoked there all day, powering dozens of drums in the tanneries.

The main source of the shtetl's income was the tanning industry. Three thousand workers of the city supplied the grocers, the bakeries, the cobblers and tailors. Every young lad dreamed of becoming a tanner — a responsible person, a bread-earner. Every visitor who comes to Krynki for the first time, will always have engraved in his memory how such a shtetl as this one has laid out the sidewalks and installed the municipal electric power: It was done by a Jewish engineer, Galinski, and a Jewish technician and collector, Mr. David Zak.

[Page 12]

The Bime [Bimah, readers platform] and the Orn-Koydesh [Aron Kodesh, Torah Ark]
of the Krinker synagogue
Standing in the center: R'Hashal Achon, the shames [synagogue caretaker] and
Orke Shimer, the gabe [trustee, charity overseer]

[Page 13]

David Gottlieb, the vice-mayor for several periods.
Efficient activist for the "Bund" and the "Tzisho"[6] schools.

Wolf Weiner, first Jewish mayor. Been active in the orphanage and "Linas Hatzedek".[15]

[Page 14]

Jewish "katsovim" [Jewish butchers] were constantly at work in the Jewish slaughterhouse by the river. People used to say that if the "kaiser of the katsovim", Leyzer Kugel, had to get things straight with his partner, it could be heard as far as the Jews on the other side of the market.

Jewish boys and girls used to spend a little time in the "shvyentar",[7] at the Orthodox church. Often, when there was a goyish wedding there, we would go inside the church to catch a glimpse of the bride and groom. In autumn, the Jewish fruit merchants used to transport their tasty apples and pears from Batyushke's orchard, which the market vendors of the shtetl would sell-and every fruit found its buyer.

Jokers of the shtetl, especially Shmuel Tenor, created popular jokes that spread to neighboring towns. Jewish automobile owners of Krynki founded the "Spulke Express":[8] 5 times a day they offered a lift that included not only a ride within the streets of Krynki, but also connections from Krynki to Bialystok and Grodno. Every few hours, the "whole shtetl" used to go to one of the automobiles to hear news, to see who had arrived and to accept newspapers.

Later, all this was nationalized, and the Jewish automobiles were no longer allowed to carry passengers. However, the Jews switched to trucks, whereupon in the shtetl Jewish commerce was buzzing again. In the summer nights, people used to walk through "Koshtshyol Street", past the "magelnik" [cemetery] to "Virion's yard". The route led them past Sime's mill and then across the wooden bridge over the "Ozyere".[9]

[Page 15]

Our "pozharnikes" [firefighters] were a reflection of our municipal administration. Twenty "pozharnikes" — all Jews, except the oldest, Vladko Anisimovich. The vice-commander was Chemya Meyerovich. The same was true for the magistrate: the largest part was made up of Jewish councilmen, with a Christian mayor, Pavel Tzarevich (who is now living in the Land of Israel!) and with a Jewish Vice mayor, David Gottlieb.

 The gentile mayor, Pavl "Tsar", as he was called, was a very friendly person. He spoke a very good Yiddish and got along well with the Jews, that is, with the Jewish leather factory owners...

The "Shomre-Shabesnikes"[10], [the guardians of the Sabbath], practiced their special activity only on Friday evenings: Before the ceremony of the "Likht-Bentshn", [the blessing over the Sabbath candles], they scattered through the shtetl's streets and caused a wave of commotion.

"Jews! Shabbath is here, it's getting late, close the stores!" And there was following a rattling and clattering of closing stores, doors and shutters-Sabbath is here!

Ben-Zion Dande used to shout all over the market, "Jews, go to shul, all of you!" And the boys echoed: "Go to shul!"

***City Council and Magistrate of Krynki In the middle is standing Moshe
Pruzhanski***

In the small "Bod-Gesl" [Bath-road][11], it begins to swarm considerably. Jews walk in and out of the bath.[11] Each had their packages under their arms. On Friday evenings, the sinful "Gang of Bale-Aveyres"[12] would go away to get shaved, and the [law-abiding] "Shomre-Shabesnikes"[10] had heated arguments with them. Very early on the Sabbath, the shtetl already looked festive. Jews, dressed in their "taleysim" [prayer shawls], used to go to their individual houses of prayer: To the Bes-Hamedresh, to the shul or to the Chasidim-shtibl.[13]

[Page 16]

The most interesting persons of the social life in Krynki were: Mr. Velvel Weiner (Velvel, "The Carpenter"), the former Jewish mayor, who devoted much of his life to social activity in the magistrate [City Council], the „kheyder haKlali"[14] and in the Orphan's Committee.

Mr. Yankel Levi, ("Yankel, The Clear"), a person full of energy in social activities, such as in the bank, in the Jewish secular school organization and in the "Bund". Also, he was an advisor in the City Council and alderman in the Magistrate. He perished in the Nazi gas chambers in Auschwitz, on January 21, 1943.

Mr. Abraham-Shmuel Zuts ("The Blind"), or, as he is referred to in literature, "Zishe, The Eternal Light". He went blind in the Tsarist prisons. However, he managed to maintain the most beautiful treasure: A brand new library, constantly updated with the latest Jewish editions.

He was continuously involved in secular activities within the school organization, in the "Bund" — and worked constantly together with young people. His room was permanently crowded with people. Together with his two sisters, Itke and Mulinke, he perished at the hands of the Nazis.

Mr. Nachum Blacher — secretary at the professional Tanners Union. There was no strike that could be settled without him. At all May Day celebrations he gave a speech in which every word was chosen with prudence — although he actually had difficulty speaking. During the ghetto period, an illegal radio [receiver] was operating in the house of Nachum Blacher, which was used to listen to news from abroad.

[Page 17]

Later, the news would spread throughout the ghetto. Nachum perished in Treblinka.

Mr. Lublinski, Baruch Mordechai Zditkowski, Baruch Stolarski (Chochem's), Alter Ayon, Motke Adinok and many others, whose names I do not remember, were very respected figures in the Jewish life of Krynki, both in the field of the Kehile, as well as in banking and generally, on the occasion of charitable actions.

And at this point, the various institutions and their services should be outlined. The mainstay of the Jewish economy was the Krinker "Volks-Bank", whose funds went to the small shopkeepers, the local textile entrepreneurs and the craftsmen, who were experiencing immense existential worries.

The main figures in banking were Messrs. Jakob-Chaim Grishtzinski, Yankele Shafir and Kananovich, ("The Passionate"). The most popular of the bank was Chaikel, who delivered the financial notifications.

The hall of the [fondly called] "Benkl" [diminutive of "bank"] was used by all organizations and institutions to hold discourses and lectures with discussions, as well as theater and cinema performances.

The shtetl was blessed with a very beautiful institution: "Linas Hatzedek"![15] It served the entire Jewish population with a doctor and a pharmacy. Poor people received medical help there for nothing, thanks to a receipt stamped by the secretary, Mr. Mordechai Shimen Grodzki, who helped intensively in the institution for many years. Recently, moreover, a magnificent "Ladovnye" (ice cellar) was established, which was a real folk treasure. After all, to get a piece of ice cream in the summer is really a big deal for a sick person! The "Linas (ha)Tzadek" was strongly supported by both the Krinkers in Chicago and the New York Relief Committee. On every Purim, they organized the "Purim (donation) campaign" for ice[16]. Later, the "Moes-Khitn" — campaign began[17] — "Matzah" for the poor. Everything was adapted to the conditions of the time and its people.

[Page 18]

A very nice activity was developed by the Jewish "yesoymem-hoyz" [Orphan's home], which maintained a daily boarding school with several dozen children. A few years earlier, before the war, the orphanage also had a tailoring school attached to it, whose director was Mrs. Blumke Zakheim. She managed that many dozens of children left the school with a recognized professional trade as a tailor.

The "Gmiles-Khsodim Fund"[18] carried out its activities quietly and modestly, in a really good way. A Jew could obtain a loan with a bill of exchange without any municipal tax; the so-called "Gmiles-Khsodim" bills were completely exempt from stamp tax; no interest (and duty) was payable on the whole. The technical secretary was Mr. Moshe Ekshtein (called Moshe Pintl), a dear, cordial man.

There was also lively activity in cultural and educational matters. Already dozens of years back, the various student groups had formed. In general, we were dealing with a city full of Jewish scholars.

These scholars were great experts in ["choosing"] the Rov [Rabbi]. Not just anyone could take the place of the Rabbi — and the last Krinker Rabbi, Rabbi I. Mishkovski, was indeed one of the most excellent persons in the Jewish-Polish Rabbinic world.

I still remember my earliest cheder years, how in the shul, on the right side of the "Polish" [ante-chamber] we were fed "knowledge" by "Yisroel, the teacher" (called "The Little Goatee"). Or, as others used to put it, they were dealt their deals, by usage of wet towels, by "Tsherne" ["The Black One"][19]— and as punishment, you had to stand in "koze" (goat pen) for a day. Later, the "Cheder haKlali" became a highly modern cheder. Jewish children from the surrounding towns such as Amdur, Brestovitch, Jalovka and Horodok, used to come to the cheder to study. And later, at the holidays, they used to go home, dressed up in their uniforms and little hats with shiny "dasheks" [visors]. The streets and the market were full of joy and fun when the children at lunchtime came out of the cheder and the Jewish school. Hundreds of children with small satchels on their backs ran home. Yes, that was the life of a Cheder boy!

[Page 19]

Tarbut-School in Krynki

For each attitude, there was a corresponding facility. The Zionists were very involved in the "Tarbut School"[20], which was a mixed institution for boys and girls. The language of instruction was Hebrew. The "Bund" also had its "niche": the Jewish-secular schools. For all Krinker Jews, it was a tradition to go to the magnificent "children's performances" on both Purim evenings, where children appeared in the respective roles of the [theater] plays: "Mekhirat Yosef" [The Sale of Yosef], "Shlumperl" [Cinderella],

"Der Sheydem-Tants" [The Dance of the Demons] and others. In the social-cultural field, the "Poale Zion"[21] stood out, but also the "Bund" and its youth organizations: the "Hachalutz",[22] "Frayhayt" [Freedom], "Tsukunft" [Future] and "SKIF" [Socialist Children's Union]. In the summer, young people and children from different organizations used to meet in the "Shalker Forest" and sing a popular song together as a warm welcome:

[Page 20]

"We are young, the world is wide,
oh beautiful world of youth,
thou world of light and freedom, we are young
and that is great..."

"Tzisho"-school in Krynki

In their blue shirts and red ties, young people from all [political] directions sang this song while marching bravely with bright eyes and proud step. Each organization found its niche. Every ideological milieu found its own special youth. In particular, it should be remembered that the communist youth carried out their activities within a limited framework and were wary of provocations. For the most part, they supported the actions of the "Bund".

[Page 21]

Jewish lectures used to be arranged in the "Benkl" and each lecture was a major event in Krinker life. After the lectures, we always saw the same: Dozens of the audience went around discussing what the speaker had said. And so it was "the order of the day" that on the Sabbath, during the "Tsholent" meal, the hottest discussions were held around the table because of political problems.

The communists often scattered leaflets. — Each one represented his individual truths, and so brothers used to have fierce disputes at the table, owed solely to party politics.

Even in the "Bote Medroshim",[13] this was commonplace, especially on the Sabbath.

Ordinary Jews were tearing their heads apart over the problems of the world. In the Chassidic-shtibl, where the contrast was particularly significant, hot discussions were held. The "Mizrekh-Vant" [the wall facing east][23] was usually 'occupied' by the factory owners, and the poor stayed by the stove. But — in the "Chasidarnia" all people are equal, after all, and Moshe-Velvl Pruzanski, the great leather manufacturer, gets an "announcement" from a tannery worker that capitalism will not last more than ten years!

On it, the other says that the Chasidic rabbi takes sides only with the poor! But a third one argues that the rabbi stands by the "bourgeois".

And so the Jewish Chasids of the "Slonimer shtibel" used to quarrel about the Rabbi, just as they later quarreled about the "loksh" [noodles] at the Rabbi's table.

A "Chazn" [cantor] — that was something for the "Misnagdim".[24] In the old "shul" — with its carved deer on both sides of the "Orn-Koydesh" [Ark], with the high "Bimah" in the middle and with the "knob" with its many lights above one's head — this was the place where "Chazonim" [cantors] sang their prayers on the "Yomim-Neroim", the ten "Days of Awe"!

Once, gifted Chazonim used to perform a "Mayrev" [Maariv, evening prayer] — against tickets.

Translator's footnotes:

1. "shaleshudes" = the last of the three meals eaten by Shabbat-observant Jews, the first is taken on Friday night, the second on Saturday day, and the third late on Saturday afternoon.
2. This sentence is ambiguous, which gives it a special charm. The Hebrew-rooted word טעמים can have different meanings: taste, flavour, reason, sense.
3. "shul", "Bes-(Ha)medresh" etc: A Bes-(Ha)medresh is primarily a house for studying the Talmud, but it is also used as a synagogue (shul). Services there tend to be conducted with less decorum then in the larger shul, whose function is solely that of a House of prayer. In an Eastern European shtetl, the shul and its Rabbi had a certain official status whereas a Bes-(Ha)medresh was more informal, sometimes privately owned and operated, sometimes attached to a Yeshiva, and sometimes serving as the location for daily prayers, whereas Sabbath services took place in the larger shul. The shul might also have a Bes-(Ha)medresh where non-prayer functions would take place. A Chasidic Rebbe residing in a shtetl would have his "Bes-(Ha)medresh", that is, a "shtibl" or "kloyz", even though the shtetl also had a shul. The Bes-(Ha)medresh term therefore can describe a number of slightly different institutions.
4. "nyemtshik (German) — tshizshik (little bird)", a children's play.
5. Khaye-Odem = "The Life of Man", popular religious book, in which one finds in brief the laws of the "Shulkhn-Orekh", a halakhic compendium from the 16th century. It was not uncommon that a Bes-Medresh or synagogue bore the name "Khaye-Odem".
6. "Tzisho" (sometimes also "Tzisha" or "Tsisho") = an acronym of "Tsentrale Yidishe Shul-Organizatsye" (Central Yiddish School Organization), a secular, yiddishist and socialist school system.
7. "shvyentar" = a Belarussian word , "priest", used here for the place around the orthodox church.
8. "Spulke" = from Polish "społ ka"= company-partnership.

9. Ozyere = from Russian, lit. lake, but here it's rather the Krinker river.

10. "Shoymer-Shabesnik" = "guardian of the Sabbath", pious Jew who keep the Sabbath and remind others in time to observe it.

11. "khevre Bale-Aveyres"= "gang of sinful persons". In general: The use of Hebrew-rooted words in Yiddish can often create a certain ambiguity of a term and likewise give it the slight flavor of irony and humor.

12. "Bod" = bath. It can be assumed that the mikvah is meant. The men in certain communities, especially chasidic and haredi groups, use(d) to go to the mikvah and practice(d) immersion before each Shabbat. But it's also possible that they took the bath just as the preparation for the Sabbath, which took place in a body of water or in the shtetl's bathhouse.

13. "shul", "Bes-(Ha)medresh" (Pl. "Bote-Medroshim"), "shtibl" etc: A Bes-(Ha)medresh is primarily a house for studying the Talmud, but it is also used as a synagogue (shul). Services there tend to be conducted with less decorum then in the larger shul, whose function is solely that of a House of prayer. In an Eastern European shtetl, the shul and its Rabbi had a certain official status whereas a Bes-(Ha)medresh was more informal, sometimes privately owned and operated, sometimes attached to a Yeshiva, and sometimes serving as the location for daily prayers, whereas Sabbath services took place in the larger shul. The shul might also have a Bes-(Ha)medresh where non-prayer functions would take place. A Chasidic Rebbe residing in a shtetl would have his "Bes-(Ha)medresh", that is, a "shtibl" or "kloyz", even though the shtetl also had a shul. The Bes-(Ha)medresh term therefore can describe a number of slightly different institutions.

14. "kheyder haKlali"= cheder haKlali, publicly licensed, Jewish-religious Primary School, reserved for boys from the age of 3.

15. "Linas Hatsedek" = lit. "decent overnight stay", a society for helping poor, sick Jewish people.

16. In the Megilat Esther, there is a commandment on Purim to give money or gifts to the needy: "...to celebrate them as days of feasting and joy, and to send gifts one to another and gifts to the needy." In the language of the Megila, "Matanot La-evyonim." In this regard, the Talmud stipulates that it is an obligation to donate to at least two poor people. Likewise, the Talmud defines that one must simply give to anyone who extends his hand on Purim.

17. "Moes-Khitn" = lit. "Money for wheat", the custom to give money to the poor so they could buy matzah for Passover and fulfill the commandment to celebrate the feast day.

18. "Gmiles-Kh(a)sodim" = Aid association that granted an interest-free loan.

19. "Tsherne" = "black", possibly the nickname of the Shames or another person, employed by the synagogue.

20. "Tarbut-School" = lit. "Culture School", secular schools with Zionist orientation which taught Jewish and general humanistic and scientific studies. The students were prepared for the necessary work in the context of an immigration to Eretz Israel.

21. "Poale-Tsion (Zion)": literally: "Workers of Zion", name of the Zionist-Socialist political movement (establ. In 1906) and the party Poale Zion.

22. "Hachalutz"= Jewish youth movement that trained young people for agricultural settlement in the Land of Israel.

23. The walls facing east were usually marked, as one performed one's prayers facing East/Jerusalem.

24. "Misnagdim" = the opponents of Chasidism, pious Jews who, in contrast to the Chasidim, were more rationalistically oriented and did not rally around a "Rabbi who performed miracles". Sometimes also used as a synonym for non-Chassidic Jews from Lithuania, the "Litvaks".

Krinik in Khurbn

Let's dedicate a special place to our beloved region "Kavkaz"[1]. The "Kavkazer" Bes-Medresh gathered his worshippers from this quarter of the shtetl.

A particularly poor part of the population lived in Kavkaz — most of them hard-working toilers. My grandfather, *R'Chaim Osher's*, the old Shames [synagogue servant] of the "Kavkazer" Bes-haMedresh, used to sit day and night studying a sheet of "Gemore"[2] — without glasses!

[Page 22]

He would often be joined by *Shmuel "The Rebetsn's"*, who studied the Gemore, as well. In general, the "Chevre-Kadishe" [Jewish funeral society] was very active here and used to gather in the "Kavkazer" Bes-Medresh.

Very dedicated in the "Chevre Kadishe" were:

R'Abraheml Benjamin Itziks, Israel the „Kirzhner" (The Furrier), Abramke the "Farbrenter" (The Passionate), Abrahamke „Brevde" [The Truthteller?][3] and Leibe-Iser Brevde.
On the evening of the Sabbath, during the "Havdole"[4] I would never fail to go to the Bes-Medresh. Because my grandpa always used to give me more wine than the others and kept letting the contents of the cup flow into my mouth. And I sensed all the tastes of the world at once. To be precise — it was the taste of paradise!

In the "Khaye-Odem"[5] Bes-Hamedresh were sitting about 50 youngsters and studied with the greatest dedication the eternally beautiful Gemore-pages; and their [devout] songs, which arose directly from their souls, frightened more than once[6] the passing by Christians, who had to go to the post office in "Gertzke's Brick House".

Jewish young men with sidelocks wound around their ears, used to eat ["esn teg")[7] at the homes of dozens of Krinker families. At every turn it was apparent that the great and good yeshiva [Jewish academy] for young men was active in the shtetl. The main "gabe" [trustee], *R' Naftali,* was exceptionally busy recruiting yeshiva students from all over the area. However, one also heard dialects of many young people from Galicia and Poland who came to study at the Krinker yeshiva, because it was considered one of the best, and quite a few graduates left the school as rabbis.

However, many of the students also left the Krinker yeshiva, especially those who had come from the small, surrounding yeshivas, and became "freemen".

All youth organizations conducted propaganda among the yeshiva students, and it often happened that anti-clerical leaflets lay between the Gemore pages.

These are memories from my youth — from those dear times. Times when Krynki lived: a city of work, worries and struggle.

Translator's footnotes:

1. " Kavkaz" = ("Caucasus"), an area in Krynki, settled by poor people, who were involved in the leather merchandise and bought their natural leather mainly from the Caucasus
2. " Gemore" = Gemara= the part of the Talmud (analysis and commentary), that explains the "Mishna" (the core text) and is written mainly in Aramaic
3. " Brevde " = probably derived from the Russian "Brevda", "Truth-Teller" or "Deliverer of Justice". in Russia, during the Middle Ages, this was a surname given to Jewish leaders who were Kohanim
4. "Havdole" = Distinguishing between the sacred and the common, ceremony to mark the end of the Sabbath or a holiday.
5. "Khaye-Odem" = "The Life of Man", popular religious book, in is to find in brief the laws of the "Shulkhn-Orekh", a halakhic compendium from the 16th century. It was not uncommon that a Bes-Medresh or synagogue bore the name "Khaye-Odem"
6. " nisht eyn mol " = not only once, but more often! In the face of the Jewish singing so deeply felt, the Christians passing by felt something like fear of God — a sudden deep touch of God's omnipresence and truthfulness that gave them a kind of fright.
7. " Esn teg " = Literally "to eat days". "Esn teg" refers to the community custom, once widespread in Eastern Europe, of supporting teachers and education by hosting yeshivah students for meals in private homes on certain days of the week — with stays probably changing from day to day.

[Page 23]

Chapter One

A day like any other weekday — but the air is filled with a silence that seems to burst apart at any moment. More people walk the streets than usual on weekdays. One passing by casts a silent glance at the other and continues towards the market, where small groups of people are standing and talking. One walks from one group to the next and listens intently to what exactly is being talked about.

It is Thursday, 10 o'clock in the morning. The police are agitated. Every moment another person approaches and tells current news. I am interested to know what is being told in the groups.

I approach one of the groups. One is talking and gesticulating in time with his hands — up and down. A small man with a pointed beard is speaking. He, a Jewish leather merchant, tells the latest news from Warsaw. Staying in this city yesterday, he had felt that the air was filled with gloom. And now he is speaking to this group of curious people, of which I am one. A policeman just passes by and orders us to disperse. Each is leaving in a different direction.

I walked toward our house, but stopped at Odinok's big brick house, which had its windows open. Inside it was full of people. Everyone was waiting for something and turned their eyes up to the big wall clock hanging above the open window.

I went in, but stopped next to the door, because I could not go further: The whole room was packed with people, head to head.

[Page 24]

The air is filled with thick, stuffy smoke. In the corner is standing a small table. On the table — a radio. Around the table are sitting quite a few people with their heads tilted far toward the radio. A quiet, sad music can be heard.

The wall clock ticks to the beat. It shows 10 minutes to 5.

The music is interrupted by a long whistle. One hand of the clock approaches twelve, the other five.

Shortly, a communiqué from Warsaw will be heard.

Everyone pricks up their ears and listens with their mouths half open. Suddenly, a word breaks the silence: "This is Warsaw, this is Warsaw!"

The faces of the people — frightened and pale.

Everyone just wants to know, as quickly as possible, what is coming at them from afar, behind fields and seas. What does he want, the one with the forelock, that Adolf? What does he want from Schmigly [General E. Śmigły-Rydz?] The radio speaks, "We don't want to give anything away! We will defend every sliver of earth, because otherwise we are doomed to perish! The corridor — this is our existence! Just as a fish cannot live without water, we cannot live without the corridor. We will not give away a single button of our military coat. Victory is with us! Justice is with us! God is with us!"

One looks to the other. One wants to say something to the other. The radio continues to speak: "This morning at 5 o'clock, German soldiers shot 5 Polish border guards — five sons of our people. We will not be silent either. Blood for blood!"

The radio is silent again. After a few minutes of silence, a long, deep moan escapes from our hearts.

People are starting to disperse. Grief lingers in the air. I go back to the street. Again, new groups of people have formed. One man joins the second, still a third comes along. Thus, a group is formed again. One talks, and the others listen with pricked ears.

[Page 25]

People run from one group to the next and listen to what this one and that one says. I walk back down the street toward our house. Now the streets are already full of people. Everyone seems to be keeping a secret, keeping it to themselves.

On the street I meet my comrade, Leizer Temkin. He tells me that there is no more work in the factories and the factory owners do not pay the salaries to the workers, but postpone this until later.

Suddenly I hear a commotion and noise. People walk in the direction of the market square, to Yosl Mostovlianski's gate. I also walk with them and recognize the poster-sticker from the magistrate walking with a smeared footstool in one hand and a bucket of glue, with the stick of the brush looking out of it, in the other hand. In this same hand he holds a bundle of pink papers — rolled up into a kind of tube. He walks towards Mostovlianski's smeared gate and stops there, casting a sad look of pity on the black huddled crowd, where one bumps into the other. Everyone wants to be the first at the gate. From minute to minute more and more people gather around.

The poster-sticker slowly, with trembling hands, takes the brush, stands on the three-legged footstool and again glances at the crowd. The brush smears a bit of the wall and then falls back into the bucket with a thud and a splash. Long fingers grab a piece of paper from the paper tube, and move to the smeared wall.

Everyone turns their eyes to the wall, and the first large black letters appear: **"MOBILIZATION"**. And after that, already smaller letters follow. I read, "Every citizen of the country between the ages of 18 to 45 is required to stand in defense of our fatherland. Everyone of this age must report to the magistrate and the police. In the event that someone does not comply withthe regulation, he must answer to the highest tribunal of the court martial. Signature: General Burtsovski".

[Page 26]

Everyone in the crowd has stopped as if frozen. No one move his lips to speak a word. One cast a glance at the other. Tears come to everyone's eyes. Everyone turns around and runs apart hanging their heads down. I quickly go home to break the news. When I come in, I find my father with a newspaper. His other children are sitting there playing. My dad asks me, "What do you hear on the street? Is there anything new?"

I stop transfixed, not knowing what to do. Should I tell the news of the mobilization or not?

I decide to tell it, "On the street, it's a sad atmosphere. They have announced the mobilization of all men 18-45 years old."

"What, what, a mobilization?" asks Dad, "a mobilization already? So soon? Did you read that yourself?"

"Yes," I say, "I read it myself. It is written there in big black words". Ringing her hands, my mother approaches, tears at the corners of her eyes running down her pale cheeks.

Loud wails penetrate the silence, "Oy, oy, my children! What will happen now? Until now we have worked and only just held the children on our laps. Black shadows have come to tear our children away from their mothers, the men from the women and the fathers from the children!"

Each of us sat there, our eyes fixed on our mother. Each of us looked to Mom with compassion and mercy — to all the mothers who now had to send their children away to shed their blood.

My older brother, Osher, approached Mom and said in a trembling voice, "Don't cry, Mom, we won't fight for those who just a few weeks ago were looking for new places for us Jews to be sent out of the land where we were born. But now we have to go to the police and report. After all, it's the day before the war"....

[Page 27]

The sky is hanging full of clouds. Sadness and melancholy can be felt in every house. The streets are full of people. Women and children are crying. Pleas from children are heard, "Dad, Dad, stay with us! Don't go away!" One image is more horrible than the other. I go out into the street. Before my eyes I see Sheyke Dreyzik. As he walks, he holds a small child in his arms. Another child is running after him. Women and children are crying. Mrs. Meyerovich is walking on the side, holding a small box in one hand, and in the other — a wet handkerchief. She speaks to herself, "My children, who will be like a father to you now?"…

Their father cries without tears, casting a glance from one child to the other. The child he carries in his arms gently strokes his dad's unshaven face. All run in one direction. Again, small groups of people are standing on the street. But already older Jews with beards are standing there, talking to each other. One recalls the war of 1914-1918.

Another says in a confident tone, "Nothing at all will come of it, for, as they say, out of gloomy great clouds falls but a little rain. England and France will come to the rescue and the 'Berlin Haman' will be quickly crushed."

Another speaks up, saying that yesterday he heard on the radio how the "Führer" shouted with an insolent voice and full of strength that "everything, everything, belongs to us, to our people". And further, with even more arrogance, "The whole world belongs to us. Our people above all other peoples of the world! 'Doytshland, Doytshland iber ales', [Germany, Germany above all]!"

And the man continues: "yes, we Jews will still have to experience many difficult days. The future can still bring us terrible things!"

I go together with all the people in the direction of the police. The street is black with people. Policemen are walking among the crowd, casting penetrating glances at everyone.

At the police station, the mayor is sitting with a piece of paper, writing down everyone's names and surname. A sound of trucks can be heard. People bump into each other as they make way for the vehicles. In several minutes the trucks are fully loaded with people who take last glances at their families and wave their hands.

[Page 28]

Gruesome scenes. Women fainting, children screaming. The police push the people away, who stand as if chained to the cars. The vehicles start moving with a sluggish sound. One after the other they drive off.

The mayor wants to calm the crying women with good words. He stands on a chair and speaks to the distraught women and children:

"You don't have to cry that your men are leaving you; they are going to defend the fatherland! Our fatherland has called us to defend every little chip. You should be proud that you send your sons to defend our and your fatherland!"

I stopped — not understanding that it was precisely that person who a month before had preached and openly proclaimed anti-Semitism: "Poland only for the Poles! The others should leave our country!"

Just now he said that we should be proud to defend our fatherland. Now, when our blood is needed, they cry out, "You are equal citizens!"

Only a short time ago, people of the 'upper echelon' ordered outright, "Beat the Jews!". And today we, the Jews, are asked to go and defend Poland.

But anyone who gets on the truck now is not going with the intention of fighting for those who are now hiding in their basements or making a nice day of it. But each of the sons and fathers who now take up a rifle goes to defend himself, to save his family from terrible murderers who want one thing above all: To drink our blood.

The last truck is driving up. I approach to say goodbye to friends. My mother is standing next to the vehicle with her sister. My cousins are carrying small children in their arms. Their husbands standing by hold one hand on the vehicle and the other on their child.

One child cries out: "Daddy, Daddy!", and his little eyes make him realize and sympathize with what is happening right around: Big, heavy tears fall on the pavement. The truck moves slowly away from the place.

The shouts of those leaving and the screams of those standing still echo through the air. The surge of waving hands rises higher and higher.

[Page 29]

They are hidden by a large grey cloud of dust, and on the sides of the pavement you can see shadows: Women who have fainted. Men are shouting, "Help!" The police disperse the surrounding crowd. Still, the sound of the trucks echo. The crying women are comforted by other people. For a few minutes it remains silent. The police no longer allow gatherings on the market square. The shtetl wraps itself in a painful evening; it is covered by a deep mourning. People are wandering the streets like shadows. From time to time, a car moves by, casting a wide streak of light, only to disappear again into the nocturnal darkness. Groups of people stand next to the houses where radios are located, waiting for the latest reports from Warsaw and Berlin. Everyone is engrossed in conversation.

Going to a window again, I take a look into the room, where people are sitting close together, their eyes fixed on the radio and the clock. The sad radio broadcast is interrupted by a long whistle; we can hear: "Radio Berlin". Everyone feels the pressure of silence and the beating of hearts. We hear: "Today, the Polish government rejected the legitimate demands of our Führer and our people; the Poles want the war. The Jews from Warsaw, Paris and London are driving the Poles to war. The Polish soldiers are provoking our border guards."

A tremble is gripping everyone' s limbs. One casts a sad glance at the other. We continue to listen:

"Polish soldiers attacked our border guards today at 2 o'clock in the afternoon. Two have been killed and six were wounded. And there is no end to their aggressiveness. We will not tolerate this any longer. They will have to pay us for all the sacrifices. Our brothers and sisters of the 'Free City of Gdansk' are reaching out to us in search of help. Our people and the Führer will come to the aid of our suffering brothers."

It is followed by a steely chant: "Deutschland, Deutschland über alles, über alles in der Welt, heute gehört uns Deutschland, morgen die ganze Welt".[1]

[Page 30]

A deep sigh escapes into the air. Everyone wipesthe cold sweat from their faces. The Jew standing next to me speaks to the crowd going out, "Yeah Jews, he wants the whole world to belong to him. Oh, how unhappy we would be if that became reality. The murderers would eat us all alive!"

And, even more passionately, the same man continues to speak: "Jews, you heard it, 'the Jews of Warsaw, Paris and London want war.' We Jews don't want war, why and for whom should we want war?"

I leave the talking Jews and go on to our house. When I enter the parlor, everyone is sitting silently and looking at me. They ask me, "What is to hear outside?" My mother is sitting at the sewing machine. Next to her, two village peasant women. Osher, my older brother, is sitting with a newspaper in his hand. His head deeply low, he gives me a silent look.

I answer the question, "There's a turbulence in the street. The air is enriched with fear, with what the next day will bring".

It is already late in the evening. The streets are shrouded in a dead silent haze. I go to sleep, but my thoughts are flying far away to the border where the dead soldiers lie. And immediately, those images come back to my mind — the numerous soldiers, heavily armed, marching to the front. Among them, I recognize many acquaintances from our shtetl who left early this morning with the trucks, leaving a last pleading look to their families. My eyes get tired and slowly fall shut.

When I get up at 7 a.m., the street is black with people. Horror is written all over everyone's face. I go out. Groups of people have formed on the street. I stick my head into a group and hear Mr. Yeshaye Glezer speaking:

"Folks, today at 4 a.m. the Germans attacked the Polish border, but Poland is resisting hard. This is war! War between Poland and Germany!"

I quickly run back, up to the parlor, and tell what I heard.

[Page 31]

Anti-Nazi demonstration on the eve of war in Krynki

The following can be seen: Messrs. David Zak, Pinye Garber, the 'zshondtse' (the manager) of the court, the engineer Galinski, David Linski, Shmuel Tenor, Gershon Pruzshanski, Motke Shteinsafir, David Shushanski and Pinye Nievizuski

[Page 32]

September 1, 1939

The youngest day of this month has brought sorrow and pain to all our hearts. The men and women who accompanied their husbands and children to the trucks yesterday, are standing wringing their hands and large, heavy tears are rolling down their pale, trembling cheeks.

I walk towards the market. The whole population is on the street and in the market. Everyone goes to the poster wall from which new black letters are shouting: "Every citizen of the city must prepare for an air raid: The windows must be well closed. No bright shine, no light must be seen. Next to each house must be a barrel of water and sand. Anyone who does not comply with the ordinance will be court-martialed!"

Police officers walk the streets with strained looks, fully armed. Again, everyone runs to the poster wall, where the "sticker" of the city authority is standing, smearing glue with his brush on the old, already read posters. Again we read a message from the police:

"Every citizen is allowed to go out on the street only until 9 o'clock in the evening. There is a state of war in the country. Everyone must submit to the decree. Signed: Police commander of the city".

I take a look at the clock. It is already 7 o'clock in the evening. Everyone is going home to comply with the government's orders, fully aware that today is the first day of the war. The streets have become deserted. Policemen walk around with heavy, slow steps. Each footstep reverberates. The sky is starry and the air is filled with a mood of mourning. The moon is hidden under a black cloak. From time to time it sticks its head out and casts a comical glance at the dreary shtetl.

Night descends and everyone sits behind covered windows.

[Page 33]

The first day of the war is over. Everyone is asking: what will be tomorrow, what might the next morning bring us?

September 2, 1939

From time to time a truck passes by, on which terrified soldiers are sitting. Some cars go to Grodno, others to Sokolka. Within the municipal government there is a tumultuous atmosphere. Several officers have stopped next to the magistrate, and a few minutes later the poster sticker is again gluing new decrees on the wall: "Everyone must deliver his horse and wagon to Viriant's yard. The ordinance goes into effect immediately!"

After a few minutes, sad people can be seen, Jews and Christians, holding their horses by the bridle, walking towards the courtyard, where several officers are standing, receiving the horses and carriages, and handing over a slip of paper, on which is written the sum that the owner has to get for his horse.

While walking, Jewish carters hold the red paper slips in their trembling hands, and their wives at their side walk with teary eyes. Every minute, more and more farmers from the surrounding villages arrive and the place fills up even more with horses. I walk out to the market and see the poster sticker again. He walks with slow steps to the smeared wall, and after a few minutes I already read a new ordinance: "Every man 18 to 45 years old must report immediately to Virian's yard to bring the mobilized horses to a certain place!"

Immediately, I go home, and report the news in the parlor. Tears stream down my mother's pale, gaunt cheeks. Two of us in the room have to leave: Me and my older brother Osher. Everyone is sad. From each house one or two have to leave. Their mothers and fathers are worried, not knowing where their children are going.

We leave, carrying a small bag of bread and water under our arms. Our mothers and sisters accompany us, looking at us with teary eyes widened in shock.

[Page 34]

We arrive at that yard. Our names and families are written down, and then everyone has to line up one behind the other in a long row to get a horse and carriage. Suddenly we hear a noise! The horses get excited, the soldiers start shouting around — the officers as well. Everyone turns their eyes to the sky. The noise gets louder and louder with every minute. And now a white, steel bird is flying above our heads! Some shout, gesturing with their hands, "Faster, hide!" Then everyone drops down, facing the green grass. A stampede breaks out. The horses neigh, and some dash in fright sideways across a plowed field, dragging the broken-down carriages behind them. Every second, the plane descends even lower and approaches the tall pine trees under which people are lying one on top of the other. Their faces are chalky white. Lying down, the soldiers keep their rifles hidden under their bodies.

Next to me stands an officer whose hand has, due to the fright, accidentally fallen into a pile of horse droppings, but he only directs his gaze to the flight of the plane, circling above the tall pines. When glancing at his hands, he says, almost laughing, "Stinks pretty good, but the place is well disguised!"

After the airplane has circled the heads of the lying people several times, a long machine-gun salvo is heard. Some of the bullets chase over the prancing horses and others over the people who at that moment keep their heads pressed low, one lying under the second, like tortoises in the furrow of the earth. After several more hails of bullets, the plane heads towards the city, from which you can already hear the intermittent whistle of the siren, which scares everyone.

As soon as it has become quiet above our heads, the colonel's voice sounds in a command tone: "Quick, everyone on the horses! We start moving!" And the pale soldiers, rising from the ground, quickly gather with us.

[Page 35]

The co-optees are ordered to pick up the scattered wheels, the shafts of the carriages, and the torn, blood-spattered horse collars from the fields.

Further away, the horses have stopped. White dense steam rises from them as if boiling water had been poured over them. Some of the horses stand on only three feet. Blood trickles from their fourth feet, and the horses' eyes plead for rescue with a mute look. Dense white foam drips from their mouths.

Each of us has grabbed a horse and quickly runs to the broken carriages. The officials are furious, shouting and cursing with every word: "Faster, faster, and if you don't have a carriage, just take the horse!"

After a few minutes, hundreds of horses are lined up in a row on the highway, with pale, frightened Jews and Christians standing next to them.

Mothers and sisters have accompanied their loved ones to the highway, wet cloths in hand. A command is heard, "Depart!" The wheels and hooves spread out on the hard highway and move away from our companions in the direction of Sokolka. We're going slowly. A cool autumn wind blows by and gets under the hair of the horses' manes.

Night falls, a black veil remains between one carriage and the other, and with every minute, the carriages that are in front of you are less visible.

So we trudge along laboriously until large, foggy clouds appear in the evening sky. A cold morning wind whistles through our bones. Many of us have no warm coats and snuggle up to the warm skins of the sweaty horses. We enter Sokolka and stop next to the barracks, where unrested soldiers walk around with their collars up.

After a few minutes of standing, another command is given by the transport leader: "Onward, forward!" None of us knows how long we'll be trudging forward like this. Some of us feel a shiver running down our entire bodies:

[Page 36]

> "Maybe all the way to the front, or maybe even further?" We drive again in the direction of Bialystok. The soldiers who accompany us, riding sideways on their horses, know as much as we do.
>
> After a 10 km drive from Sokolka, we are directed from the highway to a dirt road that leads to a dense, black forest. At the edge of the forest, we see small houses with thatched roofs, around which geese, chickens and pigs are cavorting. Deeper in the forest, by the old moss-covered trees, there are soldiers standing and sitting. Blue smoke curls out of a small fire made of dry twigs. The colonel is the first to drive up to the houses, where he dismounts heavily and sleepily from his two-wheeled carriage, and several minutes later his order goes out: "Here the horses are handed over! There will be no further driving!"

The joy is written all over everyone's face. Brothers run to brothers and fathers to their children to share their joy. Everyone is satisfied that they do not have to go any further and will soon return home, under their warm feather beds and under the anxiously caring eyes of their mother.

Above one side of the black forest, a red patch of sky appears, from which a brilliant autumn sun is forming. Its rays fall on our frozen limbs and increase our joy.

Each one goes to a small house where quite a few soldiers are already sitting at a small village table; and each one hands over his horse, one with a carriage, the other without. As a result, everyone receives two paper zloty and is no longer subject to the supervision of the military.

People gather in groups and head home on foot. One group wants to overtake the other, a merry bunch it is! From their little sacks, they pick pieces of bread and smear them with butter or take a bite from a long pork sausage (in the intestine). Others, with all five fingers, hold a piece of white bacon and eat with a good appetite. Moving forward, everyone is eating and taking another look back at where they left entire groups, spread out over the stone highway.

[Page 37]

And so fields, bushes and white little houses quickly pass by, which we didn't even see on the way there. Leaving Sokolka behind us, the spire of the Polish church of Kamenka is already visible. Aggressive village dogs run out and accompany us part of the way until they tire of the futile barking and run back to the peasant huts.

The sun is already at its zenith, moving further towards the horizon every minute. There we are leaving the suburb of our shtetl and can already see the mountain range that lies to the other side of our shtetl. When we reach the first cottages, everyone just runs faster! Everyone wants to be the first at home in the parlor. Mothers and sisters come running out of their houses and welcome their children and brothers with joyful looks, as if they just came back from the front as victors.

It is already the third day of the war. Police discipline is weakening with each passing hour. Gloom spreads through the hearts. News from the front is bad. The Germans are taking new cities every hour.

I go to an open window where there is a radio. Curious people stand at the window, waiting with great impatience for the front report.

We hear: "This is Warsaw. England and France are coming to our aid. Today England has declared war on our enemy Germany". A cheer breaks out among everyone. People squeeze each other's hands or kiss each other with joy.

"Now we're going to win", chimes the cheerful voice of a young, Polish student, "now we're going to show them what we are capable of!"

The news spreads quickly throughout the shtetl. Old and young — everyone is happy. Mothers who sent their children to the battlefield cry with joy that they will soon have their children back with them.

A happy evening in the shtetl. The third day of the war — and already such a fortune: we are not alone!

[Page 38]

The fourth day of the war begins with the sound of airplanes over the houses of the shtetl. The alarm siren forces old and young to race. The planes have flown over the shtetl, leaving a silence that lingers in the air. So, the fourth and the fifth day pass quietly.

The reports are worsening day by day. Then a rumor makes its rounds and spreads like lightning over all houses: The Germans are already at the gates of Grodno!

On the sixth and seventh day, there are ongoing news updates.

The eighth and ninth days begin with a police crowd, and like a storm, a rumor quickly spreads through the shtetl: Grodno has fallen; the Germans are already around our shtetl!

A shudder seizes the shtetl. People walk around gloomily. Pious Jews go to the Bes-Medresh reciting psalms. Some decide to fast. Women visit the dead in the cemetery to ask for mercy and help in our great need. (1)

Every minute, the rumor turns out to be more and more true. The police no longer maintain discipline. Police officers gather next to the detention center and it looks like they are preparing to leave the shtetl. There you can see carriages, ready for departure, already. The complete police archive material is packed onto them, and more and more people gather around the carts. But the police are no longer dispersing them. In a few minutes, they'll probably have to leave the shtetl. Already you can see the tear-stained faces of women crying out hand-wringing: "Who will they leave us to? Who will defend us? Who will save us from the cruel hands of the murderer?"

No one to answer that. The population now has to live in this mood of panic.

The police commander shows himself on the stairs, turning to the assembled audience with a trembling voice:

"Go apart! We are not leaving yet. We have only received an order to prepare for a withdrawal if necessary.

[Page 39]

But in the meantime, be quiet and keep order." Everyone feels the affecting voice in his speech — like a drowning man begging for rescue.

This mood lasts for three days. On the tenth day after the outbreak of war, the police and all officials leave Krynki. The entire population is filled with horror and shock. There we get the message that the Germans are only 10 kilometers away from us. Indeed, we can already hear the shots from heavy guns and tanks. In the sky, squadrons of airplanes are roaring. The siren no longer sends a signal to hide. Everything has died off. With each passing minute, the fright grows even stronger. The streets become empty. All around there is dead silence. From time to time you can still hear the heavy footsteps of Yakob Kazoltshik ("Yankl Khazer")[2], who walks all alone with a stick in his hand over the dead streets, and every step echoes. We all are sitting in the parlor with the windows covered. All around is just silence. My little sister also feels the scare. Dad instructs us to get down on the ground in case there is any gunfire. From time to time, heavy cannon shots boom, lingering in the silence of the surroundings. Slowly, I leave the parlor and crawl up to the attic, looking out of the square opening through which I can see the highway leading to Sokolka-Bialystok. My gaze reaches to the wide horizon, where heaven and earth unite. There I see Yakob Kozaltshik walking alone through the streets, holding a loaf of bread with salt in one hand, and in his second — his stick.

I shudder all over my body. The surroundings that my eyes can perceive are lifeless. No sign that there are living people here. The shutters are firmly locked. Yakob is walking ahead to the highway with long strides. A gunshot cracks through the air and echoes in the surrounding silence. My mind goes, "Where is he walking to? Why is he risking his life?" I want to shout through the attic opening, "Yakob, Yakob, don't go, you'll be shot!" But he is already too far away from me. He stops next to the well. I turn my gaze back to the highway.

[Page 40]

Small, dark figures are moving on both sides of the highway. Every minute, they become bigger and clearer. There, I see two rows of steel helmets. By now, they already have reached the first houses! With their guns ready, everyone walks forward with slow steps. I turn my eyes to Yakob: He is standing there frozen, in the middle of the street. Now they are already next to him! A shot is fired and I think that he is already lying in his blood. A tremor runs through me. Now, I already see their glances quite clearly, and each step of their nail-studded boots echoes in the dead silence. A loud shout rings out and echoes through the air, "Hände hoch — Hands up!"

Putting the bread and salt aside, Yakob raises his hands high above his head.

"No rifle?"

"No", echoes the 'wholesome' reply from Yakob.

"No Poles in town?"

"No, no soldiers", Yakob replies.

"If we're shot at from a window or a courtyard, you'll be shot, understand?"

A shaky reply, "Yes, sir!" And they walk toward the marketplace. Yakob is going in the middle of the street. The Germans' rifles are pointed at him. Each of their steps reverberates as if they were going over sheet metal. Their murderous eyes check every little corner. They disappear from my field of vision. I look down to the highway. There are small figures to be seen there, but they linger on the spot.

A few minutes later, the heavy footsteps of the Germans can be heard again; they're walking back to the highway from where they had come. They have been the scouts; about 20 people.

For an hour, the previous silence continues.

With each passing minute, the daring in all of us grows, and so everyone tries to keep their heads out of the windows. I decide to go down from the attic. But at the same time I hear that people are already moving on the street — the more audacious ones.

[Page 41]

I go down to the street, despite my mother's plea not to go, because they (the Germans) might come back again. So I go down towards the market, where quite a few people are already standing in a circle. On the side is a box with empty beer bottles. I approach and can hear Yakob, telling what the Germans said to him. "I told them that the city sent me to welcome them!"

All the bystanders burst out laughing, mixed with tears. And Yakob goes on telling us that they asked him how many Jews lived in the city. "And after that they told me: The Jews don't need to be afraid, because the Russians are coming here!"

The words are hanging in the air and everyone asks again, "What? What?"

But he swears by the health of his wife and children!

One looks the other in the eyes, asking silently: "What's wrong? Is Yakob meshugge? The Russians? Why the Russians? Suddenly? They're not even at war with Germany!" "No, Yakob, you didn't listen properly," says one of the Jews standing by.

But in a flash, the news spreads in the shtetl that the Russians are coming. The majority does not believe it. Everyone is interpreting the news in a different way. Above all, it is believed to be only a provocation of the Germans and not necessary to talk about it anymore.

And while we are standing there talking, there is a shout from the other street:

"Yakob, Yakob!"

Yakob is called! We hear the sound of a motorcycle. Quickly, everyone runs apart to their houses. In the market, motorcyclists are rattling, Krinki is once more in fear. The Germans are entering again from the other side. Sitting locked behind the curtained windows, our panic is growing with every minute. After an hour, curious people are to be seen walking around again. I, too, go back out onto the street to the market. Yakob is standing there, telling a group of Jews and Christians what the Germans said. Again, he repeats the previous words, "The Russians are coming!"

[Page 42]

In the meantime, the Germans have issued a command to organize a citizen police force that will be responsible for keeping peace in the shtetl. In addition, the Germans have ordered bread from the bakers and meat from the butchers for the next day. Tomorrow, they will pick it up. After a few hours, the (most) respectable citizens of the shtetl are already walking through the streets, wearing a red-black-yellow ribbon on their left arm, holding a stick in their hand and chasing everyone into their houses. This now is the citizen police! It consists of Yankl Khazer, Borech Tarlovski, Yosl Mostovlyanski, David Lipkes, Alter Ayon, Fishke Listokin, Motke Shteinsafir, Meilekh Zalkind, Mair Alyan, Cheikl and others.

Every now and then, a small vehicle passes by quickly, in which several officers are sitting, with their eyes piercingly examining everyone at whom they are directed. This is how we experienced the first day under German rule — without seeing a single German in the shtetl. Over and over, two motorcyclists use to come into the shtetl, riding through all the streets, only to quickly turn back. The first day remains quiet throughout.

The second day begins with a vigorous movement of vehicles through the shtetl. At 10 o'clock in the morning, twenty Germans on bicycles and an officer enter the shtetl again. Immediately they give the order:

"The whole population has to come promptly to the marketplace! There will be an announcement about the new rules of conduct for the population!"

After just a few minutes, everyone is on the move: Women, men, old people, small children; nobody dares to stay at home. All of us leave our parlors and go to the market.

The Germans are sitting at "Miriam's parlor". One sits on a motorcycle, piercing everyone he looks at with his eyes. The others are laughing at an old Jew with a beard who is standing opposite them, shaking all over.

The citizen policemen are standing three steps away and have their eyes studiously watching for the slightest peep of the Germans.

[Page 43]

A cold, murderous yelling starts from an officer who has just stepped out of his car with a long, coarse cigar between his lips:

"Is everything here yet? You bastards, damn it!"
Continuing with exactly this "melody", he climbs onto the crumbling balcony of "Miriam's Parlor". With puffy eyes, he looks down at the corpse-pale people chattering their teeth. The other (Germans) also go up. After each step, the old balcony trembles. The police, in which the manufacturers of the shtetl are represented, stand in two rows, like soldiers at the oath on the flag of the army.

A wild, murderous scream rings out , startling everyone. Each one holds their breath, and a dead silence lingers in the air above people's heads. We hear:

"Every inhabitant of this shtetl has to keep quiet and obey the orders of the German army. Every inhabitant has to obey what the police (and he points his finger at the citizen police) orders, because their members were selected by the German army. Whoever does not obey their orders, will be executed by us. There must be complete order in the shtetl, so that the Russians will find everything as it should be".

Each of us casts a glance at the other, and we have dialogues with our eyes, "What? What is he talking about?"

We are allowed to be on the street until 6 pm. After six o'clock, there will be a state of war. Everyone is going to their houses now.

Quickly, there is a jostling, a stampede. The remaining Germans, who had been standing next to the officer, are pulling hand grenades from under their belts and hold them in the air, ready to drop them on the people. This causes even more terror and increases the hustle. Woman and old people fall down on the pavement, others fall over them. The Germans go down from the balcony and run after the fleeing, frightened people with red, laughing faces. They push them with their feet, shouting wildly, "Jude, Jude!"

[Page 44]

In a few minutes, the marketplace is deserted, as if no one had just been there. The citizen police strut around like winners. Every one of them holds his head high, shouting, even if it's not necessary: "Everybody into the houses! We are responsible for everyone!"

This is the fifteenth day of the war. No one knows what is happening at the front. The majority has hidden the radios, and so the shtetl is cut off from the outside world. There are no Germans in the shtetl. People come out of their houses because it is not yet six o'clock.

Suddenly, we hear the sound of an airplane, and everyone raises their heads to the sky. The sound becomes clearer and louder with each passing moment. Now we can plainly see a white plane, flying over the shtetl. It rotates a few rounds, and then an unfamiliar sound is to be heard. We can clearly identify a star, a red star on the wing of the plane, which is getting closer and closer to the rooftops. Now it is already above us! We recognize two small faces and two hands, throwing down a pack of papers, which fly apart like white doves, driven by the wind. And there, some slips are already falling over our heads, but the wind is playing its game with us, driving the slips away, and dozens of hands are reaching out to catch them. One falls right over our heads. People jump as high as they can, all hands grab a corner of the same paper, and finally, everyone is left with just a white, written scrap of it. I, too, hold a torn off snippet and look at it. It is inscribed on both sides, but it is not legible. The place is full of people now, and the crowd is growing more with every minute. There, again a sheet of paper is flying, sailing down over dozens of hands. I jump up over the heads of the others and manage to catch it.

I quickly run home. The streets are full of people. No one listens anymore to the screams and the clamor of the just created police. I run into the parlor, my father takes off the leaf with trembling hands, and we all stand around him with open mouths. Everyone wants to gulp in a word even faster. Daddy reads aloud. We hear:

[Page 45]

> "To the citizens of Western Belarus and Western Ukraine: the Polish government has abandoned you lonely and miserable — like sheep without a shepherd. Śmigły-Rydz and Beck[3] have fled abroad. You are citizens of our peoples, and we come to your aid. Our government and our comrade Stalin have ordered the Red Army to cross the borders of Belarus and Ukraine, to guarantee your lives and property.
>
> The People's Commissar for Foreign Affairs of the Soviet Union, V.M. Molotov!"[4]

Joy arises in the shtetl! People run into the streets and fall around each other's necks, with tears of happiness and delight rolling down their cheeks. My brother is dancing with joy. Mom is crying. The little sisters are standing around, not understanding what is going on.

The streets become black with crowds of people. Some say that it is a provocation of the Germans and that we will pay dearly for our joy. People still stand together in groups, reading the same over and over again: the last words of the leaflet. Some read it in Russian, others in Polish. But in both languages, it is the same. The last words, "…guarantee your life and fortune", cause everyone to cry tears of joy.

Translator's footnotes:

1. In Judaism, the invocation of the dead is expressly forbidden. However, there is the idea that one can get in touch with their souls — from Jew to Jew — and thereby bring about a kind of mediation before the Almighty.
2. Yankl Khazer: A nickname. A khazer is a pig (or a coarse, stingy person). Yakob was a broad-shouldered, very strong man, who was called "the Samson from Krynki". We will learn more about Yakob Kozaltshik (there are different spellings of his name), later.
3. Mashall Edward Śmigły-Rydz and Colonel Józef Beck, see https://de.wikipedia.org/wiki/Edward_Rydz-%C5%9Amig%C5%82y#/media/Datei:Marshal_Rydz-Smigly_LOC_hec_27123.jpg and https://commons.wikimedia.org/wiki/File:J%C3%B3zef_beck_1.jpg
4. On September 28, 1939, Vjacheslav M. Molotov signed the German-Soviet Border and Friendship Treaty in the Kremlin, there's to find more here: https://en.wikipedia.org/wiki/German%E2%80%93Soviet_Frontier_Treaty#/media/File:MolotovRibbentropStalin.jpg

---

[Page 46]

Chapter Two

The Russians Are Coming

The streets are black with people whose faces are full with joy. The Germans are not here. The citizen police cannot restore order.

The workers gather in the professional union and decide to organize a demonstration. Everyone is already lulled into a sense of security that the liberators will arrive soon.

Suddenly there is a shouting: "People, go into the houses! The Germans are coming!" And we hear the sound of trucks. Everyone is running, again there is fright everywhere. Two or three trucks appear, with Germans sitting on them, their eyes shining like those of tigers. Everyone flees into a courtyard, the streets are quickly empty. Only the citizen policemen are standing around, pale and scared.

A vehicle stops in the market. A tall, coarse man gets out and casts a piercing glance at the empty surroundings. Screaming around, he calls two policemen to him, who stop three meters in front of him, standing with their arms hanging down like soldiers facing their general.

The German's grumbling is followed by a choppy reply from the police officers:

"Yessir, yessir!"

The German walks to the vehicle and quickly drives off, leaving behind a white cloud of dust that rises above the heads of the police officers.

A few minutes later, everyone already knows what the German officer was talking to the policemen: "No one is allowed to show themselves on the street. There must be peace and order in the shtetl. Anyone who goes out on the street will be shot by the Germans who will soon carry out a check!"

[Page 47]

Lifelessness is in the air. The joy that reigned just a few hours ago has disappeared. The women are crying again, the old people are moaning.

So two days go by and everyone keeps asking themselves whole the time: "Where are our liberators? Where are those who want to protect our lives and assets?" But no one gives an answer.

On the 19th day of the war those who listened to the radio are reporting that fighting is going on near Warsaw; the Red Army has already taken Baranovitsh and Slonim and is now marching towards us. Germany and Russia are not at war with each other. Germany has signed a 10-year pact with Russia.

After the radio listeners' report, everyone gets all aflutter and asks, "How is it possible that Hitler and Stalin, two bitter enemies, have become 'good friends' since Wednesday[1]? What is going on? What has happened in the world?" Everyone asks, but no one knows the answer.

The early morning is cold and foggy, when I look out the window. Black crows are standing in the middle of the road, rummaging through horse droppings. The "Krakra" of hungry black crows echoes as they fly over each other, from tree to ground and back.

The light footsteps of a sleepy Jewish policeman can be heard, who, while walking, keeps his hands buried deep in his pockets and sneezes from time to time. I go out into the street. People crawl out of their houses and gather in groups on the street corners.

The clock shows 7 am. No Germans here. Every now and then, we hear the sound of a flying by airplane, but we can't see it. With each passing minute, more people gather, and everyone keeps asking, "What's to be heard? What will be? And where are the liberators?"

[Page 48]

Suddenly, a man appears riding a bicycle with a red flag hanging on it. He rides straight to the municipality, and curious people run after him. His face is full of joy and his eyes sparkle. He stops next to the pole on which they raise a flag on holidays. From his chest, he takes down a big red flag and unwinds it. People run up to him, asking, "David, what are you doing?"

He answers with a smile on his face, "What are you afraid of? The Russians are coming soon! They are already in Amdur, 30 kilometers from here!"

David — this is a farmer from a village who had the chutzpah to do this — even before anyone knew when and if the Russians would come to us. But with every minute, the number of such daring people are growing, who already put red ribbons on their right arms — and they will become our police! The former citizen policemen were already quietly taking off their ribbons and hiding behind the ovens. Those who are wearing red ribbons now, are mostly workers and peasants. Farmer David who was the first to raise the red flag, has become commander of the workers' militia. Now the streets are crowded with people. Old and young, sick ones with frail bodies — all flood the streets of the shtetl. Everyone is aware that soon the liberators will arrive. I, too, am among those who wear a red band, helping maintain the order. More daring farmers from the surrounding villages are already showing themselves. They all come in holiday attire, with red flowers in the lapels. There we see an old farmer approaching, with a long white beard that he has combed wide apart. He sits on a reddish horse whose neck is draped with red flowers. Everyone walks closer to the old farmer, and in a few minutes a large crowd forms behind him. His eyes are shining with joy, and his old, shriveled face is getting younger every minute. Everyone asks who is that farmer, being so happy?

[Page 49]

After a few minutes we know that this is the old Pretitzki from the village Arkavutch. His son shot a provocateur in Vilnius and was sentenced to death. But thanks to an intervention of the Soviet government, the death penalty was commuted to life imprisonment. And the (old man) is the father of this heroic son who is now in Vilnius prison, waiting for the moment of his liberation.

The whole marketplace is full of people. Girls are standing with bouquets of red flowers and baskets filled with red apples. Their faces are beaming with joy. Quite a few young lads have gone out to the Grodner highway to greet the Red Army. The demonstrators walk down to Grodner Street with red flags. In the roundabout turmoil, one hears a far reverberating, loud noise. The earth vibrates under our feet. With every minute, the sound of tanks becomes louder and louder. People are jostling one against the other. Children are crying to be taken high in the arms. There, in front, we can see large, steel "forts" sliding down the mountain, kicking up dense columns of dust that cover the early potatoes on either side of the highway.

And now, they are already next to us, they already reach the first houses! Red flowers fall on the heads of the soldiers who, gesticulating with their hands, shout that we should make way. Their eyes shine with joy. In the great turmoil, we hear them shouting, "Comrades, we are your brothers and we have come to free you!"

A long "hurrah" bursts from all our hearts. One person wants to drown out the other. The pavement is covered with red flowers and apples. The tanks drive away one after the other and have to slow down their speed, because the large crowd is pushing closer and closer.

A lieutenant gets out of his tank. He walks dressed in leather black pants, a leather jacket and a black leather hat with half "little wheels", like "Kishkes sausage"[2], on it. He asks the people standing around:

[Page 50]

"Folks, disperse, make way, we still have to liberate many towns and villages; many people are still waiting for us!"

His words have an effect and everyone pushes back. The noise swells again, and stones pop out from under the heavy iron chains. With each moment, even more tanks pass through, accompanied by some trucks and motorcycles. People are already hoarse from shouting "hurray" and there is just a lack of flowers; the baskets are also already empty. So again, those flowers are thrown, which have already lain on the dusty pavement. The men from the Red Army throw back from the tank tobacco cigarettes and Russian newspapers. People fall on each other, and each tears off his own piece of the paper.

For an hour already, the air has been filled with the sound of the mighty tanks, and with every passing moment many more are still coming. All of them drive ahead at a fast pace. The paving stones have jumped out of their places and are lying now between the feet of the people.

My brother hangs on to a tank and the two hands of a soldier grab him; already, he is on top of the tank and slides down with his face down inside. (His) two hands wave at us, and he drives away together with the chasing Red Army to Sokolka.

For four hours already, the steel chains roll over the streets of our shtetl. The surroundings are immersed in red flags. Everyone's eyes are shining with joy. The streets and the market do not become empty of people, but, on the contrary: constantly more and more farmers from the surrounding area arrive. Everyone is dressed in holiday attire. On two poles for electric lighting, next to Mair-Cheikl's stone house, is hanging a large banner with Russian inscriptions.

After the tanks have passed, trucks come with soldiers. They wave their hands, shout and jump one on top of the other in joy. Again, flowers and apples are flying over their heads, like a big rain. From 10 o'clock in the morning to 5 o'clock in the evening, the cityscape is dominated by moving tanks, trucks and motorcycles.

[Page 51]

People are all hoarse and tired. The militia walks the streets with red ribbons on their arms. Some are already carrying rifles. The commander of the shtetl is Moyshel — Meishel Stamdler, and that of the militia is David, the farmer who first hung the red flag. On the very first day, there are arrests of Polish magistrate officials and others. They are now sitting in the new prison, which they had built themselves — for themselves!

I also get a rifle and stand guard outside the prison. Every hour, the guard is changed. The Russians themselves are not in the city. From time to time a vehicle drives by — always in the same direction. Now the workers are in power.

That's how two days go by. The stores are still closed, the factories are not yet in operation, and public life as a whole is suspended. On the second day, farmers from neighboring villages are bringing the *'Steigho(i)fer'* [landowner], who was recently appointed mayor by the government. He is bound with barbed wire and shows black spots under his eyes. He is wearing no shoes and just a shirt.

So the former mayor of the shtetl, who used to cause new grief to its residents every day, is now walking across the street, and everyone is looking at him. He is taken to the militia, and there he gets what is coming to him. Staggering, he is led away to prison. The whole population, both Jews and Christians, felt a strong hatred towards this former mayor, who was in power for only one year. But he now has to pay for his sins against everyone.

So five days have passed, and the workers remain in power. On the sixth day, a Russian commandant's office arrives, beginning to impose widespread order.

Immediately, the stores are reopened, the factories resume their activities, and everything is becoming as before. All but a few of the militias have been withdrawn. There are no new regulations. The "power" decrees that everything should be the same People are all hoarse and tired. The way as before. The factory owners should produce again, the factories still belong to them.

[Page 52]

Everyone was amazed that the labor power allowed the same system as before. The answer of the "power" is: "Everything comes in its time!"

And later this pledge will get fulfilled.

Translator's footnotes:

> 1.   On Wednesday, 23.08.1939 the "Non-Aggression Pact" between Germany and the Soviet Union was signed.
> 2.   kishke(s) sausage = stuffed intestine https://en.wikipedia.org/wiki/Kishka_(food)

Chapter Three

Life under Russian Power

The Red Army has occupied the whole of Belarus and Ukraine.

The borders are set between Germany and Russia. The war between Poland and Germany is stopped. Poland is defeated. England and France continue to fight in the war.

A few days later, the reason why the Red Army moved so quickly towards Bialystok, becomes clear to me. The German "power" that occupied Bialystok, had issued an order to its soldiers to empty the city of all goods that could be exported. But the Russian General Staff was informed about this item and ordered to quickly surround the city and to control every German vehicle driving out of the city. The Germans had already loaded a number of trucks with various textile and sewing machines, wool, copper and many fabrics.

For two days, they were surrounded by Russian tanks and could not leave the city, until Ribbentrop, the German Foreign Minister, flew specially to Moscow to negotiate over the matter. After a few days, the Germans — supported by Russians and local Jews and Christians — unloaded everything from the trucks to leave the city with their heads hanging, accompanied by stones thrown at them from all the windows and balconies. They gritted their teeth, clenched their fists, but they could do nothing: In the course of three hours, they had to be on the other side of the city.

[Page 53]

Life in the shtetl and work in the factories is going on as before. Stores are open. The money in circulation is still Polish. One does not notice the slightest difference, yet.

Thus, life flowed in the period of two months. And suddenly, on a cold, rainy early morning, there are posters on the walls, announcing great changes in urban life: "All factories and all shops will be nationalized from today!"

Immediately, new faces appeared in the shtetl — people with files under their arms — who went around the factories according to the order. The factory owners had to leave their factories and homes, immediately. The same happened to the big store keepers. It took three days to nationalize everything. Immediately, workers' committees were created, which co-managed the factories. All the special small factories were merged into one big one, which employed the whole Gabarska Street. All fences were removed so that the workers could march freely across the large yard. "Virian's Yard" has also been nationalized and its land handed over to the farmhands, who become the new owners. The same happened with the "Schalker Forest". All workers had to go back to work in the factories, but no longer for the previous owners. A Russian Jew, named Kroyman, became director of the big factory. Also, a technical director, named Lievit, joined. The former workers were now becoming masters. I also resumed my work in the leather factory and after several weeks, I was appointed master of suede[?]. The surrounding village life also changed immediately. Thus, collective farms have been created, whether the peasants wanted it or not. The discipline was getting stronger every day. A working day lasted from 8 a.m. to 5 p.m. late in the afternoon, and factories worked in three shifts, that is, around the clock, 24 hours a day. Our factory was called "Kozsh-Zavad [leather factory] Number 6" — and was one of the largest factories of Belarus, with a profitable and high-quality production.

[Page 54]

The daily wage of an ordinary worker was 7-8 rubles. Most of the workers, and urban residents in general, were engaged in black market trade, although this was strictly forbidden. Everyone in our family worked in the factory. Me, my oldest brother, my father and my youngest brother. After a few months at work, my father loses two fingers of his right hand and remains unemployed. He, no longer working, receives 300 rubles a month. Nevertheless, my mother also has to work — at the sewing machine. Life becomes more expensive day by day, and it begins to be necessary to stand in long queues to get various goods. And in the queues there are people who can get their living and earnings only by selling purchased goods for ten and fifty times more expensive than the purchase price determined by the government; for such activity one risked 5-6 years in prison. But people used to continue doing so, and every day even more, because a factory worker could no longer give his family enough money to live on. From time to time, workers in the factories or stores received various goods at government prices, about which they were, actually, happy. In general, almost everyone was satisfied, although material life was very deprived. (Finally,) everyone was asking, "Well, what if the German murderers had stayed with us?" And every day, sad news came from the other side, the German, because of the terrible suffering of the Jewish population. Every day, Jews arrived, the "bezshentses" (refugees), who told us what had happened to their families and homes. After a few months, individual factory owners and Polish anti-Semites were sent to Russia. The newly arrived "bezshentses" were also sent away to deep Russia at gun point.

Anyway, we were all happy and satisfied that we did not have to live in mortal fear of what the following time would bring. The next day seemed assured to all of us. We saw, and it was also talked about, how strong was the Red Army guarding the borders. There was no work on Sundays.

[Page 55]

The first winter is over. The war between England-France and Germany is growing stronger with each passing day, and then, breaking news that France has fallen! London is shelled with cannons from the English Channel. But the friendship between Russia and Germany is stable, and everyone is glad that we can continue our quiet life.

Summer 1941

The youth is prepared for military service. Every day after work, there are drill-units. I, too, learn how to hold a rifle. On May 2, four year groups are drafted into military service for 2 years. On May 6, my brother receives a "note" and joins the military. With him goes my cousin Menie Yelenovich, who comes back after 4 weeks with some more Jewish youngsters. No one knows the reason. They bring a taped up letter, and are sent back to the parlors. My brother serves in an army detachment near Kharkov.

A few weeks after my brother's departure, I am sent to Leningrad for training courses. I travel by train through Bialystok, Minsk, Smolensk, Oryol — to Leningrad.

A new world opens up for me as I take the very first step into the Russian city of Leningrad. I register at the given address and start studying 7 hours a day. Time to visit the city I have very little. I get all confused by the great bustle and noise. Worker's life is very hard after all. I use to study 4 hours of practical and 3 hours of theoretical knowledge. The six weeks are quickly over and the time has come, to go back to my little shtetl, Krynki, starting to work as before.

When I return, I encounter major changes in the shtetl. The former militia commander, David, has been arrested. No one knows the reason, everyone says something different. All former factory owners were sent to Siberia together with their families. The director of our factory is a new(ly arrived) Russian Jew — Fridman. After my return from Leningrad on July 15, I meet with lieutenants of the Red Army.

[Page 56]

Everyone is heavily involved with the maneuvers and somewhat concerned about our "neighbors". They all claim that they were good friends with the Germans, but they know very well that "the Jekke" is a bloody enemy of theirs and that he will still wage war with us.

On Sunday, everyone sets out to gather in the Shalker Wood, where the colonel of the city's armored division, who has taken up residence in Virian's yard, will give a speech.

It is the 20th of August. The forest is black with people. It is a very beautiful day, the sun is shining and its rays are fanning between the dense trees. The sky is deep blue. Little birds jump over the pine needles from tree to tree, chirping a sweet song. The air is fragrant, everything around is laughing.

The colonel appears, an old, gray, somewhat hunched forward man. He comes accompanied by several high officers and commissioners. Their faces light up when they take a look at the assembled audience. They hang a map between two young trees and the colonel, with a stick in his hand, approaches and takes the floor.

He speaks quietly, deliberately, choppily. From time to time, a loud cough slips out of his mouth, echoing over everyone's heads. His hand with the stick moves on the big linen map. Here he points to England, there to France, and there he shows the island of Malta and the German-Russian border. And further, pointing with his hand to the territory of the earth that is on fire, he says: "You see that there are two thatched roofs burning around us, and we are right in the middle. If only a single spark spreads to our roof, we will be taken over by the flames•. And more emphatically and with fire in his eyes, he continues to speak: "Therefore, we must all be ready and keep our eyes open".

And his last words are:

> "You workers can work with peace of mind and fulfill the government plan. But we, the Red Army, will protect you from any danger. We stand ready to defend every sliver of earth if it is attacked".

[Page 57]

These were the colonel's last words.

Chapter Four

War between Germany and Russia

Sabbath, June 20. The day is bathed in warm rays of the sun. The air is stuffy. The streets are almost empty. Every now and then someone walks by, fanning his face with a handkerchief. The workers are working as usual. However, the barbershops are full of officers and commissars. All are waiting in line to sit on the shaving chair and get under the hair clippers. Everyone asks, what's going on that there are so many officers in the barbershop in the middle of the Sabbath? And everyone gets shorn clean! The colonel is also among the waiting people and his short gray hair gets shorn smooth.

"What's that?", all passers-by asked each other; but nobody knew an answer.

Finally, in the afternoon, the shtetl already has realized why the military people were all shearing off: Sabbath in the morning, the General Staff of the Red Army had issued the order that every military man, without distinction of rank, must be shorn clean, and therefore all officers were sitting there or standing in line, waiting.

I'm coming from work and there is a happy mood in the living room. Everyone in the family is happy: a letter from my brother has arrived!

While standing and washing myself, a militiaman, Motele , enters and gives me a note: I am to report immediately to the "Voyenkom"[headquarters][1].

I, immediately, go out into the street and meet many familiar comrades who also enter the 'voyenkom' with the same slips of paper.

No one knows why we are called. But as soon as we get inside, we do know! All reservists have been called up for exercises, which will take place in the Shalker Forest.

[Page 58]

Right after that, quite a few lieutenants appear, carrying 10 rifles, grenades and two different types of machine guns.

We, immediately, march off into the forest, and first of all, the chief lieutenant gives a speech on the political situation: Thus, we have to be prepared to hold a rifle in our hands. And his last words to us are:

"Comrades, the more sweat that runs from us now, the less blood will run from us in war!"

The exercises lasted until 12 o'clock at night. Everyone was dead tired. Our legs were shaky. We parted and went home, and immediately fell into our beds.

At 6 o'clock in the morning there is a knock on the door. I open it. Again, it is a militiaman who gives me a new note: At 7 a.m., I have to be in the field!

An order is an order, and one must obey, even if the legs do not want to go through such heavy exercises again, as we did last evening from 6 to 12.

There is already a lot of movement in the streets: Everyone is sleepily walking towards the field. When we, a group of Jews and Christians, arrive at the field, three commanders are already waiting for us, who immediately register who has come. At seven o'clock, on the green, still dew-covered field, several hundred young people are already standing and waiting for their order. This early morning is very beautiful. The sun is already warming, the sky is deep blue and covered with small white spots. The air is fresh and fragrant.

We receive the order from the commander that we should all sit down in the grass. And again, the current situation is pointed out — that's why we have to be prepared and must master the use of rifles and grenades.

We are divided into four groups, each with a commander. Quickly, everyone starts marching. After that, a little bit of running and falling.

[Page 59]

"Stand up! And fall again!", and so it goes many times, until there are heavy drops of sweat on our cheeks, noses and foreheads. Then, throwing grenades follows. All of us already have our shirts stuck to our bodies. And so we go, running, falling, throwing grenades, until 9 am.

Suddenly, our exercises are interrupted by an unknown sound coming from behind the clouds. Everyone jerks their heads up, holding their hands on their foreheads, and we spot a white airplane flying high in the sky above our heads.

We ask each other what kind of aircraft this is, but our commander, immediately, confirms that it is ours, a Russian one, and orders us to continue our exercises.

However, suddenly, we hear a machine-gun salvo, and large clouds of smoke are lingering in the air.

"What is this shooting?" we ask the commander.

He replies angrily that this comes from our maneuvers and starts shouting that we should march on quickly.

But suddenly, we see two Red Army soldiers running in our direction. They are dressed in full war gear. One runs to our commander and stays there for a few minutes. His face is white, his tongue is rising and falling, he is breathing frantically. He talks fast, with choppy words:

"Comrade, it's war!

The commander leaves the place with a jerk and runs along with the others, throwing a few words at us:

"Comrades, be ready! The moment is here to defend our borders!"

And quickly he runs away. At first, we all stand still as if frozen. But quickly a few comrades start to run in the direction of the shtetl, and I also run along. A loud sound of tanks reaches us, and when we arrive at the marketplace, the tanks are already chasing, all one after the other, in the direction of Bialystok. The colonel is standing with a red flag in his hand, his teeth visibly clenched firmly. Each of its limbs moves in a special way.

[Page 60]

He shouts, "Faster, faster, ahead! Ahead!"

And the tanks chase one after the other, leaving behind dense gray clouds of dust that fall on the pale people standing around, who do not even suspect what is going on.

After half an hour, everyone is already informed that Germany has invaded the Soviet Union.

On a pole of the electric lighting, in the middle of the market, is hanging a loudspeaker, around which now have gathered black crowds of people, straining their ears. Meanwhile, we hear a soft, choppy music, but soon, the music is interrupted by a speaker, announcing that Molotov is about to give a speech. After a few minutes, the voice that gives the floor to Molotov, answers again.

We hear a shaky, quiet voice, filled with sadness. The market is black with people. Old and young, women and children — all stand around, their eyes turned to the black "bugle". Everyone likes to be higher than the other to quickly catch the words. We hear:

> "Citizens of the Soviet Union! Men and women! Today, at 3 o'clock in the night, the German fascist bandits attacked our peaceful borders, without any declaration of war. Fascist planes immediately dropped bombs on our peaceful cities, such as Bialystok, Grodno, Minsk, Kiev, Kharkov, Odessa and many others. Our government has mustered all its forces to avoid bloodshed. Our people are ready and determined to defend every sliver of earth until the victory over the bandit fascist army! Our armies have counterattacked on all fronts and have broken through the borders in some places.

[Page 61]

> Citizens and citizens! All to the gun! Everybody has to defend his city and his village! With us is the International Working Class! With us is victory!"

The "Internationale" is heard, and then the loudspeaker is silent. Everyone stops as if frozen, as if their feet were fused to the stones. A deep sigh escapes from each, gets caught in the hot air of the surroundings, now filled with the smell of gasoline and with dust. We hear the roar of an airplane again. The militia yells, "Quick, everyone to their homes!" And suddenly, the siren, which is on the roof of the highest stone house, starts whistling. Its choppy sounds evoke terror in the population. The plane flies two rounds over the shtetl and disappears on the blue-white horizon towards Grodno.

The streets are black with people again. Trucks drive there and back. The Red Army soldiers are disturbed and angry.

There, an order from the headquarters: MOBILIZATION!

Everyone receives a slip of paper and must place themselves next to the headquarters. My age group is also called. A great wailing begins. Women run around screaming: "My husband! My child!" It's the same scenes as a year and a half ago.

At 5 o'clock all the drafted people are already ready to march off. There is great confusion at the headquarters and militia. Everyone is angry and upset. The 1921, 1922 and 1923 cohorts are mobilized to defend our shtetl. Each of us is given a rifle. We are now standing next to the militia, and each of us is already holding something in his hand. We are divided into small groups, each of which is assigned a Red Army soldier who is the commander of the group. We receive orders to go to the Polish church to prevent anything from being looted from it. Our group includes 12 people, among them Jews and Christians. So we go to the Catholic church; the keys are held by our commander. Everyone, including the priest, is strictly forbidden to enter the area around the church. Every two hours the guard is changed, and in that time anyone can go into the city and help at the 'voyenkom' [headquarters].

[Page 62]

The few age groups that were mobilized are led away in closed rows to Gross-Berstavitz, 14 km away from our shtetl. Night has fallen. I have finished my watch and am going back home. The streets are already empty and there is a melancholy mood. Every now and then a few vehicles drive by, their headlights covered. All of them are moving in the same direction, towards the leather factory. I want to know if we will work tomorrow or not. The factory is in operation, its machines roaring. The windows are already covered with black plywood.

I enter the factory. The director, Fridman, and the technologist, Lievit, meet me and give me the order to color all the electric lamps green. So I stay in the factory and start working. The faces of the director and the technologist look upset, their eyes are red. I work until early morning, and all the electric lamps have been already colored. When I had to go to my guard post at 2 o'clock in the night, I was stopped by patrols who demanded special permission from me to be on the street now.

The movement of tanks, trucks, and motorcyclists was much stronger than during the day. Everyone was hastening away in a single direction. The sky is starry, the air is cool, a small wind blows over the warm stones of the pavement, lifting dense clouds of gray dust into the air. The houses are shrouded in blackness, no trace of a light can be seen, everything is shrouded in darkness.

My eyes are sticky with fatigue. I go back to the factory and decide to wait until it gets light so I can go to the changing of the guard.

Meanwhile, I take a nap on the hard work table, placing a bundle of finished leather pieces under my head.

[Page 63]

At dawn, the technologist, Lievit, comes to me and informs me that he must leave the factory and go off to the front, together with the director.

I ask him, "Comrade technologist, what happened? Why are you leaving? Who will continue to work here?"

> "The situation is serious," he answers me, "we must control the front! In some places our front has been broken, the enemy is attacking strongly. We leave the factory and you will continue to work! We will be in telephone communication with you!"

After listening to the technologist's speech, I decide to go out on the street to hear what's going on around us.

It is 8 o'clock in the morning. The workers are already at work, as they are every day. Their faces all look a little somber. I prepare more dyeing and go out to the market. The whole market is crowded with people. Next of the headquarters are several vehicles on which large, thick books from the headquarters archive are loaded. The old colonel is upset. He hastily runs in and out.

Nobody knows what's going on. The militia and the NKVD [People's Commissariat for Internal Affairs] are all in the marketplace; everyone is distracted. A truck arrives and quite a few lieutenants get out of it, asking for directions to the hospital. On a second truck, several wounded lie next to each other, wrapped in blankets. Their faces are chalky white. They are coming from the front — and now, everyone realizes that the front is near! Meanwhile, the trucks that were standing next of the headquarters have left in the direction of Grodno.

The colonel leaves the headquarters, walking towards the market, which is now full of people.

Everyone has their eyes on the colonel. He stops next to a truck that has just arrived. On this truck are lying wounded soldiers. He talks quickly and excitedly with the lieutenant and then walks with quick steps back to the headquarters.

After a few minutes, the colonel is already sitting on a truck, around which many people have gathered.

One of them asks the colonel: "Comrade Colonel, what is heard at the front? What's the situation? What should we do now?"

[Page 64]

He casts an upset glance at the assembled audience and replies: "You must defend your shtetl! Everyone with a rifle in hand, even with a knife! Women and children — everyone must fight for each house! We follow the order to leave the shtetl and go to the front!"

The vehicle moves from the spot. The colonel's eyes fall on everyone, standing around: "Comrades! Be heroes! Defend every sliver!" These are the last words of the colonel, who has now left for the front.

The commander of our group also left the same day, and our group was still active until 8 pm on Monday. But there was no discipline anymore. The director and technologist — had already departed. Now the workers are no longer working, but they guard the factory.

Monday, the Second Day of the War

The whole shtetl is in fear of what is to come. Everyone asks the other: "What happened to the strong Red Army? Where are all the planes?"

From time to time a plane flies by, but a German one. The airspace is already dominated by German planes, which in low flight bombard every tank and every vehicle.

Monday evening, at 10 pm, there is a strong movement of tanks, trucks and pedestrians. All run sweaty, upset and angry. One shouts at the other. The stones of the pavement are jumped out, lying around under the heavy steel tracks of the tanks. The soldiers ask for the way to Minsk. No one stops, everyone just moves forward quickly. A tank has stopped there! Red tongues of fire burst from its 'pipes' and after a few minutes, the flames are already spreading around the market. The fire is getting bigger and bigger. Three Red Army soldiers quickly rush out of the flames and shout to the people who come running: "Run away, run away, artillery rounds are about to crash in!"

[Page 65]

And right after these words, we hear several strong impacts. After half an hour, the fire is extinguished by the municipal fire fighters. But the movement is getting stronger with each passing minute.

That night no one from our parlor slept. Everyone stood at the window and looked into the night, how the tanks were passing by and throwing long tongues of fire into the darkness. So we all stood at the windows until gray streaks appeared in the sky, getting brighter and brighter until it was as bright as day everywhere.

I go out into the street, where people with sleepy eyes ask each other how things will be.

It is already the third day of the war. The militia and the NKVD have finished packing to leave the city.

No one knows where the front is. People, passers-by, coming from the Bialystoker highway, say that the Germans are close, only no one knows where exactly. There comes a truck, loaded with sitting and standing women and small children. These are the women of the Red Army soldiers. With each passing minute, more trucks arrive, all heading quickly in the same direction — to Minsk.

Soldiers run by barefoot, carrying their boots on their shoulders. And there are running pilots who left their planes on fire at the Bialystok airport. The youth of the shtetl gather in the market and divide into groups of 6, which, joining the running army, set off. Together with a few more comrades, I also decide to flee. We agree to meet at the marketplace. Everyone goes to his home to take food for the way.

I come into our parlor. My mother sits on the porch with teary eyes and says to me, "My child, what shall we do now? Just see, how the Red Army is retreating more and more with every passing moment!" "Mom," I say in a trembling voice, "I want to leave together with the Red Army to Minsk!"

[Page 66]

"No my child, you mustn't go, stay with us", my mother replies in a tearful voice, with tears streaming down her pale cheeks. My little sister Manyele[1] is also crying. Her small heart is beating very fast. Her eyes look at me pleading: Don't leave us behind, stay with us!

I go into another room and think: What should I do now? Should I wait until the German murderers come back? But then our fate would be sealed! Shouldn't I better go away with other young comrades and fight against the murderers? I don't want to leave my sick parents alone with the little children — but I don't want to stay with them until the murderers come and kill us all! So what should I do?

I decide, to leave together with the Red Army and the comrades who are waiting for me at the market.

Mom sits on the porch, with Manyele in her arms, and cries. Dad is on the street. My young brother digs a pit as a shelter during air raids.

I quickly go to the kitchen and take some food in a white sack, and with shaky steps I go out the back door, casting a last farewell glance at my mother and little sister. I jump over a fence, and from the neighboring yard I run with quick steps to the market.

Neighbors follow me with their eyes. Women wipe their tears with trembling hands. Finally, our house disappears from my sight, and I arrive at the marketplace, where groups are already standing, ready to leave.

Translator's footnotes:

    1.   "voyenkom" (voyenkomat-военкомат) — means military commissar. However, to concretize the Russian term, the author puts behind it the Yiddish word "shtab" in brackets, which means "headquarters"
    2.   Later, she is called "Sonyele"

[Page 67]

Chapter Five

On the Way

In the market are standing both civilians and military people, most of them with backpacks on their shoulders. The movement of trucks and tanks is getting stronger every minute. I walk with quick steps and arrive next to the NKVD [People's Commissariat for Internal Affairs], where three comrades of mine are already standing and waiting for me. The armory is open to all; anyone who sets out, takes what they want: a rifle, a revolver, grenades. The soldier working at the armory calls everyone from the street in and hands out any weapons that are requested. The four of us go in, and each of us takes a revolver and two grenades to go with it.

The armory man squeezes our hands and wishes us to use the bullets well: each bullet should hit the enemy's head. We are very pleased that we have received weapons, and thus something to fight with. As well as looking at the revolvers and the grenades, our courage to fight grows.

Around us, it is black with people. Mothers accompany their children with tears in their eyes. Deep sighs escape the fathers from the depths of their hearts. I see my father next to me. Sadness is written all over his face. His lips tremble as he speaks the first words to me: "You're going with everyone, too!?"

"Yes, Dad, I'm going with my comrades," I answer.

"Take Peretz with you. Let him go with you and save himself!• my father says.

"All right, I'll take him with me. But it's already late. We still have 50 kilometers to go today!"

[Page 68]
"I'll go and bring him, wait there!", Dad replies.

"Don't tell Mom! She wouldn't be able to stand it!", I yell after Dad, who quickly leaves in the direction of our house.

After 5 minutes, my younger brother, Peretz, is already standing next to me, with a small sack under his arm. I quickly run into the armory and take out a revolver for him.

We take one last look at the crowd standing around us. My dad's next to us. His last words to us are: "Go, go, save your lives!"

We take the first steps of the road toward Wolkowysk-Slonim-Baranavichy-Minsk.

In front of us, we see a white highway; on both sides there are large fields with half-ripe ears of grain.

Behind us, our shtetl disappears from view. We take a last look at its houses and enter a forest.

We hear the echo of an air raid alarm, and above our heads three German planes are flying very low in the direction of our shtetl. A machine gun salvo echoes towards us. These are the projectiles of the planes aimed at the moving trucks and tanks. On the white horizon, black smoke curls, from which large tongues of fire reach up to the sky.

We lie down on the ground and wait until the planes have flown through.

For several minutes, we hear the whistling of the bullets and the loud noises. We are lying in the ditches of the highway. A little further from us, are lying Red Army soldiers who had to leave their trucks and tanks on the highway. A bit away from us, on both sides of the path, there is a dense forest, in which many soldiers are now lying, looking up to the sky to see where the sounds are coming from. In this way, we have lain for half an hour, until it became quiet.

In the surrounding area, white smoke has curled from burning houses, from which we are separating. And just now, we already lose sight of the last little houses. In front of us is a green, white speckled field, which stretches to the dense pine forest.

[Page 69]

We decide to go quickly, not stopping for a single minute, because every moment is precious. We take off our shoes and throw them over our shoulders. With our pants rolled up, we follow the highway into the dense forest.

The road is full of moving trucks and tanks. On the sides, frightened people, civilians and soldiers who have lost their regiments and are now going to look for them. The sun is not stingy to send us its hot rays. The sand and the stones under our feet are burning.

We walk fast, meanwhile driving all those who walk ahead of us. We do not look at each other, each walks with his head bent forward, eyes fixed on his feet; and on his shoulders, tied with a rope, each wears two shoes or boots, plus a white sack on a knotty stick from the forest.

With every minute, all the things we carry with us, become heavier and heavier. One of us is already throwing away his heavy winter coat that his mother gave him, so that "the child, God forbid, should not catch cold on the way".

Still we are the fastest of the pedestrians. Everyone looks at us and says: "go slower, then you will get further!" But we don't listen to their advice. We do what we want and what we think is right. One is pushing the other, shouting, "Ahead, ahead! We still have 100 kilometers to go today!"

The four of us walk the full width of the highway: Me, my brother and two comrades. We mark a path on which we can reach our destination more quickly — and our destination is Minsk!

Because in Minsk, they said, the Russians would be able to maintain a strong resistance — and we would be on the Russian side.

We are already drawing up plans to return to our shtetl and free our parents, and our courage to fight is growing within us with every passing moment.

[Page 70]

We have already walked 20 kilometers, but none of us feels tired. Everyone is shouting, "Faster, faster!"

Suddenly, we hear a voice from the forest: "Comrades, what are you running for? Come, sit down, rest a little!"

We see three people in front of us — on the left side, under a dense green bush — three Russians! They ask us for a piece of bread and a cigarette. We stop and give them bread and some tobacco.

They ask us who we are and where we are going. We sit down next to them in the grass and after a few minutes, we are already friends! They are the Russian pilots who lost their plane at the Bialystok airport, and now they are leaving together with all the fugitives.

They ask us, if we want to come with them, they would lead us to the destination as straight as the crow flies. Each of them has a map, a compass and full backpacks, which now are lying under their heads, in the grass.

We decide to join them. Firstly, we will be more comfortable, and secondly, they know the way well, which does not lead along the highways — where it is very difficult to walk now, because of the frequent air raids and the dense traffic of trucks, tanks and motorcycles.

"Well, comrades, let's set out and get moving!" orders one of the Russians, a lieutenant.

We already know the names of all of them. We are now seven people in total. The lieutenant's name is 'Kuzin'. He gives us a short speech: we should be disciplined and walk as fast as possible. We are to protect and help each other. We have to avoid villages and farmers because the Germans have landed parachutists there, disguised as farmers and soldiers.

> "So, comrades, on the way! We must quickly reach Minsk, and then to Berezina, because there on the river Berezina, the front will line up".

So the lieutenant tells us, and we march right away across the fields where grain and potatoes have been sown. We crawl among the golden ears of corn.

[Page 71]

The path is much more burdensome to walk than the main road, but it is much shorter, and every minute is precious.

We come to a small river that flows silently between the fields and quench our thirst; one drinks from a top, the other directly from the river, with his nose in the water.

The sun is already setting, and a cool breeze brushes our sunburned faces.

"Ahead! Ahead!" shouts the lieutenant from time to time, and the others assist him. Some of us get tired and already drag their feet like heavy blocks. We put our shoes back on because of the sharp stones that prick our feet like needles.

My brother gets tired and asks me to rest a little; but to rest the lieutenant has to give an order, we can't just do that, because the others would not wait for us. And we do not want to stay alone again as before, because we are now somewhere between fields, forest and sky. We do not know where there is a village or a town. But the Russians are also getting tired, and the lieutenant suggests that we sit down and rest for 10 minutes. This is quickly implemented by all — by us Jews even faster, because we were indeed all exhausted. At this point, we notice the consequences of the first 20 kilometers that we had virtually "flown" to show our strength — which we now have already lost.

We are lying among tall ears with ripe grains. The lieutenant takes out the map and the compass, and we immediately know where in the world we are, namely in the vicinity of Slonim. We see the city on the paper and draw a line to bypass it.

The gloom of the night has embraced us like black liquid, blocking our way in its flow. But the luminous pointer of the compass is guiding us through the darkness. We are now walking with slow steps, there is already no more shouting "Forward, faster!"

We leave the grain and enter a large area where potatoes are growing. And after the potatoes, comes a field of oats.

[Page 72]

Here we are in a small, young grove, and every now and then one of us bumps his whole body against a little tree [that is swinging back?], and they both "kiss each other off."

So we walked until a bright, gray streak appeared on the vast, dark horizon, slowly growing wider and wider, pushing away more and more of the surrounding blackness. We reach a new green field where the softness of the earth bothers us from hurrying further at a fast pace.

It's already light, a cool breeze blows by and dissipates somewhere away into the wasteland. We are now marching in single file, one behind the other. The first to go is the lieutenant, the last is me. In front of me is walking a Russian, who turns to me after every few steps.

> "Comrades," the lieutenant warns us, "a swampy area is coming, and everyone must be
> very careful not to sink into the thick mud!"

The sky becomes clearer with each passing minute, and a red streak appears, extending from the bottom to the top.

We go on. Everyone keeps his tired head lowered to the earth. We walk barefoot. The black mud splashes out between our toes and against our pants. We splash each other full of mud. The lieutenant decrees that we should take off our pants and go on half naked, this will make it easier for us to walk over the swampy path that still stretches on for a long time.

Again and again we think that we are already getting out now, into the "dry". Soon we reach the sky that lies over yonder before us, merged with the earth. But heaven plays its little games with us. The closer we get to him, the further he runs away from us!

Just now, one of us puts his foot in a black mud pit and can only pull it out again by summoning up his last reserves of strength.

We hear a loud sound of planes flying over our heads in the direction of Minsk.

The lieutenant orders: "Everybody lie down!"

[Page 73]

We throw ourselves into the swamp, and I get up to my head in the mud. Three planes approach in a row.

They fly very high. We are all lying there with our heads hidden behind each other.

> "Mask the white sacks, or they'll notice us!" the lieutenant exclaims. Everyone reaches for
> their provision sacks and hides them under themselves or in the mud.

The planes have disappeared in the distance and out of our field of vision; their noise is still reverberating in the silence of the surroundings.

We rise, taking our little sacks and shoes on our shoulders. Trickles of mud run down from everything; our faces are sweaty.

But it's essential that we get through the swamps faster and arrive in Minsk to be out of danger. We, who are in between heaven and earth, do not know what is going on around us at the moment. We don't see anyone to ask. Each and every one of us only knows that the sooner we arrive in Minsk, the safer and better it will be for us.

Everyone marches with slow steps, silently. All think only one thing: When will this end? When will we finally get out of the swamp and onto dry ground, so that we can tread firmly and safely again?

But the road is still long and difficult. Many will lose their lives along the way. Others will reach the dry path — and a path of joy and happiness.

"Ahead, ahead, comrades! We must be in Minsk tonight! Tomorrow morning we must already arrive in the Berezine!", the lieutenant is motivating us, already himself with a weak voice. He is also already tired and can barely lift his feet, which have heavy clumps of mud stuck to them that won't fall off.

One comforts the other: Soon we will reach dry ground, then we can rest a little and continue to the marked destination.

I go last and step in where another has already left his footprints. I am walking, so to speak, on a "well-trodden path".

[Page 74]

And just now, I put my foot down and feel it sink, deeper and deeper into the black swamp. I muster all my strength and want to pull it out, but now the second foot has no solid ground under it either and I sink deeper and deeper into the dense, black muck.

My comrades have hurried ahead and have not noticed how I, sinking into the mud, have remained behind alone. Just now I have found myself in the swamp up to above the knees, and now even deeper! With every moment the mud reaches me higher and higher! All my efforts are in vain. I'm already stuck up to my neck. Only now does a desperate cry escape me, "Comrades, save me!" But no one answers my call. Everyone is already far away and I don't even see them anymore. Again, I try to free myself by mustering all my strength alone, but in vain. I'm already stuck up to my chin and now even the liquid, black earth is already creeping into my mouth.

I try to shout one more time, "Comrades, save me, save me!"

I hear the echo of my comrades' voices in the silence of the surroundings.

"Hey, hey, Alyosha, where are you?" — that's the lieutenant and two comrades, who come running to me! They have recognized my situation and quickly have called the other comrades, who have stopped, waiting for the lieutenant.

Now, everyone is already standing next to me, and everyone is trying to pull me out, but in vain. They are also sinking into the depths of the swamp.

"Give me the rubber boat!" shouts the lieutenant.

The boat, which was folded up in one of the backpacks, is spread out next to me. Two comrades have taken the sleeves of four jackets and have tied them together to use as rope. I have held on tightly to the rope, and the comrades have already started to pull.

After pulling hard three more times, accompanied by : "Ra-az, dva-a-a, tri?! [One-two-three]!", I have already lain on the rubber boat, covered all over with mud. They have taken off my clothes, wiping away the muck with a shirt.

[Page 75]

We fold the boat again and continue our way. Now, I'm walking second behind the lieutenant, and all the comrades are laughing and making fun of me for being such a jinx.

The earth begins to get harder under our feet until we reach completely dry ground. Now, we can already march with firm steps. Who cares that we are splattered with mud from head to toe!...

I go in my underpants. I threw away my long pants where I entered the swamp, and that's where they have remained.

We enter a forest and all drop into the grass, dead tired. In this way, we remain lying for a whole two hours. With each of us, the legs are heavy as blocks, and no one wants to be the first to remind that we must march on. The sun is baking and roasting. We are all hungry and thirsty. We grab our "white" sacks, which are now all black from the mud.

We all eat together, but we have nothing to drink. Anyway, no one wants to go out to look for water.

The lieutenant has already stood up, wondering, if we don't want to march on. Some of us have already fallen asleep, but the lieutenant wakes everyone up. Everyone yawns, their sleepy eyes still half closed.

"Well, comrades, let's move on! Now the way will be easier for us," the lieutenant encourages us.

Everyone asks if we can lie down for another minute, but eventually, we have to go.

We stand up. Our feet are heavy and swollen, but we must go on! We have to reach our destination and time is precious.

We do not know what is lurking around us.

We march out (of the forest) with slow steps. The sky is deep blue, the sun is sinking. The evening is getting closer and closer, with every step we take ahead.

[Page 76]

Night has fallen. We have left the forest and come back to a field with high, half-ripe ears of corn, where we have to put on our shoes over our swollen feet for the walk over the stones.

The lieutenant takes a look at the map and the compass and sees that we are already not far from Minsk. All in all, there are still 40 kilometers to go. We have already crossed the old Polish-Russian border and are now marching on Russian soil.

Looking across the wide field, we spot a village with a few scattered cottages on a small mountain. We decide that one of us should go to the village, ask what's going on, and bring water for all of us.

It is the lieutenant who goes to the village. We all remain in the field among the potatoes. After ten minutes he comes back, bringing a full wooden bucket with water. Still far away, he has already waved his hand that we should come to him.

We run up to him and all ask in the same breath: "What's going on?"

"Comrades," he shouts in a trembling voice, "drink the water quickly. We have to get out of here, immediately. The Germans are very close to us!"

"What, Germans?" everyone asks in astonishment.

"Germans, Germans, parachutists!" the lieutenant answers in a quivering voice, "faster, comrades, faster, they are here in this area."

All of us take out our revolvers and put them in our pockets.

My revolver is lying in the little sack. We all wipe the mud off our revolvers and load them with new bullets.

Thus we go on, around us dark gloom. At every snort we hear, we stop with our revolvers drawn.

We reach again a long, open meadow, overgrown with tall green grass. The grass is cold and wet; we put on our shoes again. Those of us whose feet are swollen, just wrap them in rags. And so we march ahead, though very slowly, because we have to be careful. We do not know what is hiding behind our backs.

[Page 77]

The lieutenant informs us about a farmer who told him that this morning there, in the field around the village, parachutists landed, shooting at anyone they met, whether civilians or soldiers. Thus, on the other side of the village, there would already lie many dead civilians and soldiers. Today in the morning, they were suddenly shot at with machine guns from the cornfields.

The lieutenant chooses a swampy path on which we can make our way to Minsk, or somewhere beyond it.

We turn right and walk as the lieutenant leads us. I walk next to the lieutenant and familiarize myself with the map and compass.

The third night is cold. A damp wind whistles around us and we march again across a field where the foot does not meet the smallest piece of solid earth to tread firmly. We are careful and go slowly again, one behind the second.

The earth is swaying like large ice floes in spring, floating on the water.

The lieutenant takes a look at the compass, points with his hand the direction in which we have to go, and shouts again: "Ahead, ahead, comrades! We must reach our destination! Pay no attention to your tired feet! If you go ahead faster, we will achieve the goal we have set for ourselves!"

The lieutenant advises that those who find it too difficult to carry their trousers or coats with them, should just throw everything away so that they can walk more easily. The majority of us follow him right away, dropping anything that is just an unnecessary burden.

"Ahead, ahead," sounds the voice in the darkness of the surroundings. We are all cold and we find it difficult to take the next step. But the inner momentum drives us. Death chases us from behind, tirelessly like a shadow. Everyone knows what to expect when they fall into the hands of the murderers. Thus, nobody feels anymore, how swollen and lame their feet are. Now, nobody has any strength to keep going.

[Page 78]

Only their inner impetus and their fear of the "shadow" that lurks on all sides is driving all ahead, ahead to save their lives.

The path becomes heavier and more dangerous with every step, but we don't stop for anything. Our feet pull us down, we would love to lie in the mud and rest for a minute!

"Ahead," cries the lieutenant, and his eyes gleam like those of a wild cat that is just on the prowl for mice, or else fleeing from a vicious dog. We hold on to each other because we don't want to lose anyone in the gloom of the night. Just now, we think that in the vastness of the night we saw a forest with tall grass where we could sit down, but when we get there, we are disappointed: what we had marked as "forest" is just an open field.

Two of the rearmost comrades become limp and can go no further. But there is not a single piece of dry earth where they could rest and sit down. It is very dangerous, because we are not sure who could suddenly come out of the darkness.

Two strong comrades take the weaker ones on their shoulders and walk with them until they themselves get too tired and have to surrender both of them to others. We don't want to leave any comrade alone in the dark night in the swampy terrain! After all, we promised each other mutual devotion, and we intend to keep that until we've made our way to our destination.

The sky is black. The stars twinkle and show us the way. The glow of the crescent moon shines on us and gives us light in the dark surroundings.

In one corner at the edge of the sky, a large streak appears, growing rapidly in length and width into the surrounding black. The twinkling stars slowly go out, leaving dark gray patches in their place. A cool breeze blows by and penetrates our wet, sweaty bones. Everyone walks silently, no one speaks to the other, even as if there were complete strangers walking. Everyone is deeply immersed in his thoughts and fantasies, which paint us the most beautiful achievements — solid earth under our feet!

[Page 79]

We hear again a soft sound of airplanes, which comes closer and closer, and now, we already see in the deep, foggy clouds whole flocks of flying steel birds, which carry a special charge for healthy, peaceful people: death, instead of bread!

"Faster, ahead, ahead! We have to hide, they will notice us and machine-gun us," the lieutenant yells, waving with his hands and nudging everyone to go faster. The comrades who had stayed behind had already begun to walk a little apart, but now we all begin to walk in long, quick strides. But it is impossible for us to escape the planes, and the lieutenant gives the order to lie down on the wet, muddy grass, because the planes are already very close to us. They are flying in the gray haze, one next to the other, bold and proud, as if the earth already belonged to them. They are carrying a heavy load. In a moment they will spew out pieces of iron, filled with dynamite — and hundreds of people will be dead.

"Oh, where is my plane?" exclaims the youngest pilot, now lying grudgingly next to me, his fists clenched, his eyes fixed far upward at the flying planes.

A second one speaks up: "Soon we will get airplanes, and then we will also swarm out like this in the sky towards Berlin!"

The sound diminishes. We rise and receive a strict order from the lieutenant: "Comrades, quickly forward! It is already getting light. We have to get out of this swampy area faster! According to the map, we are very close to Minsk, so the forest must be coming soon, that big old forest that stretches from Minsk to Bialystok!"

"We are meeting forest, comrades! Run faster, there I see forest!" shouts the lieutenant, who goes ahead, waving towards the rearmost comrades.

[Page 80]

His eyes are full of joy. A large pine forest spreads out in front of us, and now we have already reached the first tree.

In a moment we drop to the ground, over which dry needles and leaves of blueberry bushes are poured. Oh, how good it feels to lie down for a bit, legs up in a tree, so that the blood can distribute itself throughout the body again! The feet are hot and the tips of the toes sting as if needles were pricking them. Everyone falls asleep right away, even before the provision bags are brought out.

When we wake up, there is great commotion and noise around us.

The edge of the forest is occupied and covered by Red Army soldiers, lieutenants and higher officers. Everyone is worried and upset. We see many people without weapons, but others carrying two rifles or machine guns at once while loaded with hand grenades. We stand up. Our legs are swollen and heavy like lead. The lieutenant asks us to muster all the strength we still have and set off for Minsk. We are already no more than 9 kilometers from the city.

The lieutenant not only asks, but also helps each of us up with the words: "Comrades, we have already passed the first hurdle. And with courage and faith in our victory we will achieve everything!"

We begin to take the first steps into the forest. The further and deeper we get into the forest, the more soldiers are around us. Some lie hungry and overtired in the grass and sleep, some lie wounded and with dried lips — and nobody gives them sanitary help. There is no discipline at all anymore. Soldiers no longer follow their commanders, commanders no longer follow their lieutenants, and so it continues all the way up to the colonel.

In front of me walks a young soldier leaning on his rifle. His pants are bloodstained and torn. His face is pale like a dead man. His eyes are deep in their sockets.

I ask him: "Comrade, what about you? Are you wounded?" "I took three bullet holes in my leg, and my comrades were all killed in battle. The Germans are scattered across the length and breadth of Belarusian soil," he says with tears in his eyes and asks me, "don't you have something to smoke, comrade?"

[Page 81]

I hand him some tobacco that was still hiding in my pocket, mixed with pieces of bread.

> "I want to smoke another cigarette and then — die", the wounded soldier tells me as I pour the tobacco from my pocket into his hand.

> "Where is the front, comrade?", I ask him.

> "The front has spread everywhere," he says, "our soldiers are in a bad situation. We have to see if we can get over to Minsk faster, because the Germans may arrive any minute from the air with parachutes."

We are now walking absentmindedly through the forest. Soldiers are lying against every tree with their heads hanging down. There we see a truck where colonels are standing and studying a map. The sun is baking strongly. The sand burns under our feet. We are now walking to a village located on the edge of the forest.

The village is besieged by military of all divisions. One can see Russian infantry, cavalry, tank drivers, pilots and a great deal of Cossacks with their big, hairy tippets, sitting on their small, skinny horses, or lying on the grass with their little horses standing next to them, holding their heads bent low to the ground. The horse, too, feels the danger that is approaching every moment.

In the village, there is a wooden well overgrown with green moss. Above the well hangs a long beam made of oak. Two heavy stones are tied to one end of the beam. At the other end hangs a heavy, wooden bucket. Soldiers and civilians are standing around the fountain. Women with small children in their arms stand at the side with teary eyes, asking to get a little water in a tin can.

[Page 82]

But no one pays attention to the women with their children in their arms. Everyone is busy with himself. Everyone's tongue is burning like hot coals, and everyone wants to cool it as quickly as possible. Soldiers form a line, and now they all stand, one behind the other, looking at the one who holds his head in the bucket and doesn't want to stop drinking or even pull his head away from the bucket again.

We from our group are also all in line, one behind the other. We have to wait a very long time for the bucket to come to us too, because those who go to the bucket without a tin can or a ladle have to push their heads into the bucket together with their hands, and half the water pours out onto their feet. Then there are fierce arguments, and a few times there are also fights and finally even that one shoots at the other with a revolver.

All the soldiers and officers here are angry at one another. Many ugly and indecent words are heard. Even the term "prodatel" (traitor) is used — and after this word there is a heated quarrel and there is no one to separate the quarrelsome people. No one is bothered by what the other is doing.

Four comrades from our group get tired and leave the line. Three remain standing, I am among them. In front of me is a lieutenant who can't keep his mouth shut. He does not stop shouting and ranting.

The lieutenant, a tall, strong young man with a red, sunburned face, wears an unbuttoned shirt as if he had just come from a great sword battle.

"Comrades," he says to the bystanders, "there is no reason for us to fight anymore! We have lost the war. The Germans are already in Minsk. Let's all go into captivity together, because there is no point in fighting any more". Everyone looks around at the lieutenant, who is now speaking to the soldiers.

With each passing moment, more people gather around him. From the sides confirmations are heard, "it is true what the comrade lieutenant is telling us. In fact, it no longer makes sense to fight. It's just unnecessary bloodshed!"

[Page 83]

Hearing that he is getting supporters for his plan, the lieutenant becomes bolder and bolder and now continues to speak:

> "Comrades, let's all go into captivity together. I will lead you all and there we will have enough to eat and drink!"

Among all the gathered soldiers, a younger one stands sideways, and his eyes fix intensely on the lieutenant's face.

Now I see how this small soldier quickly leaves the group and runs with quick steps to the next barn, where several colonels and political commissars are standing. And at the same moment I see this soldier already coming back, behind him two soldiers from the NKVD and a major. They stop next to the gathering of soldiers who listen with open mouths to the words of their "rescuer" who wants to lead them into captivity "where there is a lot to eat and drink"...

The major stops next to the lieutenant.

> "Passport?" he asks the lieutenant in a loud voice. The latter is not embarrassed, but takes out his passport with an implied smile.

> "From which regiment?" the major continues to ask, simultaneously waving his eyes at the two soldiers standing to the lieutenant's right and left.

> "Who is the colonel of your regiment?" the major continues to ask. The lieutenant, who used to have such a red face, has suddenly turned white like a piece of red paper that you smear with white paint.

> "I, I forgot the colonel's name...I don't remember it so well...because...I just came from a big battle, and I forgot everything, Comrade Major!"

The major gives a wave to the two soldiers, and at the same moment the hands of the brazen lieutenant are turned firmly downward, and they immediately take from him his passport and his revolver, which (he) has not stuck in the leather scabbard, but has been stuffed under the passport, as the majority carry these weapons.

Page 84]

A loud shouting can be heard from the lieutenant, who is now being led away with his hands twisted backwards.

Everyone goes after him, like after a funeral. He has been led down the hill to where the barn is located, by which many officers are standing with maps unfolded. They do not pay attention to the incident at all.

The red-faced lieutenant, who has just been so proud, has his shackles removed, and the commissar, who has been standing in the middle of the group studying the maps is approaching now, taking out his revolver. We are hearing a bang that echoes. The bullet hit the head next to the neck, and the tall, strong man has now fallen down like a sawed-off oak. Immediately, a stream of red blood has stained the green grass. The lying lieutenant has given another gasp, which is immediately interrupted by a final death moan.

The commissar, who has done his duty, has ordered two soldiers to take off the dead man's clothes and search everything thoroughly.

A large number of hands are immediately busy with the lieutenant's body. One pulls on a boot, the other on the sleeve of his shirt. In a few seconds, the shot person is already lying in his bloody underwear, and everyone who has stood there gives him a kick with his foot, like kicking a ball that is lying in a large puddle of mud.

The commissar and the major are standing and reading the papers that fall from the pockets (of the clothes) onto the ground. Next to me are two soldiers who feel every seam of the pants. Suddenly there is a scream from a soldier who has felt a piece of hard paper in the rim of the trousers. Immediately, the commissar and the major are running to him, undoing the seam. A piece of folded, thin paper has fallen out. Everyone looks with strained eyes and wants to be the first to read what is written on it. But the major exclaims something and at the same time, he gives a pat on the shoulder to the young soldier who was standing there so quietly before, listening to the lieutenant's "beautiful speech".

[Page 85]

> "Comrades, he was a German spy! A parachutist, who posed as a lieutenant in a Russian
> uniform! Bravo, comrade!" shouts the commissar, holding the paper in his hand.

Everyone has stopped and simply cannot believe that the lieutenant, who spoke Russian as well as a real Muscovite, was actually a German!

We gather again as a group next to a tree, where several soldiers are still lying with swollen feet, and our lieutenant says:

> "Comrades, we have to move on. We are already somewhat rested and now let's go on our
> way again!"

Some soldiers have been sitting next to us, listening to the lieutenant's words.

> "Comrades, where are you going?" asks us one of the soldiers, lying there with his feet
> propped up on a tree.

> "We want to go to Minsk and continue towards the Berezina," our lieutenant answers.

> "How are you going to get through the city? All the roads are closed. The Germans are
> already in Minsk with a strong incursion".

Listening to the soldiers' report, all of us have been sitting frozen.

"We have to wait here in the forest until night falls, then we want to go on the attack and fight our way through the city. Right now we cannot go, because the air is dominated by German planes that fly over our heads, just as soon as we go out into the open field".

"Is that really so, comrade?" the lieutenant asks again, and we all are listening intently to hear what the soldier might answer.

[Page 86]

"Yes, comrades, it's true! We have already tried to go on ourselves, but the field leading to Minsk is already covered with dead soldiers!"

"Comrades, get up! We will go alone and see for ourselves!", the lieutenant says to us, and we are already standing ready on the way. The sun is already sinking. Its evening rays are shining through the dense coniferous branches into the dark forest. Pieces of the sky are peeking out from between the branches.

In the depths of the forest, we all march in a line. The whole path is covered with soldiers. One is sleeping, the other is sitting and looking for something between the seams of his shirt.

"Where are you going, comrades?" we hear the voice of a reclining major beckoning us toward him.

We all go towards him and stop around him.

"We are going through Minsk to the Berezina," the lieutenant answers him.

"Don't you know that the road is blocked off and no one can go any further?" says the major in a cold undertone.

We are silent. One of us glances at the other, and our eyes ask: "What will happen now? Where shall we go now?"

"Lie here, comrades, until you are called, then, when it becomes dark. We want to do everything we can to open a path so that we can get to the front on the other side of the Berezina!"

We have stopped and do not know what to do. To go further is impossible now. We decide to wait until it gets dark and the enemy planes disappear from the sky. Then we want to go out to fight against the few dozens of parachutists.

We sit down next to a "free" tree and take our provision bags, which are almost empty.

In the forest, more and more soldiers and civilians arrive every moment. Everyone remains sitting on the grass and we wait for the moment to go out into battle.

Suddenly, we hear a loud sound of an airplane flying very low over the trees.

[Page 87]

"Put out the fire," we hear officers commanding from all sides to those sitting by the fire.

All are lying, their heads hidden behind the other. One person runs confusedly from tree to tree, not knowing where to lie down and where to find a safe place.

One of the soldiers, who is not far from us, has shot up with his rifle to the plane that was flying overhead. At the same moment, the plane has let out a cloud of white smoke that is hanging over the forest; above our heads!

"Faster, comrades, flee! They are about to shell the forest!" shouts the lieutenant, who is well versed in interpreting the signs of aircraft movements.

We get up and walk bent over, one behind the other, to the village, which is not far from the village.

"Trach, tararach!" Pieces of earth and fiery splinters explode and fly in the air, down to the place from which we have just fled. Again "trach, tararach!", and red, fiery splinters shoot up between the trees and the lying people. We hurry quickly in the direction of the village. Parts of branches fall on us, pieces of earth with grass fall on our heads and get into our eyes. People are screaming. Another artillery round and the people, who have climbed the trees in fright fall down one by one.

There we see parts of roots, earth and torn people. And flying through the air are a hand, a head, a foot, still wriggling in the air.

Now we are in the village. The shooting gets stronger every moment, always coming from the same direction. It is fired from heavy cannons, which the Germans have captured from the Russians.

We are lying in a deep, stone cellar, one on top of the other. One shouts, "Save me, I'm wounded!" but no one looks around for him. Everyone is lying in confusion with their bodies twisted. Every single limb is trembling.

[Page 88]

All of our group are here. No one has stayed in the forest. The shooting is continuing. Right now, an artillery round explodes in the village! A shout goes up, "help, help!"

The village is on fire. The women who are among us are crying and wringing their hands.

"No one leaves the cellar!" shouts a colonel lying by the window. His face is pale, his hands are shaking.

The shooting dies down, but no one wants to leave the basement. The village is still on fire; the fire is spreading more with every passing moment. There are large cloud fields in the sky. Bundles of straw shoot up to the sky and immediately fall onto a second thatched roof, from which large tongues of fire are already blazing toward the sky.

The shooting has stopped. One by one we leave the cellar. The whole village is now on fire. We hear the cries of burning cows and sheep, which are mixed with the cries coming from the forest — from the wounded soldiers and civilians.

We walk back to the forest; no one puts out the fire. The farmers from the village who have run out of the burning houses are now confusedly moving around, not knowing what to do first.

There is no water. The only well is now surrounded by great flames and no one can get to it. The forest is covered with uprooted trees and looks like a plowed field. People are swathed under roots and branches. Some are lying quite still like pieces of wood. All that can be heard is a crying scream, intermixed with tears and pain:

> "Comrades, save me, save me!" — But no one comes to help. We don't know which one to go to first. From under every tree the same shouting can be heard, everyone is calling us to them.

The night is fallen. We set about pulling the wounded out from between the branches. Others lie buried under the earth, still gasping softly. The colonel, who had been in the cellar with us, walks among the uprooted trees, revolver in hand, and shoots the soldiers who have their hands and feet torn off, or even their stomachs ripped open. His eyes glisten moistly, and the hand in which he holds the revolver trembles after each shot that hits the wounded man's temple. The lightly wounded are pulled out and placed to the side. Several nurses are standing there, not knowing whom to help first.

[Page 89]

Every moment, more and more soldiers and civilians arrive, and the rescue operations intensify. Our group is now scattered throughout the forest, and everyone is working beyond their strength. We do not feel the pain in our feet, which are still swollen from the long trek.

Among the people, a colonel rides a black horse and give commands to everyone what to do. The dead, and those shot by the colonel, remain in their places. Everyone is very busy carrying out the wounded who can still be helped.

It's getting darker and darker now. We carry the wounded and have to walk with every step over the fallen trees and the dead.

Several trucks have arrived on which we load the wounded. After two hours of hard work, we have pulled all the wounded out of the branches and have loaded them onto the trucks, which have now left — to who knows where.

The colonel on the horse rides around shouting something to everyone. We are to gather in a group.

The forest is again black with soldiers and civilians, new ones keep pouring in, but all are apathetic and upset. The same mood prevails among all of us: "Lost, defeated!"

Quite a few tanks appear, stopping between the trees that have been torn out. It's getting pitch black. We no longer see each other, but we are not allowed to make a fire. In the darkness, we hear only screams. Everyone gathers in one place to form a group. Anyone who resists or disobeys the order, will be shot on the spot. And it no longer impresses anyone that on the earth, under our feet, people are lying like pieces of wood. A few soldiers are still standing by some of the dead, pulling off their boots and searching in all their pockets for tobacco or anything else.

[Page 90]

The colonel, who had been riding around on his horse, now stops in the middle of the crowd:

> "Comrades, we must prepare for the attack," he says, now standing with his feet on the horse as he speaks to the soldiers.

Half an hour later, thousands of soldiers are ready to attack. There are two or three tanks in front. The Lieutenants and officers line people up side by side, each with a rifle or grenade in hand. The colonel has been riding ahead on his horse, with a glistening sword in his hand, reflecting a light into the surrounding darkness.

I and my group are also standing next to each other, not far from the tanks, which are already noisy and ready to go. The sky is starry and the crescent moon smiles down. The forest is fragrant, a cool wind blows across your face. It is quiet, nly the sound of the tanks can be heard.

> "Comrades, be ready! For our fatherland, ahead, ahead!" exclaims the colonel, who has already ridden ahead first.

The whole crowd has started to move. Everyone has the grenades and guns ready.

Now we are already next to the first houses of Minsk! All around is silence. In long steps we go forward to the city.

Suddenly, from both sides of the main road and the field, a barrage of machine-gun fire and a hail of grenades hit the marching crowd. We throw back with our grenades. Under a flurry of gunfire from all sides, soldiers fall at our feet like flies.

We run ahead. Now we are already in the city, but we are being shot at from every house!

[Page 91]

The battle is getting stronger. Red fires are flickering in the surrounding darkness. There! A bullet hits our lieutenant in the chest! He falls over backwards. People run over him and hurry on. The hail of fire from all sides becomes more and more intense. People lie on top of each other. Yells are ringing out, "Ura, Ura, ahead!"

A shell hits not far from me, and a splinter hits me in my left leg. I fall to the ground and feel myself getting hot. I feel the wound with my hand and feel weakness and pain in my body. I want to get up again, but in vain. The remaining soldiers run back to the forest. Still more fire everywhere. I can still hear cries of wounded lying next to me.

With my hand, I squeeze the iron splinter, which has not stuck deep into my leg. A sharp pain under my heart runs through me. I hit the ground with my whole body, and then I don't know what's happening to me.

Chapter Six

In Captivity

When I have opened my eyes, it has been already light. Soldiers and civilians were lying around me, all wounded, one lighter, the other heavier. My whole body is shivering with cold. I feel severe pain in my leg. I tear a piece of linen off my shirt and tie it around the wound. I squeeze out a piece of splinter, wipe the blood with my shirt and wrap it around my leg.

I want to rise, exerting all my strength, but I cannot. My feet are swollen, and after every movement the pain radiates to below my heart, and my eyes go black.

I hear the noise of trucks that are about to drive up to the people lying on the ground.

Russian paramedics are standing around the trucks. And suddenly I see Germans! The Germans are standing there with their rifles pointed at the medics, and their murderous eyes are glistening in all directions. I can hear them yelling:

[Page 92]

"Faster, damn pigs!" And the paramedics drag the wounded onto the trucks and drive away.

The Germans stop around us, rifles pointed at us.

I exert the last of my strength and want to get up, but every effort is in vain. I look for my revolver and my grenades, but nothing is left. Soldiers are still lying around me, each one groaning deeply from time to time; one is lying there completely still like a log.

The trucks return, and now they are already next to me. Two paramedics come running, put me on a stretcher and carry me onto the truck. One of them stays next to me, wraps a bandage over the wound, washes off the blood and puts on some more gauze.

We have been taken to an open field between two forests. The grass is wet. Germans with machine guns are standing around — every two meters a German. The whole field is occupied by soldiers and civilians. Not all of them are wounded. Many are lying broken and despondent on the grass.

Soldiers lie around me, their eyes deep in their sockets, their faces yellow, each looking as if he had already died.

I don't know where my comrades are, where is my brother, where are all of them? I search among the crowds of soldiers, but I can't find anyone. Every soldier is despondent, depressed. No one talks to the other. Each is lying on the grass with his face to the ground, absorbed in his thoughts.

The whole territory that my eyes can see is full of soldiers. Some sit around a fire where paper and rags burn. I unwrap my bandages and look at my wound, which is still bleeding. My neighbor advises me that I should put "green leaves" (chicory?) on it, then the wound will heal quickly, because it is not deep. He brings me several leaves and bandages the wound. I feel the wound cooling down that was burning like fire before.

[Page 93]

A truck is arriving, on which several shot Russian horses are lying, from which a smell emanates already from a distance. The horses are now lying on the grass, and the Germans order to eat them. A few dozen Russians are going for them right away with knives, cutting off pieces of the horses.

Soon, they roast pieces of meat on the fire and eat them half-raw.

The first day is over.

The night is cold, a rain drizzles and we lie under the open sky.

On the second day, very early, several trucks with Germans arrive, and next to them stands a young man dressed in black, holding a folder in his hand.

A German speaks to him, and soon you hear whistling and shouting for everyone to gather in one place.

I already feel significantly better than yesterday. The leaves have helped me a lot, I already have no more pain. I exert all my strength and try to stand up. It works! I can already stand and take a step forward, but not a firm one, like with my healthy leg.

I go closer to the trucks, where now almost the whole camp is already standing. The place where we have been was a collection camp, and from there people have been taken to other camps.

The man in civilian clothes is now standing on the truck and speaking to the prisoners. His first words are:

"All Jews should line up separately, Russians too, Tatars too, Uzbeks too," and so on.

Immediately, there is pushing and falling. One steps on the other. There are shouts: "Russians — here!", "Tatars — here and there!"

And there are several dozen Jews standing there shouting: "Jews — here!"

What should I do now? Should I go to the group of Jews? No, I decide, I will not go to the Jews. I know only too well what the murderer will do to them. When you are among the Jews, there is danger. I decide to stand among the Tatars, who are similar to the Jews and also circumcised.

[Page 94]

I am already standing in the back row, between the Tatars. No one is paying attention to me. Everyone is only busy with himself. I see two tall Germans standing around and their intoxicated eyes sparkle at the groups, which stand apart from each other.

Right now, their murderous gaze fall on me.

They go from group to group , looking at everyone from head to toe. Now they are with the Jewish group. It gives me a stab in my heart. A murderous voice is heard, spat out like cauterized pieces of lead:

"All Jews on the trucks!"

One after the other, the Jewish soldiers, officers, commissars and many civilian elderly people run, driven by the Germans, who beat the heads and backs of the refugees with their rifle butts.

My last glance falls on the remaining Jewish comrades, who are now being deported to who knows where.

Immediately after that, the same trucks come again, and now the murderers shout in German, and the man with the black suit in Russian:

"All officers from the First Lieutenant to the colonel, have to come out of the group! All political commissars are to come forward as well!"

A few dozen men came out. Among them the colonel, who had been on horseback and was the first to enter the battle.

Immediately, another order follows: "Everyone on the trucks!", and they drive off in an unknown direction, leaving behind clouds of dust, swirling up from the wheels. The trucks disappear from our view towards the dense pine forest.

Another day has passed.

[Page 95]

I feel a strong hunger and thirst. I have not eaten for three days. My lips are dried up and cracked. The Russians dig in the earth with spoons and draw out a little dirty water. But to dig a whole hole, they do not manage.

I already feel much better than before. The pain is gone. I change the green leaves on the wound every hour. There are enough of them in the field.

I see a Kyrgyz, sitting and frying pieces of meat, which are impaled on a long, rusted wire. He pulls out a piece of white meat from his pocket, and places it in the fire.

My hunger grows even more when I see the Kyrgyz with the watery little eyes take pieces of roasted meat and put them in his provision bag.

"Comrade, give me a piece of meat! I haven't eaten for three days," I say to the Kyrgyz.

He gives me a look with his small eyes and then answers nasally: "Go and bring me paper or wood, and I will give you a piece of meat!" I have jumped up, keeping one foot raised a little, and have searched around and between people, pieces of paper, rags, and old, torn shoes.

After I have brought him all this, he has torn off a piece of black meat, which is only a little burnt on the surface, but inside red and hard as bone. But I accept it, and with hungry teeth I tear off pieces of raw meat.

"Well, did you like it?" the Kirghiz asks me.

"Yes, certainly, now everything tastes good!", I answer.

"If you like it, I'll give you another piece!" he tells me. I accept it and hide it for later.

"Comrade, what kind of meat is this? From a horse or a cow?" I ask him.

"It's human flesh," he answers me with a smile.

"What? Human meat?", I ask him again, and immediately spit the bite out of my mouth, which is already the last of the first piece.

[Page 96]

"Yes, yes, comrade, this is human flesh. I cut that from the dead lying there."

I stand still as if frozen. I have eaten human flesh! I want to spit it all out again, rip it out of my stomach along with the intestines! "But is that really true, comrade? Is it really human flesh?", I ask again, thinking that he was just making a fool of me.

"Yes, it's human flesh," he repeats, still laughing at me for being so startled and turning pale as lime.

"Come on, I want to show you where I cut this off".

We approached the dead, who were lying one on top of the other in the middle of the field, and now I see the Kyrgyz shouting something to me and pointing to a foot with his hand: "From this Polish woman I pulled off a piece of soft flesh!" My eyes go black as I watch:

The Kyrgyz is back on the dead, cutting off pieces of flesh from a second soldier.

I fell on the grass with my face to the ground, and great tears poured out of my eyes onto the green grass.

> "Today they cut pieces of meat from a comrade, and tomorrow from me! No, I don't want to stay here anymore. I can't stand the man-eaters and the murderous faces of the drunken Germans anymore. I must find a way out, do everything to escape. Either fall from a bullet or be free!"

[Page 97]

Chapter Seven

The Escape

For six days already, I have been in the same field camp. Everyone is now allotted 100 grams of bread a day and a liter of water mixed with black flour.

I can already stand well on my feet. The wound is getting better every day. The man who stood with the Germans and spoke to the prisoners in Russian is in the camp all day. His face has Jewish features. I decide to make his acquaintance and actually have stopped him the same day, asking him for a piece of bread. He has given me a piece of bread and turns back to his work. Later, already towards evening, he has met me next to the kitchen. He has stopped me, asking if I would like a piece of bread. I have taken a piece of bread from him and we have both talked to each other.

"Comrade, you must be very careful! I know who you are," he tells me. "I, too, am a Jew, I'm from Minsk. My family is in the city, and here I work as an interpreter."

I have turned pale when I hear his words that he has realized and knows that I am a Jew.

"You don't have to be afraid of me. I will not betray you. I will help you with whatever I can".

I'm not saying anything. My teeth are chattering. What will happen when I am handed over? I ask him with tears in my eyes: "Where have the trucks been taken with all the Jews?"

He looks around and answers me: "They are not alive anymore. They were all shot in the forest".

I have known in advance what awaits the one who puts himself as a Jew into German murderous hands.

[Page 98]

> "Comrade, if you want, I have a good job for you, where you will get so much bread every day until you are full".

"What kind of work is that?", I ask, making sure not to be overheard what we are talking about.

"I will give you a bag of flour every day, and you will go with me to our house. My parents, sisters and brothers are starving, and I cannot carry anything out alone".

"Well, what about the guard?", I ask him, thinking he's playing me for a fool.

"The guard — I've already taken care of that. I have already arranged with a guard that he will receive something from me and I will take something from the kitchen every day, but I alone cannot carry it. Besides, I have to have a person from the camp with me for whom I am responsible.[1] If you want, you can be that person, only you must remember that I am responsible for you!"

"Yes, and if I am seized, what shall I say?"

"No one will seize you. I have also already made an arrangement with the officer. It's just that I'm not supposed to carry (the sack) myself."

"I'm going to get bread for this?"

"Yes, you will receive bread, and I will also give you tobacco."

"Ok, I will go," I answer.

We agree that in half an hour, he will carry out to me a bag of flour and sugar. We are three kilometers from the city.

Yes, I will go — and see to find a way, not to come back. The half hour is over and the interpreter comes to meet me with a paper cement sack filled with flour.

"Well, comrade, you take this sack now, walking behind me. And all will be well!"

I walk with the sack on my shoulder and my legs buckle. And already, I fall down onto the way. The interpreter walks thirty meters ahead of me. Right now he has already stopped next to the German who is standing on guard by the machine gun. I take smaller steps until I see that I am being beckoned to go forward.

[Page 99]

And there, I am standing next to the piercing eyes that are examining me from head to toe. I pretend that I am not even there. I am already above the bearing line, ("Lager-Linie") walking on a free field! A long, narrow path is lying before me. The interpreter turns every minute after me and waves with his hand that I may follow him faster. But in the way I have to walk, I can't do so. My legs are weakened and the wound, from which blood is still running, is large.

Now we are already between the first houses of Minsk. The streets are empty, as if nobody is living there. Everywhere is dead silence. Only the reverberation of fast passing vehicles can be heard.

We are walking in a narrow alley. A hungry dog walks by and stares at me with its eyes. The interpreter is thirty meters in front of me.

I decide to put the sack down and hurry into the first courtyard. But there, he just looks at me and waves, that I should go on.

I put the sack down on the ground and quickly run with my last strength into the opposite courtyard. I jump over the fence and find myself in a large garden. It is quiet around me. I don't know whether the interpreter has already seen that I have fled.

I'm lying on the lawn of the garden for a while. My heart is beating wildly — it's about to jump out. Sweat runs down my entire body. I quickly run on one leg after having felt a strong pain in my injured leg.

Through an open window, I enter a stone basement. Now, I am already lying on the stone floor of the cellar. It is dark. My heart is racing, and with every rustle I think that I will be taken back to the camp and left to death — because the camp also means certain death, only a longer one, by starvation.

Translator's footnote:

1.   I think, in the sense of having the authority to give instructions.

[Page 100]

Chapter Eight

In the Woods

I stayed in the basement all night. Big mice jumped on my feet and I did not sleep all night. When I calmed down a bit, it went through my mind whether I am really free. Various images appeared before my eyes: There I see my comrades and my brother, being on the other side of Berezina and preparing to go into battle to liberate our families languishing under the murderous bondage. It sent shivers down my spine, when I thought of the little Kyrgyz man, cutting off human flesh with his dull, rusty knife and having his pockets full of roasted people's flesh. People who were still among the living yesterday. People who had gone to fight for freedom and had fallen as heroes in battle. I also ate from that meat. There are still pieces of undigested human flesh in my stomach. A shudder goes through my body. I spit out and continuously clean my tongue — in case a piece of human flesh still has remained there. I am lying on the wet cement, and my eyes are turned to the small open window, from which a thin stripe of gray light comes in and falls beside me. My pants are wet and stained with blood. My jacket is torn. First, I must see to acquire clothes, so that I can leave here. My plan, which I have worked out, lying on the cement floor, is:

I must escape to the forest, and there I will be free as a bird. There are weapons in the forest, and with a weapon I will get everything and feel bolder and braver.

[Page 101]

The large stripe becomes brighter and brighter. It is already daytime. The street is wrapped in a dead silence. The last stars go out. A rooster has crowed — and soon a second. I get up and try to go to the window. My gaze falls on the garden, which is covered with dew.

Looking around, I see black clothes hanging in a corner, on the wall from the basement, on which the stripe of light now falls through the window.

Yes, clothes! Clothing from a railroad worker with brass buttons. Everything is present: Pants, a shirt and a coat; a hat lies on the ground. The coat is a little smeared by the white lime of the wall. I clean it and dress like a railroad worker.

Now I decide that when it gets later, about 8 o'clock in the morning, I will go away from here towards the station, to which the forest is very close. I am already ready to go out, but my shoes are torn and very dirty. There is nothing available with which I can clean them. I rub the mud off with my discarded pants. Now, I go to the window and take a look at the garden. All around it is quiet; from the street only moving trucks can be heard. From the position of the sun I conclude that it is already about eight o'clock in the morning. Now is the right time to go out. It will not be noticeable when I go to the railroad.

I am already standing in the garden, on the other side of the window. One jump over the fence, and I'm already on the street. It is silent. Several old women walk around, their heads covered with headscarves, whispering among themselves. I'm about to leave, my gaze turned to the front. Now I have come to the wide road that leads to the railroad.

[Page 102]

Several railroad workers walk with fast steps in the same direction as me. Nobody pays attention to me. I take long steps. I don't feel the sick leg at all. There, I already see the train station, and on its left the forest, to which my gaze is turned. I want to get into his arms as quickly as possible, because then I'll be saved. I turn left, leaving the train station to my side. Several more quick steps, and I have reached the forest! I walk between the tall pines. The path is littered with rifles. Trucks are lying with their wheels up, and around them are empty and full barrels of gasoline, empty and full boxes of ammunition. There is a tank with a thin copper wire around it. No one is coming toward me. The forest is deserted; only the sweet song of a bird and the murmur of the trees can be heard.

Where should I go? In which direction? I do not know. I go where the eyes lead me, somewhere further away from the city and deeper into the forest. I know that the forest is very large. It stretches three hundred kilometers from Minsk to Bialystok. So I have walked for two hours, until I feel a strong pain in my leg and an increasing hunger. I have not eaten for a second day, already. Now I feel weakened and decide to look for an opaque place where I can hide and stay until tomorrow. Then I'll see what to do next. When I opened my eyes, it was already dark around me. The forest instilled fear in me. With every rustle of the branches, I thought that someone was approaching me.

All night, I was sitting in one place. The cold crept into my bones and I could not fall asleep. Various images came to my mind as I sat leaning against a tree and letting my eyes wander into the darkness around me.

The night has seemed so long! I already was thinking that it would last for all eternity, and I would sit leaning against the tree forever. I don't know what time it is because I don't have a watch and the sun is not visible now. During the day, I estimate the time according to the position of the sun. A gray stripe stretched across the forest, and with each minute it became brighter until I could already see the surroundings.

[Page 103]

Birds have woken up from sleep, dancing and singing happily, flying from branch to branch. There, I see a squirrel jumping from tree to tree, squeaking to a second one that is on the opposite tree.

Hunger has overwhelmed me now, in the early morning forest air, and I have seen black streaks before my eyes.

Bread. A piece of bread, that is my only request. I want to get up, but the legs are weakened, and in my head, everything is turning. Everything is spinning before my eyes. With each passing moment , I'm feeling worse and worse. Now, I am going to faint, and soon I will perish. No! Don't despair! Get up! Get up!

I talk to myself, giving myself courage. With my last strength, I get up and stand on my legs, which are wobbling, not being able to hold my body. It pulls me down to the earth. I'm already falling, but (quickly) take another step. (Better, to) rest a little on the thrown apart boxes. I sit down on a box and a cold sweat is gripping my whole body.

A bird has flown down and stands in front of me.

"Oh bird, oh bird, bring me a piece of bread," I murmur to the bird, which has noticed me and has disappeared — back into the dense foliage.

Not far from me, there is a large, broken box, next to which are lying small, tinny cans. I lie down on the grass and crawl with my whole body forward to the box! Oh, maybe, maybe there is something there to eat, to satisfy hunger, to stay alive!

Just now, I am next to the box. I take one of the cans in my hand, on which is written in Russian, "meat". And there, an open can is lying! I tear off pieces of meat with my fingernails and stuff them into my mouth with both hands.

After I have eaten the first can, I have lain on the grass, my eyes turning to the piece of blue that shows itself between the branches. I feel better and the hunger is satisfied. I can get up already. Now, I have to get a gun. A rifle or a revolver, to defend myself in case they try to catch me.

[Page 104]

Guns and grenades are lying around every tree, but all are without locks (bolts?)[1]. The locks had been taken out in time by the Russians. I take a machine gun[1] in my hand , thinking: This will be my comrade, but where can I get a lock? A lot of bullets are scattered in the forest, but the main thing is missing — a lock!

I decide to go in the direction of Baranovitsh (Baranavichy). But I'm going to walk only at night; during the day, I would better lie well hidden and sleep.

On the third day, next to a gasoline tank, I found a dead Russian soldier sitting there, holding the "cog" (1a) in his hand, with a deep hole in his chest. Next to him is a machine gun and a lot of bullets. First, I took the machine gun and quickly walked away between the dense trees.

Now, I am already more jòyful and I feel bolder, holding the rifle with which I will defend myself and fight for my survival. I have thoroughly cleaned the lock and have inserted a full magazine of bullets. I have also filled my pockets with bullets. In a military sack, I've packed several cans of meat. Now I am full, having in my hand a comrade, who gives me strength to live and fight. I go to find a well-hidden place where I can sleep.

Already in the evening, I have woken up. Every time I take a step, I fall down with my whole body on a tree, hitting my nose. The sky is covered with stars. A cool wind is moving the branches and leaves are falling to the earth.

I walk and feel bolder and braver now. My only goal is, to find a group of partisans and fight together with them. It is the third night that I am in the forest. But now, the darkness no longer frightens me. I feel braver and bolder. With every rustle I hear, I already have the machine gun ready, with my finger on the trigger.

In the same early morning, I see a startled rabbit hobbling by. Immediately, I have taken the machine gun, aiming and hitting it. The rabbit was lying there with a torn belly.

[Page 105]

This was the first shot in my life that I fired at a living creature.

So, I was walking slowly ahead through the forest, and when I noticed a beaten path or a path where horses had been walking with wagons, I quickly moved away from it. My "path" only led along between dense trees where there was no path or trail.

I lie hidden during the day and march ahead during the nights. On the sixth day, I found a dead Russian soldier, who was already black as a "glovnye"[2] and from whom a strong smell emanated. I approached him, holding my hand over my nose. Next to the soldier, there has been a piece of moldy bread with yellow flies crawling on it.

First, I took the bread and then started searching in the pockets of the dead soldier. I was looking for fire and tobacco. I found a lighter, but its gasoline had already dried up. I pulled off his boots, which came off his feet with great resistance. Only after fierce efforts, I managed to pull them off. I left my tattered shoes next to the dead soldier. His boots fitted me well.

Now, I became warmer on my feet. I also found a blanket in the forest. And all this was my current inventory. Henceforth, my goal was to obtain gasoline so that I could start a fire, if it was possible (safe).

You only could set a fire when it was very foggy so that the smoke was not visible. Foggy mornings had been very frequent, and there was no lack of and wood and paper. Just the main thing was missing, fire! I already have a lighter, but I still had to get gasoline.

The next early morning, I found a barrel of gasoline, of which I poured a bit into a military bottle, which I also found that morning.

[Page 106]

The whole path was covered with various military accessories, which had been very useful to me. I found tobacco and paper and in the time when I would not sleep, I used to smoke and clean my "comrade", which I guarded like gold.

I often used to shoot birds and roast them on the fire, and then, with a full belly, I went to sleep. I usually found bottled water, or I drank rainwater. At times, the thirst has been so great that I tend to stand there with my mouth open when there is even a little rain — but with the result that the few drops of water tend to make me even thirstier. I also packed a helmet, which served me as a pot for cooking. I usually found snails and frogs in a stream. These I used to fry or to eat raw. Bread, on the other hand, I had very little, my only food was meat. I did not see any potatoes.

So I became accustomed to solitude and almost believed that I had been among birds in the forest all my life, separated from people, from towns and villages.

Once, after three weeks of living in the forest, I left very early in the morning to look for water. My tongue seemed to me like a wooden board, and it had been several days that I had run out of water and no rain had fallen.

Suddenly, I noticed an open field where grain was sown. I was trembling all over: "That means I'm close to a village and need to leave the place quickly!"

But the thought that I might find water on the other side tempted me to go through the tall grain.

The field was among the woods.

A strong smell of rotten horse is penetrating my nose. I enter the cornfield and notice a large, white parachute, close to which a German is lying, with his face to the sun. He is black as coal and his face is covered with yellow flies. Next to him lies a machine gun and two grenades hang from his belt. Also, A revolver hangs at his side. I hold my nose with my hand. The smell is so strong that I feel nauseous from the first minute.

[Page 107]

His body is swollen. He looks as if there were a pile of stone coal lying there. On one hand, which is stretched almost completely under the body, I discover a watch. The bracelet has dug deep into the flesh. I try to take it off, but I can't. The flesh around the leather strip is rotten. I took the revolver off his belt and stuffed the cog (of the wheel lock) under his watch. That's when it fell off the leather strap. On the second hand, he had a large compass, the sight of which gave me a big smile. I quickly took off the compass and ran back into the forest with joy.

This was the first German I had seen lying with his head shot through. This made me very satisfied and happy. First, because I saw a German, lying in a rotten state with big flies eating him with relish , and secondly, because I got a good revolver and a compass with a watch. The clock and the compass worked well. I set the time according to the sun. I already had a map and now I knew exactly, where I was and where to go next. My joy at winning was so great that I even forgot about my thirst.

Now I had found a good place between young, dense trees. I hid myself well with branches and lay down to study the map with the help of the compass. According to my calculation, I was in the area between Slonim and Baranovitsh (Baranavichy). My further plan was to go in the direction of Bialystok, because partisans had to be there. My only goal was, to meet them. I had already gotten used to the forest, the darkness and the loneliness, as if I had been there and lived there for years.

[Page 108]

Sometimes, when I am lying there, my eyes turned to the blue sky, various thoughts and images used to come to me. There I see my Mom, my Dad and all of the family, sitting there, mourning and crying over me, because I am (supposedly) already among the dead. And there, I see my brother, lying shot near Minsk, and flies are eating him like that German. But I also see other terrible pictures: In our shtetl, the Jews are locked up in the camp, waiting for the day when they will be liberated. And there, I see our shtetl with its happy, proud youth, walking to the Shalker forest on Sabbath, after the "tsholent" (meal). All this seems like a dream to me now, as if none of this had ever existed, as if I too had been born from a stone, without a mother and without a home.

At times, when the rain is already drenching me to the body and the wind is sweeping through my bones, a thought tends to take possession of me, to put an end to my life; to hold the revolver to my temple, to press the trigger — and finished!

For what should I continue to live such a lonely life, without a tomorrow, not knowing what else will happen?

> "No, I want to wait one more day, maybe I will find a comrade, then I can share my melancholy with him", that's how I used to talk to myself to convince myself to wait one more day.

On a day, when the sun would rise again, when the wet clothes would dry and the limbs ("bones") would tighten again, I used to reflect:

"That world is so beautiful, with its bright sun, with its free forest. And you want to end your life yourself and leave the world forever, not bringing any benefit to the world?"

I don't want to do that! First fight for life, and finish the fight!

But after several days, when thirst or hunger would torment me, the thought would come again: "stop, full stop, finish!"

One day after another went by and I was slowly moving forward, not knowing my destination and where to stop. So I drag myself along for 5 1/2 weeks. My leg was already significantly better. Every day, I used to put leaves (on the wound) and they helped to heal. I used to keep my "inventory" with me at all times while I sleep. I often put the machine gun and bullets right under my head, and sometimes, when I wake up from a bad dream that someone is standing next to me and wants to pull the machine gun out from under my head, I used to quickly grab the machine gun, looking around with sleepy eyes.

[Page 109]

Lying under a tree that just had a lot of birds on it, I felt like shooting a few and waiting for fog so I could roast them.

I take good aim at them and shoot into the flock of birds. The shot has echoed loudly and two birds are falling to the ground. Both have been hit by the same bullet and have torn bellies. It was evening now. I plucked the birds and hid them for tomorrow morning; maybe it would be foggy and I could make a fire.

In fact, as if God himself was with me, the next morning a thick fog fell and I made a fire, roasted the birds and boiled some rainwater that had collected drop by drop during the night. I sat down to eat with a good appetite, drunken from the water. A bird sang to me in a tree and I was happy that everything had gone so well. The main thing is that I had enough to eat and drink. Even if the meat was without salt and half raw, I considered that good. Because very often, I used to eat something completely raw. Now, I was in a good mood. After the meal, I rolled a cigarette and took a deep drag, as if I had just finished a lunch at home.

Sitting there and leaning against a tree, my family comes to my mind, as they all sit there hungry, looking for a piece of bread. I see Mom sitting and crying for me, and my older brother, being a soldier in Russia. Oh, if only the birds, so numerous around me, would carry a letter to my mother that I am alive, fighting for my survival, and that I am healthy and feel free, really as free as the bird(s) around me. Thus, I decide that I will approach our shtetl and enter our house by night to take my father out with a number of comrades. Then we'll be together in the forest, fighting together.

[Page 110]

According to my study of the map, I must now be in the area between Volkovysk (Waukawysk) and Zelva. It's not far from the town of my birth, Krynki, only about 40 kilometers. I'll be there in five or six days, and then I'll work out a plan for how to go in or otherwise connect with family and comrades.

I've been in the forest for six weeks and went through everything early on: I was in the hands of the murderous Hitlerists already, I saw a dead German, and I've been between the forest, air and sky for six weeks. While lying there, I mentally work out various plans on how to get into our house during the night and then quickly flee back, taking the youth of the shtetl with me. Then we fight for our survival and against the murderous bandits who condemned us Jews to death.

That night is rainy and a strong wind shakes the trees. I'm sitting right now wrapped in the blanket, which is already wet. Suddenly I hear footsteps! I quickly get up, holding the machine gun ready to fire.

There is dense darkness around me. I can't see my own hands in front of my eyes. Leaning against a tree, I hear (again) footsteps. Small twigs break under each step. Leaning against the tree, I kneel down and look in the direction from which the steps are coming. I hear someone approaching me.

I ask in Russian, "Who is there?"

"Parol!"[3] someone answers me in Russian.

"Who are you? What are you doing there?", I hear a voice again.

"I am one of you!"

"From which city?"

"I'm from Krynki."

"Did you know Levit[4]?"

"Levit! Levit!", I shout loudly in a joyful voice. "Of course I knew him!"

"Well, that's me. I am Levit!" the voice answers me and the person approaches.

[Page 111]

After he arrived next to me, lighting a headlight, he fell on me and we kissed as brothers. This was Levit — the technologist from the factory where we had worked together.

We sit down next to a tree, and I tell him about my journey, how I got here, and how I escaped from the death camp. I tell him everything in detail, how the Jews were taken away on trucks into the forest to be shot, and so on. Levit tells me his experiences and that he is now in the forest with a group of comrades. There are 32 of them; many are former employees of the governing institutions of Krynki, such as the secretary of the "raykos" (party committee), the chairman of the NKVD and the director of our leather factory, Fridman.

My first words to him were, "comrade Levit, you must include me in your group!"

"I can't decide that on my own. We have a commander, and he will decide about. I and Fridman will see to get you accepted into our group. We are here, in this area. Wait until tomorrow at the same time, and I will tell you the answer. Now I have to go, because it is already late, and I have to be back in the bunker at 5 o'clock."

We said goodbye until tomorrow. The whole day seemed to me like a year. Every moment I looked at the clock and could not find peace. Finally, night fell, and at the appointed hour Levit appeared in the darkness, reciting his watchword that we had determined yesterday.

"Comrade Alyosha, you will be with us!" were his first words when we met. My joy was so great that I danced like a child.

Levit patted me on the shoulder, and after half an hour we were already standing at the entrance to the bunker — a hollowed-out tree.

When we entered, there were already ten pairs of eyes on me. I, immediately, introduced myself to all of them. I put all my "inventory" down on the ground, and sat down on a box that was full of mines, grenades and revolvers.

[Page 112]

The commander, an old man of 60 with a sharp look, has a wrinkled but serious and stern face with a short-shaven red beard. In terms of stature, he is tall and a little inclined. The rest are young people; the youngest is 18 years old. Everyone is sitting on the floor, where moss is piled up and several blankets are spread out. There are 10 people here, the rest are distributed in two more bunkers of 11 people each. The bunker is two meters high. Several linens hang over the heads, to prevent earth from falling on our faces. There are two couches next to each other in a row; different clothes, civilian and military, are lying thrown together. On the side, by the entrance, there is a gasoline barrel filled with water. In the other corner is standing a second barrel, which serves as a stove. The smoke escapes somewhere underground, far away from the bunker. The air is stuffy. The first few minutes after I came in, I felt very bad. I was short of air. But later, I got used to it, like to everything else. The activity of the comrades consisted in playing cards, cleaning the rifles and puttering around the mines and grenades that had rusted after being exposed to rain in the forest.

Buried deep in the earth, there was a barrel full of meat, which was piled with salt and onions. The light came from a gasoline-powered generator, sitting on top of the stove, with its acrid smell stinging the eyes. No one was bothered by this anymore, except me. My eyes were watering, and if I hadn't been ashamed of it, I would have asked to be guided outside, into the fresh air.

But on the second and third day, I could already stand it significantly better. The food was very good, there was also bread. I don't know, where this all comes from, and I still feel like a "greener" (inexperienced). The commander introduced me to the group rules. Discipline was very strong, much stricter than in the military. I was not allowed to leave the bunker for a single minute. Inside, there was also a barrel, the "paroshka", into which everyone "relieved" themselves. And when it was full, the contents were carried with a bucket to the river, which was three kilometers away from the bunker.

[Page 113]

The first week, I sat inside by the fire, telling all about the Germans, murdering the prisoners in the camp. My first activity was, to carry away the paroshka to the river in the evening, together with a comrade. During the first week, the other comrades left several times at "12 o'clock" (midnight) and returned at dawn, bringing with them various food, clothes and tobacco. The bunker was guarded all night, and at night, everyone used to either sleep or tell each other stories and jokes. The commander often made political speeches or sat, tinkering with grenades and mines. They really liked my revolver, and the commander took it and played around with it. There were many revolvers lying around, but all of them were rusted or had bad locks. There were also many grenades and mine launchers, as well as rifles — two for each person. Each rifle was stored separately, and they were very well guarded, cleaned and lubricated.

After ten days, I was already assigned to keep watch around the bunker, and I was already much more familiar with everything. Actually, I had "oysgegrint" (acclimatized) myself. I was already taken to work in the villages, which I liked very much. We used to scare a whole village so much that no one dared to take a step out (of their house). Thirty of us went to work. Three stayed there to guard the bunkers.

Our group was not yet in contact with anyone. We did everything on our own initiative. Our goal was to first accumulate a lot of food supplies for the winter and then start attacking the enemy by detonate the railroad, the bridges, and so on.

[Page 114]

To the villages that were 10-12 kilometers away from us, we all went well armed from head to toe. We used to start marching at 10 o'clock at night and returned, fully loaded, at three o'clock in the morning. In the villages, we were the bosses. Mostly, we take (goods) from the rich, bad farmers, or we take, what the village magistrate has accumulated for the Germans.

We used to get along well with the farmers and, usually, meet no resistance, only moaning and groaning. But this does not deter us. We act concretely, boldly and quickly. The peasants don't care to report (the incidents) to the Germans, because we tell them sternly, "If you report it, we'll leave the whole village in smoke and ashes!"

A few times, we come across very good food to take home, but it is usually very exhausting, until we have hauled all this to the bunker.

We are very careful with the excavated earth. When we dig a pit in the bunker to hide food, we carry every bit of earth away in a bag to the river and mix it with water there. This work is always done by those who had been standing guard.

Every weapon we find in the forest is a treasure for us. The commander takes care of cleaning them and putting them in order for later use. With each passing day, our inventory grows larger and more extensive. We cook only once a day, because the smoke in the bunker is very strong, and we would not have been able to sleep otherwise; our eyes would water and burn.

In this way we lived together for two months, and it felt like it had been two years.

Levit was my personal comrade. We once reminisced about how we worked together and how he lectured to me. Levit now [lit. "only"] requested permission from the commander to go to Krynki and to detonate the leather factory. But each day again, the commander refused to accept it. We were standing about 30-40 kilometers away from my birth shtetl.

[Page 115]

I kept talking to Levit that we had to go to Krynki to take the youth out, but the commander did not allow it. He didn't want our group to increase because we weren't doing any fighting activities yet. We were just preparing for it. First, the commander wanted to get in touch with the partisan staff and then carry out actions according to a plan. It should bring more success that way.

Once, about ten o'clock, all thirty of us left, and entered a distant village, where we had never been before. But the farmers of the villages where we had been before, used to point out to us that this village was very rich and that no Germans were there.

It took longer than two hours, to get there. First, we usually surrounded the village, so that no one from there would come out, and then we went to the first farmer, usually a poor one, and asked him about everything: "Where does the village magistrate live? Has he accumulated food for the Germans?" and, "what is his relationship with the farmers?" And so on.

This time I stood guard around the village. The rest of the comrades were gone, and after half an hour, a revolver shot was heard. After that it was quiet again. This night was very bright. The moon was also shining, and one could see each other well.

After an hour, the comrades came back, bringing a cart with a horse harnessed in front of it. There were various things in the cart, and the commander moved the guards away. We made our way to the bunker with quick steps.

When we had to turn on the path towards the forest, the horse and his cart stopped. We unloaded all the stuff and everyone took something. However, we could not grab all the things, so we left the rest and camouflaged it a little with branches. We steered the horse with the cart towards the village and let it go to run back to where it had come from. The path was very difficult to walk, the trees were very close together.

[Page 116]

Anyway, we reached the bunker, put everything down for now, and the commander ordered us to leave again quickly and get the rest of the things. So all thirty of us left, and when we got to the spot, it was really light out, about 4 in the morning.

Suddenly, we hear the clatter of horseshoes. We prick up our ears and the sound approaches. The commander carried a lorgnette[5], and after his first glance, we hear his command: "Everybody up in the trees! Three to four men to a tree each!"

Quickly, we were all among the branches, all in one place. The commander was sitting on the tree opposite me.

"Everybody get the grenades ready!" he orders. We all sit there, holding the grenades and revolvers in our hands.

"There are Germans, riding horses", we hear the commander's voice, "wait for my order! When I say 'fire', attack!". And while speaking to us, the commander's eyes are looking strained through the lorgnette.

A hundred meters from us, the Germans stopped and tied their horses to the trees.

We see them shuffle themselves from tree to tree, and then start a blind shootout in the woods. Only the German lieutenant is still riding on his horse and shouts something to those who run from tree to tree.

Suddenly, one of them notices a sack of flour, and immediately, almost everyone comes running around the sack, and the lieutenant shouts loudly:

"The bandits must be here! Fire heavily at every tree!"

We are sitting strained, nestled against the branches, everyone is holding ready the grenades. There, we hear a shout: "Ogon! (Fire!)"

Through the air, shells are falling on the Germans. A black smoke rises to the sky. The horses neigh, and shots from machine guns hit in our direction. We quickly jump down from the trees.

[Page 117]

Our commander is the first to run to the black smoke — and all of us after him. Each (of us) throws a grenade and fires shots from our revolvers and 'machine guns' ("oytomatn"). After 50 meters that we have sprinted forward, we stop. The Germans have scattered, leaving behind their horses tied to the trees.

Immediately, the commander gives the order to shoot the horses and all wounded Germans! We quickly take our three wounded comrades leaving five dead. The battle has cost us eight comrades and the German murderers have lost 18 dead and wounded. Their wounded we killed immediately and took their weapons, which they left behind. And with quick steps, we run away to the bunker, without the food, but with many German rifles, machine guns and clothes.

Everyone was drenched in sweat. When we arrived at the bunkers, it was already nine o'clock. Immediately, we covered all the tracks and headed down to the bunkers. Everyone tiredly fell onto the couches. The wounded were screaming and begging to be shot. Two were lightly wounded and one seriously, and he was really shot the same day. He remained lying in the bunker together with us. We had already lost six comrades! We were in a sad mood, the cries of the wounded grew stronger, but we had nothing with which to heal their wounds. Among us was a military doctor, but empty-handed even he could not help.

For four days we did not leave the bunker. The doctor asked for various medicines and suggested to send two people in civilian clothes to the city to get various medical and pharmaceutical items from a doctor there. The commander determined that I and Levit should go. We agreed and decided to go to Krynki. There, I knew doctors from whom I would receive everything needed. I was also drawn there to see my family and get information about them.

[Page 118]

We took two revolvers and set out on our way. It took us two days, to get to the Shalker Forest. Here, Levit was to wait for me for a whole day until I would return in the evening. I handed my revolver to Levit and we said goodbye to each other.

I left for a well-known farmer and asked him everything about the Jews, where they were being now and where they were working. I got a lot of information from the farmer. All the Jews were already living in the ghetto, being in a bad situation. Very many Jews had been shot by the German murderers.

The farmer tells me about a Jew, Berl Tevel, who was led to be shot along with another twenty people. Berl was the only one who was not shot. The bullet passed next to his lungs and exited under his arm. He got up and walked with shaky steps back to the shtetl to the first house, and now he is in the ghetto, "he is alive", the farmer tells me.

I told the farmer that I came from Grodno, not knowing how my family was. Together with the factory workers, who always walked united to and from work , I entered the ghetto.

When I opened the door of our house, my mother fell over on the ground. My sisters around me were crying. I did not recognize my Mom and my Dad. How terribly they had changed!

When Dad saw me, he wept silently with joy. I told no one, where I had been and where I was standing now. This was a secret, and even my parents were not allowed to know.

I learned a lot of new things concerning some friends and comrades, (also?), who had been shot by the murderers. I was also told that 50 Jews were working on the highway. All my friends came to me; they had already suspected me among the dead. My cousin, *Libe Jelinovitch Levi,* tells me how they tormented her while she was moving into the ghetto. The killers photographed her with a broom in her hand and her hair tousled, and ordered her to roll around on the ground while they took pictures. Jews who wore beards were also tormented in various ways.

[Page 119]

That same day I could not leave the ghetto. All the things that our doctor had written down for me, I got from a Jewish doctor, Lichtenshtein. I decided to leave the ghetto early in the morning without telling anyone. Only my Dad I wanted to let know, because when I came, he asked me why I was not with the partisans, but back in the claws of the murderers.

I had not answered all the questions, but decided, to trust my actual situation to my father, and to tell him that I would go back to the forest again. I had hidden the medication well, and I had already worked out a plan, to leave the ghetto without going through the gate.

In our house, I met my younger brother, Peretz. He had returned from Minsk with two other comrades, and, not being able to get through this city, his group had to retreat. My brother told me, how he had lost me, being already sure then that I had fallen in battle. The day I was in the ghetto, I felt like I was locked in a cage, like a caught bird.

For a whole day, our door did not close, because many curious people came to see me, trying to get information, where I had been all the time. Everyone asked me about their children or men who had fled with me, along with the army. I just said that I didn't know about anyone, because I had been lying in the Grodno hospital.

The hour approached, and I decided to make my way to my comrades, who were waiting with great impatience for my arrival. The screams of the wounded comrades who ask to be shot, are still very present to me, as is the commandant's clear commanding voice that we should not be late, but return as soon as possible, because we were on a very important mission — namely to save three comrades!

[Page 120]

I told my father that I was leaving for the woods and that after several weeks, I would come to get a lot of people out of the ghetto. Nobody noticed, when I left. It was quiet in the ghetto; the streets and courtyards were wrapped in a cloak of sadness.

I take my backpack that I had hidden under the stairs and walk to the fence of the ghetto, opposite the Christian church. I take a glance to the other side; it's quiet, the narrow street is empty. I quickly jump over the fence and walk straight across the field to the Shalker Forest, where Levit is impatiently waiting for me. Just now, I'm leaving sideways the "Elektrownia" (power station) and take quick steps through the "Alshinkes" to the forest.

Suddenly, I hear the sound of a motorcycle. I let myself fall to the ground and at the same time, a bullet is flying over my head. I've thrown my backpack aside. I hear a German scream:

"Halt! (Stop!)"

The motorcycle has stopped and heavy steps are approaching me. I am lying tense, with my face to the ground.

"Hands up!" I hear a cold voice and get a boot kick in the side.

Being pale, I get up and already have put my hands up.

"What are you doing there, you damn Jew?" — another boot kick in my stomach. At first, I am too upset to know what to answer.

Suddenly, the gendarme takes out a chain, and immediately my hands are cuffed. This is followed by a kick in the back and a shout: "Ahead!"
But soon he notices the backpack and grabs it with both hands.

"Oh, I already know, why you were hiding! You damn Jew!"

[Page 121]

The motorcycle was a dyad, equipped with a sidecar. I was immediately thrown into the sidecar and taken to the gendarmerie. There, I was immediately thrown into a cellar, where it was very dark and wet. I fell on the wet cement and did not understand what was going on. Fumbling at my pocket, I look for my revolver. Where is my revolver? Levit is waiting for me, and I am lying there, in the murderous hands of the Germans. At the first moment, I don't know what is happening to me at all. What should I tell them, also in terms of who the medication is for? Or should I say that the backpack is not mine? No, I'll say that I'm carrying it for the Jews who work on the highway, and that I myself also work there. That will be the best excuse.

I hear the rattle of keys on the iron door. It opens and two tall assassins appear at the entrance, with guns in their hands. Both are drunk and almost unable to hold themselves up straight. " Get up, cursed Jew, damn it!"

I get up and stop, my gaze turning to the two red faces with their watery eyes.

"Ahead, to the government office, quickly!" And a thrust into my side with the butt of the rifle is following.

When I entered the office, the two companions stopped next to the door, and I — in the middle of the room. At the side, by the window, sat a tall lieutenant looking at me. His gaze pierced me up to the heart. He had pushed his large glasses up onto his forehead. Piles of papers lay on the desk. I decide not to give my real name. I will give the name of my brother who is in Russia.

"What's your name?"

"Osher Soyfer."

"Who were you carrying the drugs for?"

"For the Jews who work on the highway".

[Page 122]

That's when I see him pull my backpack out from under the table and dump it all on the table.

"Who did you get all this from?"

I remain thoughtfully standing and do not know what to answer.

Suddenly a wild shout and a bang on the table so that everything jumps into the air.

"Who handed this to you, damn, dirty Jew? Damn it! The Judenrat, huh? The Judenrat! Well, we'll see about that!"

He picked up the phone, and after ten minutes the "Judenältester" (Jewish elder), Yosl Goltz, came in. Being pale, he stopped, casting frightened glances both at me and at the gendarme, who was now smoking a coarse cigar.

"Do you know this man?"

"Yes, I do," the Judenälteste answers.

"Did you give him medicine for the Jews working on the road construction?"

The Judenälteste stood there with his eyes wide open, not knowing what to answer. My heart began to beat harder; I would have liked to shout out, "Say that yes, say it, and save my life with it!"

But he only raised his shoulders, shook his head, and a silent "no" was heard in the air, which was suffused with death and life.

"Oh, now I already realize for whom you were wearing the backpack!", and heavy footsteps approached me, "now I already know exactly who you are! Tell me quickly, who are your comrades, these bandits, the partisans?"

And a heavy, hairy paw fell into my face. I saw only black dots in front of my eyes, and my legs gave way under me. A second, violent blow near my heart robbed me of consciousness, and a cold sweat broke out all over my body.

[Page 123]

I don't know what happened to me after that. When I opened my eyes, I was lying there soaked, with a swollen face and stains of dried blood on my shirt. My whole body felt like it was riddled with holes. Every single limb hurt me. My body felt swollen, blue patches of flesh that were hot like fire.

I woke up as if from a dream. " Where have I gone in this world? Where are my comrades? Where is my revolver?[6] Has it all been just a dream? "

So I lay there for a whole day and a whole night. A small square window with an iron grille was located in one wall of the little room, which was the size of a step [in diameter]. In a corner lay my jacket, wet and splattered with blood. It was difficult for me to move a foot or a hand. My feet felt like heavy oak blocks.

So I lay there for two days and nights. On the third day, the two murderers came and ordered me to get up. I was not able to do that. They then poked me in both sides with their boots, laughed insolently at each other, watching their victim, who lay on the wet cement, writhing, unable to get up.

I said a silent prayer, "Shoot, shoot, shoot, shoot me!"

A cold laughter, filled with fun, was the answer: "Shooting you would be far too little, you dirty Jew! We will keep cutting pieces of your flesh, until you'll tell us where the bandits are, for whom you carried the medicine!"

A push with the boot in the side, which I have no longer felt. Every bit of flesh on my body has already been an aching wound.

"If you tell us where the partisan bandits are, we will release you."

[Page 124]

I don't answer and keep my eyes closed to avoid seeing

those murderous red faces. "But if you don't say anything, we'll shoot you like a dog!"

I don't answer and wait for the bullet they have just threatened me with. Oh, if only they would shoot me now! That would be a good thing to finally stop writhing like a snake on the wet cement!

I get kicked, they spit on me, and while shouting "Jew pig!" they leave. I hear the door slam shut.

My tongue is burning, my lips are parched. There is not a bit of saliva in my mouth. I lick the wet cement with my tongue, which feels like a board.

On the same day, the guard brought me a little water in a tin ladle with a piece of moldy bread in it. I was not able to get the bread into my mouth. Every muscle of my palate pricked like needles. The water I drank in one go.

I didn't know what day of the week it was, or even if it was day or night.

After I got the little bit of water the next day, I could already move one foot and one hand. I also looked at the window and saw a piece of blue sky watching me. The same day, I could already slide on my knees to the wall and take my jacket. In its pocket was a handkerchief, with which I could wipe some of the sweat and dried blood from my face.

I tried knocking on the wall, maybe someone from the other side would answer me. But all around me I heard only a dead silence.

I knew exactly what the verdict would be like and was just waiting for it to be executed as soon as possible. My only desire was that I could just inform my father in the ghetto and send him, or my brother, to "my place" to Levit[7].

[Page 125]

In the evening of the same day I was brought some water and a piece of bread. I asked the guard, a Pole, what day it was. He answered that it was Friday. I asked him to let them know about my situation in the ghetto, but he immediately refused.

On Sabbath morning, Yakob Kozaltshik[7], the then-commander of the Jewish police, came to the small door window, and shouted in to me:

"Don't be afraid, I will save you!"

Now I was sure that they already knew about my desperate situation at home.

Oh, why didn't I say goodbye to my mother and the rest of my family! This was God's punishment for that.

I feel the excruciating pain in my bones much more than I did yesterday and the day before.

"Where can I get a revolver?" is my only thought. I want to die in battle, together with a German murderer. I know very well what is waiting for me, but I am at peace with myself, because I had strength and courage enough to endure the terrible blows and to remain silent. Let them do what they want to me, the fight for freedom will go on! In fact, with even more determination and even more loyalty! For each victim, those cold, predatory murderers will pay dearly! And in this awareness, it is easier for me to die.

I have been lying in the dark detention room for 4 days. Without the small window, I would not be able to distinguish day from night.

Lying on the wet, cold cement, various images come before my eyes. Just now I see our group, all sitting cross-legged, playing cards. The old, gray commander sits next to the stove, cleaning a rusted grenade. And now, I see the German murderers lying there with their mouths open and their bodies torn open, staring at us with their eyes wide open, begging for mercy.

And there, I hear the cries of our wounded comrades as they plead with tears in their eyes, "shoot, shoot us!"

[Page 126]

Has it all been just a dream? As if none of these things in the world really happened? These thoughts are going through my mind now, as I lie there, bleeding and broken, because for so long, so long a time, I have been living in the wet darkness now. With every rustle that can be heard from the other side of the iron door, every limb of mine shudders. Now, I hear the heavy boot steps of the murderers. And there again, I see their red faces drenched in blood, their cold, steely laughter stabbing through my heart and my whole body.

It's Sabbath today! I remember Sabbath days of yore, when we were sitting happily together and playing in the sand, or were funny playing hide and seek. And later, after the tsholent meal on the Sabbath, we went out to the market, [carefully] combed and with polished shoes, and made our rounds around the stores, walking behind girls who walked ahead and made the street resound with merry laughter. Summertime, Sabbath evening, we are walking on the highway behind the shtetl, lads and lasses. Our sounds pour over the green fields, covered with a wet veil.

More and more images come to my mind now of those Sabbath days and the holidays, when our proud, heroic youth marched so boldly and bravely across fields and forests, wearing blue shirts and red ties, and all were united under the red flag that flew in wide, blue heights. I am still so young, and in the middle of my bloom, I am torn away from the juicy roots of life. Today me — and tomorrow others. The verdict on the future is in for everyone, but there is a way out: to fight and fall like heroes in battle. That is how we were taught.

I will go to the iron bars of the windows and shout all this to heaven, perhaps a little bird will carry my cry to those, who will be in the same situation tomorrow as I am today. The sky that shines into the window gets darker and darker. I am lying with my eyes turned into the darkness. Suddenly, heavy footsteps approach the door again, and iron keys rattle. The door has opened and two German murderers have entered.

[Page 127]

"Get up, damned swine Jew!" — a kick in my back with a boot.

I try to muster my last few strength and stand up with trembling knees and lowered hands.

"Into the office, to the boss!" And once again a kick and a push.

I take trembling steps. My body rocks to the right and left. There, I already fall next to the door.

No, do not fall, gain strength!

With several pushes I have been led into the government office, where my legs immediately gave way under me.

A stern, piercing look has fallen on me from the lieutenant, who has sat at the desk, holding a large sheet of paper.

"Stand up for judgment! Listen!" the lieutenant yells wildly.

I again exert all my last strength and stand up, leaning against the wall. I hear him reading the verdict off the paper:

"In the name of the law, 'some number', the Jew Soyfer Osher is sentenced by the German military court to the penalty of death by firing squad! The sentence will be carried out on 'some date'. Do you understand?"

I don't answer, and large, black balls approach my eyes. I fall to the earth. When I open my eyes again, I have been lying on the wet cement in my dark cell again.

The next day, Sunday, I lay there all day, with my eyes turned to that patch of blue sky, and my thoughts flew far, far out.

My only thought was that I didn't want to die like a little lamb, I wanted to resist, even though I had nothing in my hands. In the evening, heavy footsteps could be heard and the rattling of keys. The door opened and two gendarmes entered with their rifles.

[Page 128]

"Get up!", the drunken voice of one of them can be heard. With the last of my strength, I stand up on my trembling legs.

"Get out of the detention room, you damned bastard!" — A shove is delivered to my back. With trembling legs, I left for the yard, under the open sky.

A cool evening wind blew over my face. I stopped, as if drunk by the fresh air and the brightness.

The two gendarmes brought me a spade and ordered me to take it on my shoulder. The gate opened and the wide, empty Kościelna (Church) Street spread out in front of me. I'm walking with shaky, short steps towards the cemetery grounds, where the gendarmes lead me. My gaze falls on the shuttered windows, which look as if they are shrouded in a death veil.

Going ahead, I think I'm about to fall, my legs caving in after each step. Right now I see a curtain being pulled open at a crooked window, and a person's pointed head peering out onto the street. Every step of the nailed boots is echoing in the silent surroundings.

We walk in the direction of the Polish cemetery, down Mill Street. On one side, there is the fence of the ghetto, on the other side, ruins of houses.

Just now, we are crossing the bridge and I feel that any moment I will fall on the pavement.

Suddenly, I hear heavy, running footsteps behind me. They come closer and closer with every passing moment. I turn my head and see Yakob, the commandant of the ghetto, panting and sweaty, with widened, big eyes. Walking between the two gendarmes, he talks to them in a mixture of Yiddish and German.

My mind is spinning. My temples are throbbing like heavy hammers, and I don't understand a word they're talking about. I'm taking even smaller steps.

[Page 129]

The gendarmes no longer chase me, as they did before, and my gaze is fixed on the ripped-out stones of the road. Just then, a frightened chicken runs past me and looks at me with a merciful glance. It feels my pain. I turn around to the back and see that Yakob is holding something in his hand, which the gendarmes are looking at intently.

I don't know what's going on. Maybe it's about my corpse, that it shouldn't lie in the Polish (Christian) cemetery, or is it about something else?

I can already see the stone wall of the cemetery grounds. The green trees are standing there, looking at the tormented Jewish lad, who is so quietly and alone going to die there. As we get even closer, a black cloud of flying crows lifts above the cemetery grounds, as if to accompany me with a funeral dance.

That's when I hear shouting, "Turn left!"

I enter the green grass next to the stone wall. One of the gendarmes has stopped on the way, and the other, together with Yakob, comes running up to me and grabs my spade. A small pit has formed next to me, into which Yakob and the gendarme have thrown a few large stones from the wall, and I hear Yakob shouting: "You are saved!"

A shot bounces on a small mound of freshly dug earth, which is between the green blades of grass. The sky is covered with black crows, the air is filled with (the smell of) powder.

I don't know what has just happened there. Standing leaning against the wall, I don't know if I'm alive or if I'm under the freshly dug mound.

The two gendarmes have stopped on the way, and Yakob has ordered me to hide between the crosses until 12 midnight. Then a person with a horse and cart will come and take me to Grodno. I must not show myself in Krynki as a person who stayed alive.

Yakob and the two gendarmes went away to the city, and I remained lying as if in agony. It was pounding in my head like hammers. My whole body trembled with joy.

[Page 130]

So I lay there until dark, with my head nestled in the grass, waiting for the person to come and get me.

It was impossible for me to get up alone and go away to the forest. The pain in my whole body had now become much stronger than before.

I could not fall asleep. Every rustle of a bird or a branch appeared to me as if the murderous Germans were coming to me again.

Suddenly, in the nightly silence, I've heard the tapping of wheels and horses' hooves. Next to the cemetery grounds, the horse has stopped, and a shout is heard in the darkness: "Avromel!"

I was lying in the grass and at first, I was afraid to pick up my head, but later I eased up and answered.

The wagon driver was an old Jew, Yitzchok Brevde. I got on the cart, and we drove away. The night caressed my aching body. Our way led along between fields, which slowly calmed my mind.

Translator's footnotes:

1.   In general: I think that by the Yiddish term "oytomat" the author does not mean a modern machine gun, but an "automatic weapon/rifle". a "shlos"= a lock, the lock is the mechanism for igniting the propellant charge of a firearm. Anyway, also the term "bolt" might be meant here, a lock being an archaic element of a gun firing mechanism, see https://en.wikipedia.org/wiki/Machine_gun 1a) "redchen"= the cog, part of a wheel lock https://en.wikipedia.org/wiki/Wheellock

2.   glovnye= main, głownia= torch, głowacz= bullhead, old carp (see "fulshtendik Poylish-Yidish verterbuch", A. Mark)

3.   He asks for the watchword, password

4.   We learned to know this man on page 63, but there, his name is spelled "Leviet" or "Levyet".

5.   lorgete, lorgnette: I think that here in the text, it is a special telescope for military purposes https://en.wikipedia.org/wiki/Lorgnette

6.   see page 118: "I handed my revolver to Levit"

7.   "to my place" = maybe he wanted to send his father or his brother there, to take his place in the partisans.

8.   Yakev Kozaltshik/Jakob Kozolchik/ Jakub Kozalczik, "The Hero of Krynki", please read: https://www.worldcat.org/title/jakub-kozalczik-the-hero-from-krynki-in-block-11/oclc/54611960

[Page 131]

Chapter Nine

Back in the Ghetto

We arrived at the Grodno Ghetto. There I stayed with my relative, an elderly woman who had lost one of her sons in the first days of the war. I was bedridden. The life of the old, sick woman was very difficult. She had already sold her last pillows and clothes for a piece of bread, and now she had to take care of me, as well. The Judenrat did not give out any bread for me.

Later, with tears [in her eyes] she managed to beg 100 grams of bread a day for me. There were neither potatoes nor wood. Thus, old, broken pieces of furniture were already burned, which had stood moldy in the attic.

Every day it got worse. For the first few days, I just lay there, unable to turn to the other side. Every single blow [that I had received] hurt me especially now. Once the doctor visited me and prescribed cold compresses.

After two weeks of lying in bed, I became healthier and could already walk around the room with trembling steps.

Every single day, there was a different incident in the ghetto. Both the Germans and the ghetto commissar demanded more and more. Every day, the population experienced minutes and hours, when they were scared to death. Today, girls are taken to work and no one knows where they will be sent. And tomorrow, gold, fur and other things will be demanded from the Judenrat. There was no "enough" for these bandits.

[Page 132]

From the leather factory of Krynki often a truck used to come to get special materials for work and take (valuable) things for the commissioner.

My family knew where I was, and every time the truck came, I got a letter from my parents.

The situation in the Grodno ghetto continued to worsen every day. Suddenly, posters were put up, saying that everyone had to report to the Judenrat. Understanding very well what that meant, I wrote a letter home about how I should decide; what should I do next? Going back to the forest would have been very tough for me. Finally, it was already cold and in my current state of health I would not have lasted long.

From home, I received the answer that I should return with the factory truck to the Krynki Ghetto. There, I was to appear under a different name, because I had given my brother's name to the gendarmerie.

[So,]I hid well on the truck among the bags of selected things, and arrived at the factory. From there, I went to the ghetto, together with the workers.

The first meeting with my mother will remain in my memory forever. Maternal despair mixed with tragic joy sprayed from her good, teary eyes. Even before that time, my appearance had changed a lot. I had become anemic, my eyes sat deeply buried in their sockets, and my clothes were torn. My younger brother, along with other boys and girls, had been assigned to dig peat. The situation in the ghetto had worsened a lot. As in Grodno, in the Krynki ghetto, too, new decrees and new suffering were created each single day. The Jews were walking around like shadows, getting weaker and sicker every day.

The Judenrat was composed of the following persons:

Israel Kalinovitch, Yosl Goltz, Tale Goldshmid, Yankl Levi (The Clear), Yankl Grosman, Mair Kaplan, Notke Mastovl(y)anski, Yosl Mastovl(y)anski (Representative of the Commander) and Yankl (Yakob) Kozaltshik.

[Page 133]

The ghetto stretched across one part of the shtetl, starting from one side of Mill Street, encompassing the second, [reverse?] Mill Street and Bath Street, which ended as a dead end at the river where the ghetto fence stood, crisscrossed with barbed wire at the top. Moreover, in the ghetto there was Gabarska Street, over which a bridge spanned to connect both halves of the ghetto. The bridge was located next to the brick houses of Yoshke Garber and Alter Kugel.

Further on was the shul's courtyard, which the Nazis had occupied as a place to repair their tanks. Gemina Street led through the ghetto up to Grosman's factory; the ghetto fence ran the entire length to the power station. The "tsverke" [the chapel at the Russian orthodox cemetery] stood outside the ghetto. The fence of the ghetto ran near "Shteiner's" fence. Both "Tserkovne" Street and half a side of "Amdurer" Street were in the ghetto. This was the area that the ghetto had taken. The other side of the shtetl had been destroyed.

The ghetto commissar and the "Amtskommissar"[1] used to take their "walks"[2] through the ghetto a few times a day, and then the few narrow streets died away, as if there were no living people there.

The houses were crowded with people. One square meter per person was prescribed. Three to four families lived in each house[3].Three or four women used to stand by the fireplaces, and while blowing into them (to start the fire), tears would run from their eyes, both from the bitter smoke and from their bitter, hard lives.

And despite the narrowness, more and more Jewish families were brought from the surrounding shtetls.

The shul and the " Bote-Medroshim " (study houses) were overcrowded with people, and one can imagine how depressing the sanitary conditions were in the ghetto. There was, as well, a hospital in the ghetto, but it was also overcrowded.

The food consisted of each 100 grams of bread and potatoes per person. No one caught sight of fat, except those who worked outside the ghetto. And these persons used to smuggle in, with great difficulty, a piece of butter, wrapped in a broom, or twisted into the hair of women. Woe to whoever was caught participating in this activity. By the gates, the bribable Polish policemen were standing, together with a gendarme. And at the side, a Jewish policeman used to stand with a stick in his hand, demanding his share of the goods smuggled in. The Judenrat became a full government force with a president, police, and even its own prison, where those who would break the ghetto's strict discipline or would refuse to go to work were imprisoned.

[Page 134]

The children and friends of the Judenrat officials did not go to any work. In opposition to this, the commander, who held dictatorial power over the Judenrat, waged a strong struggle. Often, brawls broke out. One particular story is about a pool (pond) that the commissioner had built for himself and his followers ("clique"). Every day, thousands of women, men and children used to be driven to (work on) the pool. It was a "mil fun beyner"[4] there. People kept falling down while carrying the heavy loads of earth, and leather whips ("nagaikes") beat down on them from all sides, mainly by the hands of the venal, bandit Polish police.

Factory workers, too, after finishing their hard day's work, used to be forced into work again. At the gate of the ghetto, the bandits used to wait already together with the ghetto commissioner, and instead of letting the workers into the ghetto, they were taken away at gun point to the pool. And that's where they really felt what it meant to work under duress. The completely exhausted workers used to barely manage to drag themselves back to their homes — to arrive to an empty pot and nothing edible on the table, where the little children begged, with tears in their eyes: "Dad, bread!", "bread, Mom!", only to fall asleep hungry.

In the ghetto, people were informed about the daily news at the front, but they received this information from only a few people.

Nochem Blacher's son, Simche, had a radio built into an empty barrel in his cellar, and every day, *Bome Fridman* would stay there to listen to the news from London, Moscow, and Berlin.

[Page 135]

For this, the death penalty of hundreds of people was threatened, and therefore, this matter was kept very strictly secret. Mostly, the youth had been divided to do [different] work. A few dozens were sent to dig peat in "Padbonike", and others to saw wood in the forest. There was an incident that the partisans in the forest took the picks and saws from this group, sending them back to the ghetto, not wanting to take them with them.

When the partisans of the area met a Jew in the forest, they generally took everything from him, telling him to go back to where he came from. The reason for this was that the Germans used to send their spies, disguised as Jews with yellow patches on their backs, into the woods. These later announced where the bunkers were located. For those who dug peat, it happened that they were visited by partisans. Some young people, including my brother, wanted to go with them into the forest, but the partisans strictly forbade it, threatening that they would shoot them.

The Germans spread great fear among the Christian population. They were forbidden to give even the slightest support to the Jews. The Jews who left the ghetto to go to work, were strictly guarded by the police and gendarmes.

Those, who have remained alive, will forever remember the word "Feldfebl" (Feldwebel, sergeant). This man instilled fear in everyone. He was a tall, coarse German with large, piercing eyes. His job was to keep the main road to Bialystok clean. For this purpose, he often visited the ghetto, and the Jews then had to feel the blows of his "nagaike" (whip) on their backs. The worst time was in winter, when the main road was covered with high snowdrifts, and the Jews had to remove them as quickly as possible.

The "feldfebl" used to drive into the ghetto with his truck, herding out several hundred Jews. They then ran ahead, and he drove behind and impelled them with his truncheon.

He made no distinction, but forced everyone, women, men and even old people, to work. Once, he went in drunk, and, although he was always drunk, this time he really seemed like a wild animal. First, he shot into the windows, then he ran into the houses, took out several dozen girls who were still lying in their beds (it was 4 a.m.), and herded them in their nightgowns through the ghetto to the main street. In the evening, he brought the girls back. All of them had frozen feet and hands. The sadist had raped several girls and brought them, half-dead, back to the ghetto in his truck.

[Page 136]

When he used to drive several hundred people out of the ghetto, as well as generally in the execution of his sadistic and brutal plans, he was assisted by the thuggish police.

The production of leather and shoes flowed exclusively to the Germans.

It happened the day before Passover, 1942.[5] It was a gloomy day and the wind was blowing over the ghetto. As happened every day, early in the morning the work troops stood in front of the gate, waiting for permission from the ghetto administration to march out. This time both the ghetto commissar and the "Amtskommissar" stood at the gate, preventing elderly Jews from leaving. No one understood the significance of this measure; everyone speculated on something else. According to the order of the ghetto commissar, the Jewish police ordered all young people to leave for work.

I then left the first day together with the leather workers. At ten o'clock, the ghetto gate was opened and one hundred and fifty German murderers, armed from head to toe, entered the ghetto, singing the "Horst Wessel" song: "Wenn's Judenblut vom Messer spritzt" ("When Jewish blood spurts from the knife"). They scattered around the ghetto houses and shooting was heard, mixed with crying and shouting. Yakob ran across the streets, his shirt unbuttoned, his eyes full of tears. He yelled without cease: "Jews, hide yourselves. They are going to shoot you!" He begged the Germans tooth and nail that they may not shoot, but the shooting did not stop. At the same time, "negotiations" were held in the Judenrat with the murderous officer of the death squad ("toytn-grupe").

The officer demanded 300 Jews to be shot. After an hour of "negotiations", and for the price of a large amount of gold, leather and other valuables, the Judenrat managed to "bargain down" the demand: Only those with beards were to be shot, that is, several dozen Jews.

[Page 137]

The massacre lasted two hours, until 12 noon. Until [early] evening, the number of those shot could not yet be clarified, because the victims were hidden in different places.

In the [later] evening, 33 people were recorded as having been shot, among them the persons listed below[6]:

Leibke Segal Munye L(y)evin Moshe Lapate, Muntshik Wolf (The grandson of the blacksmith) Yankele Wolf, Motl Kravyetski (Bashke Spodvil(y)er's son), Moshe L(y)ev the baker, who stood up heroically against the murderers not to get shot, Motke L(y)evi Arbultshik, the tailor, Henoch Nogidman (Israel-Hertzske's son), the blond "Moyre-Hoyroe"[7] of the Hasidic shtibl, Blak (Blok), Mones F(P)itshebutzki

Alter, "The Rooster" Veirokh, Natovitsh, Rabkin, Sender Shapir, Abraham Brevde, Pinye Gendler (Pinye Munye Feigl Yehoshua)

Women:

Shoshke Lasher, Yisroel Hertzke's wife-Nagdimon, Akon (stabbed in bed by a sword), Ilin, the wife of old Mendl

It was no longer allowed to take the dead out to the Jewish cemetery, so all had to be buried in the ghetto, next to the [house of] "Linas-Hatzedek"[8], in a common-grave. The Hasidic "Moyre-Hoyroe", called "The Blond", had his beard burned off alive, then he was nailed to the wall of the Hasidic shtibl.

The entire ghetto was enveloped in mourning. All around there was dead silence. The ghetto commissar forbade us to bewail the dead. They were buried with their clothes on, in the presence of the ghetto commissar and the "Amtskommissar". The first Seder in 1942 was transformed into a Seder of destruction, mourning and torment.

The ghetto was divided into two parts, which were connected by a large bridge. Under the bridge ran Gabarska Street, on the sides of which was the ghetto fence. Until 9 o'clock in the evening, one used to pass from one part of the ghetto to the other.

[Page 138]

Material life was deteriorating day by day, all supplies had run out. People became paler and weaker. Mortality increased enormously, so that the empty piece of field next to the "Linas-Hatzedek" was already full of graves. The hunger spread more and more with each passing day. Very little could be smuggled into the ghetto. The majority lived with the hope that it would not be long before their liberation. When such people as *Yudl Kaplan, Isaiah Glezer* and my father came and held the opinion that we had to seek the way to our liberation alone, and that we had to go into the woods with rifle in hand to fight the enemy, others used to come along, such as *Zeidl Filippski*, and preach that we had to remain in the ghetto and wait, until the "Amolek vet hobn dem sof fun Homenen"[9].

The days passed by. I worked in the factory, because none of the able-bodied in the ghetto were allowed to remain without work. To return to the forest was too early for me, because I still felt too weak after my experiences, besides I did not know the exact place where my comrades were staying now. The forest was large, and I had no rifle. So I decided to wait and later, together with my brother, leave the ghetto for the forest.

Winter was approaching, and the majority in the ghetto had no wood. A rumor came that the Krinker Jews would be transferred to another ghetto. People were already packing bags and preparing for the move.

In November 1942, the black day came for the ghetto. Christians told that they had been ordered to come to the marketplace with their horses and carts. Immediately, the ghetto was extremely heavily guarded, so that it was almost impossible to leave.

The labor troops, who worked on the main roads in the surrounding villages, were brought into the ghetto. Everyone already knew that the ghetto would be transferred to another city.

[Page 139]

However, no one knew where. There was only conjecture. Even the Judenrat did not know the truth, And so heavy, black clouds gathered over our pain-stricken heads.

Translator's footnotes:

1. "Amtskommisar" is a German title that is difficult to translate, it is a kind of mayor for a special district/county.
2. In the original Yiddish text, the word "patrol" is deliberately not used. The Yiddish word "shpatsir", in English "walk, stroll", seems to me like bitter humor.
3. "shtub" is primarily to be translated as "house", but can also mean "room", "parlor," "apartment." One should keep in mind how small most of the houses were.
4. "Mil fun beyner"= in German "Knochenmühle", "bone mill", a synonym for extremely hard, physical work
5. The following incident is also mentioned in the Yizkor book "Krynica (Krynki) Wieś", https://digitalcollections.nypl.org/items/30129f40-7525-0133-6825-00505686d14e under the title "der blutiker Freytik".
6. a complete list of the victims' names can be found here: https://www.jewishgen.org/yizkor/krynki/kry305.html#Page318 Please note: The spelling of some names in these two lists differs considerably. I proofread the list of the original "Krynki Wies" and except for a few minor details, I read it exactly as in the existing translation. I point out that in the "Krinik in Khurbn", there are some spelling mistakes as well a strongly faded places, where the letters are hardly or no longer readable. Also, people were often given different nicknames. Please note that not all names are given in "Krinik in Khurbn".
7. Yiddish = moyre-hoyroe, Hebrew = mo-re hora'ah, lit. "a teacher, who teaches", a judge, a rabbi, a teacher, who gives religious instructions and is allowed to answer questions of the rabbi
8. Linas Hatsedek, lit. "decent overnight stay", a Jewish society for helping poor, sick Jewish people
9. "biz der 'Amolek' vet hobn dem sof fun Homenen" = The nation Amalek wanted to destroy the Jews, as well as Haman, b.t.w. a descendant of Agag, the King of Amalek. I think that this Yiddish phrase can be interpreted in this way: The Jews wanted to wait until the German's ("Amalek") would experience the end of Hitler ("Haman") - who like Haman, would deliver himself to the gallows cause of his hatred on Jews.

Chapter Ten

The Liquidation of the Ghetto

Fall was approaching. The situation in the ghetto became worse and more desperate. Twenty butchers were imprisoned for smuggling a cow into the ghetto. They were taken away to the prison in Bialystok. Nobody knew what happened to them, and there were different rumors about their fate. Among the butchers was also a member of the Judenrat. After a few weeks, it was confirmed that all of them had been shot. The ghetto commissar promised that he would supply the population with enough potatoes and wood during the winter. In the meantime, I had also received information about the sad day, when the Germans bombed the city. At that time, all the people had run to the field. The German planes threw down leaflets that the population should put on white headscarves. So they did. All the Jews were sitting together in one place of the field, and the whole shtetl was on fire. After the bombing, a few Jews ran to check on their houses. In the evening, an airplane suddenly flew through overhead, letting off a white streak of smoke. At the same moment a firing of cannons was heard, and the artillery rounds fell on the gathered Jews. After two shots, there were 76 dead and many wounded. Whole families were killed while they had been sitting together in one place. People went mad and ran around the field. The first victim was Mr. Leibl Zak with his wife. Furthermore: Hershl Borowski. The family of Israel Kirzner — except the father. [But] Shloime, Chane, Neche and so on. The pharmacist Zhuchowski perished with his two children, Roza and Tanya, and his wife went mad.

[Page 140]

The days passed. In Virian's yard, the pool had already been finished. Now, everyone went to work at the ruins. The economic commissioner opened a tailor and furrier workshop. Work was done here exclusively for the use of Germans, who went to Germany every day carrying their looted goods.

So everyone lived and waited for the day of liberation. The 2nd of November 1942 arrived. The ghetto was surrounded with machine guns, it was no longer possible to leave. The ghetto Commissioner and all the other Germans took from the Jews all the ordered works, though they were not yet finished. For a whole day already, people were not let out to work, and at dusk, the rumor spread that everyone from the ghetto would be transferred to another city. All night, everyone was already sewing backpacks and preparing for the move…

The next morning at 6 o'clock, the ghetto commissar announced that everyone would leave the ghetto in one hour. Farmers' carts were already gathering at the market. Then, at half past six, armed Germans appeared, together with officers and Gestapo. The gate was already open for going out. After 10 minutes, there were hundreds of people already standing, young and old, with luggage on their shoulders. Just as they started marching out of the gate, a crowd of German and Polish bandits began beating the Jews on their heads and backs with clubs. People fell to the pavement streaming with blood. Children cried. Feathers from pillows covered the pavement. The whole Gabarska Street up to the market was covered all over with pieces of luggage and battered people. Children lost their parents and ran between the feet of the murderers, who struck without stopping, shouting, "Faster! Faster! Ahead!"

The officers, standing with cameras, took photographs of the gruesome scenes while laughing at the running victims.

My father had taken nothing more than tobacco leaves with him, when he left the ghetto. His eyes were full of tears.

[Page 141]

My mother strode ahead, with her small children around her. When walking, Grandma's legs buckled after every step.

I walked alongside and looked at the officers' murderous faces. The whole street was black with people and the noise of wheels, rattling on the hard stones, was to be heard. We were already among the last to leave the ghetto.

Suddenly we heard a shouting from the murderous director of the leather factory:

A group of Krinker Jews from the ghetto being driven to work

All the workers of his factory would have to gather to the shul's courtyard! Mom asked me to go there and stand with the tanners. However, I objected because I did not want to separate from my parents again, although I knew that this was already the last way... But Dad also asked me, with tears in his eyes, to leave. So I accepted. I took the last look at everyone from my family. When I was already in line, my sister, *Sonyale*, came running to me, bringing me a warm jacket. Tears were running from her black eyes and her heart was beating wildly. In front of me, a murderous policeman gave her a push, and my sister fell to the sidewalk. The others had already gone away to the carts on the market. I took the last look at everyone. The clatter of the wheels echoed in the surroundings. The murderous director, together with the Jewish representative, *Yankl Shinder*, was still sorting out those who remained standing. Those who were removed from the line, ran to the market to look for their families. Only the tanners remained, 170 people and all professionals. The "Amtskommissar" had the Judenrat put in addition, as well the best shoemakers, tailors and (female) dressmakers. A total of 350 people were then left standing. The clatter of the wheels became quieter with each passing moment. A gust of wind whirled the feathers into the air. The men who had to send their wives and children away, stood with tears in their eyes. A few more times, they enumerated us and wrote down. The director strutted around haughtily like a general. His murderous eyes gleamed like those of a wild, angry tiger. Formed in lines of 5 people each, we were led off to the factory. Several old wounded people were still lying on the pavement. A [mood of] deadly silence emerged from the ghetto. The heavy kicks of the killers echoed in the air. The [ghetto] gate was wide open.

[Page 142]

We marched with our heads hanging down. At the side walked the policemen, their rifles ready to shoot. We walked to Tarlavski's factory. Here, we were led into an empty brick building with wet walls. Everyone fell to the floor, and a fierce crying escaped our hearts.

[Page 142]

Chapter Eleven

The Factory Camp

The remaining tanners stood on the wet cement, burying their faces in their hands and crying. Screams and sobs were heard: "Why didn't I go with them?! Why did I leave the family alone?! The atmosphere was as if we had just come from a funeral…

The tailors and shoemakers were taken to a second factory, at "Grosman's", in the Krynki ghetto. We, in the leather factory, were 70 people, including quite a few girls and women for cooking, all the others were professionals, which the factory urgently needed.

No children were left, except Zeidl Filipski's daughter*[1], *who was the only (two-year-old) child who remained in the factory camp. He, Zeidl, did not want to separate from his wife and child, and since he was one of the best locksmiths and specialists in the technology of water pipes, the director was forced to accept Filipski's wish. But yet another reason compelled the murderous director: He needed Zeidl to have his residence finished. The second camp, where cobblers, tailors, quilters, and a few other needed professionals were housed, was called "Grosmans Fabrik-Lager" (Grosman's Factory-Camp). Any kind of communication between the two camps was strictly forbidden. There were also several members of the Judenrat who remained with their families, for example, the chairman of the Judenrat, Yosl Goltz with his wife. But their three children were deported together with the others.

[Page 144]

Because it was implemented, as it was announced before, that all Jews must leave the ghetto. But at that time no one knew that after all the above-mentioned people would nevertheless be staying. Therefore, Yosl Goltz had already prepared a good hiding place in a double wall. He had remained there with his whole family until two o'clock in the morning, but then went out to find out what's new. But as soon as he appeared on the street, he was caught and taken to the gendarmerie. His wife was waiting with their children, getting restless when he, the father, did not come. At 5 o'clock in the morning, she decided to go out and check on him. But as soon as she was on the street, she heard heavy footsteps of the German guards; so she ran into a cellar to hide. The children waited for another hour, but when their parents did not come, they decided to go out into the street to look for them. Immediately, when they went outside, they were caught and taken away by truck to where all the horse carts had gone with the other people. Their father was taken to the factory camp in the morning, and his wife stayed in the cellar until late at night. When she came out on the street, she was immediately caught and the next morning, she was also taken to the factory camp. Both were out of their minds when, after two days, they learned of the fate of their three lost children.

The factory we were in was fenced off and strictly guarded. The director often visited the camp and introduced strict discipline. The commander of the camp was Yakob Kozaltchik, who had remained alone. His wife and two children had been transported out of the ghetto together with the other Jews. After a few days, we learned that our families had been taken to a camp for former prisoners of war near Grodno, to Kelbasin (Kiełbasin). Fifteen thousand Russians had lived there, and after a short time, they had all been killed. In their place, they now brought the Jews from Krynki and the surrounding shtetls. People lived there in mud-huts, in very poor conditions. It was impossible for outsiders to come into contact with people of this horrible death camp, Kelbasin. The mortality there grew with every hour, and the dead were not allowed to be taken out of the camp.

[Page 145]

We had sent quite a few peasants to bring bread there and to give a greeting. But everything was in vain. The camp was cut off from the outside world.

Winter was approaching. The frosts brought temperatures of up to 35 degrees below zero. Each attempt to flee into the forest was doomed to failure. A few youths ran away, taking with them picks and shovels. But two days later they all came back, with frozen hands and feet. Knowing, that we would not remain in the factory camp for long, we started to make plans to escape or to hide in a bunker. After some deliberation, a place was chosen in the Jewish cemetery, in a cement pit where "sheymes"[2] were kept. Only a few people knew about this. Our work had to remain strictly secret. The initiators of our following activity were *Shepsl Kushner* and *Yudl Kaplan*.

Every night, around 2 o'clock, we would bribe the policeman, telling him that we would carry bread or other food into the camp. Then we went to the cemetery and prepared everything there. Each time, two people went and took what they could: rusks, meat, water and other food. There had to be enough room in the bunker for 20 people. Yakob, the commander, knew about our plan and helped us a lot. We had to be very careful and only walked when there was heavy snowfall so that our footprints would be covered right back up. I also went there several times, together with Yudl Kaplan, and when we lowered ourselves into the pit, we could see there the sacks filled with rusks and various cookware. Everything worked out very well. The pit was large, with plenty of air; it was to be entered through a tombstone[3]. Our activities were carried out at night, when the wind was whistling and we were sinking into the snow up to our knees.

[Page 146]

Everything was almost ready. Also a woman should be there with us to prepare the food. Once, when two comrades came to the place, they found the pit empty. Everything had been taken out. As we learned later, these had been little non-Jewish rascals who had found human footprints in the snow very early in the morning.

So, our hard work had fallen through. We started to make new plans and decided that in case our camp would stay in Krynki, a group of us would escape to the forest.

After 6 weeks the sad news reached us about the fate of our families: they had been deported to the hell of Treblinka. And now we too knew exactly what was waiting for us. In the second camp, where the cobblers and tailors were, a group had also prepared to escape. Among them was a very energetic young

Russian fellow named Mair. It was also plotted and studied here where, possibly, to hide in the period after the garbage was sent out[4]. A few people then set up a place for 6 people in a boiler in the bathroom, where six people were actually hiding later: *Chaim-Mair and Yosl Goltz with his wife, Soreke, Mair and Chaimke Gendler.*

Some of us tried to go to a village to a known farmer and ask for a future hideout there. But the peasants did not know anyone, nor did they want to provide a hiding place, because the rulers acted vigorously against those who wanted to help Jews, even threatening to shoot them. Once in the evening, when we were already standing at the entrance of the factory waiting for the whistle to leave, suddenly the door opened and the director came in. This moment, I was just smoking a cigarette. This was strictly forbidden and meant sabotage! Immediately I ran away through the back door, and disappeared into the yard. Since it was already dark in the factory, the director had not been able to recognize my face. Immediately after that, the whistle sounded and everyone went back to the camp. However, at the same time the director came running out of breath, demanding to know the name of the escaped person who had been smoking. If not, he would call the Gestapo and insist that 20 people were to be shot.

[Page 147]

Before he left, he gave 10 minutes respite. I reported to Yakob, the commander, that it was me. Immediately we went to the director, and Yakob made such a racket, hue and cry that the director became quite confused. He shouted, "I've already paid him back!", and at the same moment, Yakob gave me a light slap. But then, the director got up from the chair and went to me. From the first blow he gave me, a pool of blood immediately formed on the floor. That was enough. Then he pronounced my sentence: I was no longer allowed to work in the factory, but from now on I was a "penal prisoner," a detainee who had, all alone, to do the hardest work in the camp.

This improved my situation in two ways: firstly, I no longer had to get up as early as everyone else, and secondly, it gave me enough time to do some work for realizing our plans we still had in mind. However, the director always had it in for me. As soon as he set foot in the camp, he shouted, "Where is the wood sawyer?" (he called me that because sawing wood was considered the hardest work). The director was an old German, a rager. We called him "Malakh Pyatsh"[5]. This was the name of the bad angel.

The new year was approaching. And there, we entered already 1943. The frosts did not let up, and the mood among the older workers was very depressed. Most of them lay awake for whole nights crying. Zeidl Filipski organized religious lectures every Friday evening and used to prove to us, by means of figures and "facts", that we were already close to "salvation" and Messiah would come shortly on his white horse to liberate us. During the lectures, quarrels would arise with the young people, who vigorously fought against such harmful propaganda. The speaker also used to bring examples of Jonah, the prophet, who was swallowed by a fish. After he prayed into its belly, the fish spewed him out unharmed. This meant that if we behaved in the same way, we too would come out of the situation just as unscathed. Therefore, some workers used to sit and recite psalms all night long.

[Page 148]

The food in both camps, ours and the cobblers and tailors, was good. All the food that remained in the ghetto had been transported to the camps. Several women worked by the discarded clothes that had been collected at the Bes-Hamedresh (Jewish House of Study). The better things used to be sent to Germany by the ghetto commissar, who was "the master over all". He used to sell the leftovers to the farmers who came every day from the surrounding villages. They would stand in line to get hold of Jewish belongings that were splattered with our blood. The girls, who worked as sorters, had to watch the selling of clothes and pillows of their families and loved ones. A group of Jews worked tearing down the ghetto fence, and in fact Christians from the villages had already taken up residence in some Jewish houses.

In the first few days after the deportation from the ghetto, a number of Christians had gone into the empty ghetto houses and stole everything. A gendarme, named Gaver (Naver?) noticed it and shot several of these Christians.

During the whole time in the (tanner) camp, I could go to the cobbler camp twice. Also, my uncle and aunt with their two children were staying there. When I got there, my aunt was crying hard, remembering her other sisters and families. She begged fervently that I could stay with them, so that whatever came, at least we would be together.

My uncle Yisralke, however, disagreed. He used to argue that we had to organize ourselves and get weapons. We would have to escape into the forest, no matter what the cost. Although Yisralke had two small children, he had the courage to flee into the forest. But the freezes fought with the greatest ferocity against any attempt to realize this.

We now hoped to hold out until Passover and then fight in the woods.

[Page 149]

But the power holders did not sleep and had already planned the day of our deportation. On January 17, the order was issued: "Krynki must become 'judenrein'[6]!"

Right in the morning of January 18, our two camps were already surrounded by policemen and the gendarmerie.

During the night of January 17-18, some people escaped from both our camp and the other camp.

Of us, 18 men and women fled. The former chairman of the Judenrat, Yosl Goltz, fled together with his brother, Chaim-Mair. They hid in the boiler of the bath. The 18 who fled were: Peretz and Yoshe Pruzhanski, Velvl Wolf, Yitzhak Zutz, Moishele Kagan, Abrahaml Vacht, Kushn(y)er, Mair Gendler,Chaim Veiner, Motke Shteinsafir, Sore'ke Goltz, Sore'ke Gendler, Leah'tshe Wolf, Perl Levi, Fridke Zalkind, Mashke Kaplan and Itshe Wolf. "They"[7] were later caught and shot. Some others ran to known farmers, the rest into the forest.

Yankl (Yakob) Kozaltshik (center), commander of the Krynki Ghetto

[Page 150]

From the survivors, I learned the terrible fate of those who had frozen to death in the forest. My cousins, Peretz and Yosl Pruzhanski, had been caught and tortured to death.

The Russian engineer, Dimitrov, hid in his house two girls, Perl Levi and Leytshe Wolf, who stayed with him until the day of liberation.

We, the remaining ones, were led out to the marketplace. There, sleighs were already waiting to take us to the train (26 kilometers from the shtetl to Sokolka).

Everyone was allowed to take only one backpack; we had to leave everything else in the camp. Several Germans came to the factory courtyard and demanded that everyone hand in their jewelry. In case they still found any more of it on someone, he would be shot.

Soon, more assassins appeared in the market, lining up around us at gunpoint. Again, people gathered, who sifted through our clothes and took everything they found there. As we were already driving out of the shtetl, a second group appeared and threatened to fire if jewelry was found among the unfortunate victims. On the way, we were accompanied by dozens of gendarmes and Polish police. There was a heavy frost, and the people sitting on the sleighs immediately froze their feet off. (We) all walked on foot.[8] As we left our shtetl, peasant women with tears in their eyes came to escort us. A girl, Fanye Roitbard, had left her four-year-old boy, who could not speak Yiddish, with a Christian[9]. The mother, Fanye, had come from Russia with her child, and had already been shot by the Germans. When we were just lined to march off, the Christian brought the little boy to us and instructed him to go with us.

[Page 151]

We were taken to Sokolka and there, we were thrown into dirty cattle wagons for horses with shuttered windows. They packed 50 people into each wagon. *In each wagon there was a soldier who prevented us from looking through a small window. They threw in some bread and locked the door. *The train started.[10] Thus our shtetl became "Judenrein".

Translator's footnotes:

1.   I have connected two sentences, marked with ** that were torn apart in the original text
2.   sheymes, שמות: torn off single pages from religious books, especially pages where the paraphrase for the name of G-d appears, and which, for reasons of respect for the sacred, aren't allowed to be thrown away. Usually, sheymes are kept hidden in a safe place, for example, in attics or Jewish cemeteries. BTW, the word is spelled the same as the Hebrew "shemot" שמות, which translates to "names": a) Sefer Shemot, the name of the 2nd Book of the Torah, the biblical "Exodus" and b) name of the 13th week section of the Torah.
3.   "matseyve"= gravestone, but another meaning is "monument"
4.   The phrase can have different meanings, so I'm not quite sure of the translation here
5.   "Malakh Pyatsh" = "The 5th (pyatsh) angel", I think, he means the angel Abaddon
6.   "judenrein"= German Nazi term, "cleansed of Jews".
7.   There are small stylistic "bumps" in the text, so I think better to translate here as "Most of them".
8.   I find the passage to be somewhat contradictory.
9.   The sentence is somewhat unclear. Did the child really not know Yiddish, or could it just not converse with the Christian in Yiddish? (Later, we learn that the child spoke Russian with the Jewish people). In my opinion, however, rudimentary knowledge of Yiddish was usually present even among the Christian population. But in any case, there were language problems between the child and the Christian.
10.   I put one sentence back here

Chapter Twelve

The Last Way

Together with my aunt and uncle, I fell into a wagon. Besides me, there were in the same wagon[1]: Yakob Kozaltshik, (Yankl "Khazer"), the former commandant of the camp, Berl, Blumke and Rochele Zakheim, Henech Muglos with his daughter Mertshe, Israel Kalinovitch, his wife and two children, Abraham'l Efraimson (Shiskhes')[2] with his wife, son and daughter. Dode Kirpitch with his mother and his brother Zundl, (who threw himself off the train), Moishe Skovronski, his wife and two children. Furthermore, as mentioned above, my uncle Israel Skvoranik ("the Africans"), his wife Peshe and two sons, Lozerke un Hershele, Nyomke Skavranik and his wife — Dvore (Deborah) Maniches, Hershl Abramovitch, (who threw himself off the train), Motl Kirzner un Yudl Kaplan. After sitting down in a corner, various thoughts and images came to my mind. A few Jews recited psalms, and the women wept.

In addition, the remaining Jews from Sokolka were squeezed into our wagons, so that we were 1200 people in total. We stood at the station for a few more hours until the train started moving in the evening.

Everyone was sure that we would be taken to Treblinka via Malkin[3].

[Page 152]

Yakob broke open the small window, and a group of young people prepared to jump out. The train flew along at full speed. I, too, decided to jump. We lined up in a row. First to jump was Shepsl Kushn(y)er's boy Moishele — and then his father himself.

And so one by one jumped out of the train, which was running at full speed. A mother encouraged her two children to jump and helped her little son at the window. But finally, the main initiator was Yakob, who stood at the window, helping everyone to throw themselves off the train. When I went out of the window to pull myself up to jump out, my aunt rushed to me and tugged me by the sleeve. With tears in her eyes, she asked me not to jump. I should go together with them, staying with them at all costs, whatever might happen to us. Also my two cousins held me and asked not to jump. Meanwhile, the train was just passing Bialystok, and I stood bewildered against the wall out of the wagon, unable to make a decision. Yakob stripped down to his shirt and threw his clothes out the window. He now wanted to jump himself. However, his corpulence did not allow it; the window was too small for his oversized body.

Realizing that all his efforts were in vain, he took out a vial of poison and drank it off. But the toxin did not work sufficiently on him; his heart was stronger than it, and he now was lying on the ground and roaring like an animal after the slaughterer's cut, with white foam on his lips. None of us had water, we could only scrape the frost off the boards, but we actually managed to save him with it. We were now approaching Malkin. Again, some Jews, with tears in their eyes, started reciting psalms. Zeydl Filipski put on his talis (tallit, prayer shawl) and tefilin[4]. Our hands and feet were shaking: In the next moment, we will be in Malkin, and our lives will be put on the line! But, there the train flies past Malkin station in a flash, without stopping! We felt an inexpressible joy! The pious Jews claimed that their psalm prayers helped us: Now, we would be led somewhere to work, as the director of the factory had promised us; we "would work and live like in a palace". My aunt came to me saying, "Well, I told you not to jump! Now you will be with us!"

[Page 153]

I didn't answer, just sat there in silence and looked closely at everyone in the wagon. There were the beautiful children with their black, lively eyes-how they snuggled up to their mothers! And now I hear Valodke, the boy whom the Christian brought, asking in Russian: "Will we survive? Won't they shoot us?" And his lips are trembling.

My two young cousins, Lozerke and Hershele, stood beside me, their hands high on my shoulders, and asked in their sweet voices, "Avroheml, where are they taking us? You won't jump, Avroheml, you will stay with us!" A deep sigh was my response. I comforted my cousins, if only with my eyes, for the words stuck in my throat. We're traveling in the direction of Warsaw. It is already dark, but no one is asleep. In the deep gloom, heavy sighs and knocking noises from [cold] feet can be heard. The frost is very strong, and therefore, the walls in the wagon are white. We scrape off the frost with spoons and use it, as a substitute for water, to quench our burning thirst.

The first night is over. Early in the morning we arrived in Warsaw, where we stopped for a whole day. Nine people jumped out of our wagon, here I give their names: The first was Moishele Kushn(y)er. Then followed Shepsl Kushn(y)er, Yosl and Chaim Braverman, Leibl Naliber, Hershl Abramovitch, Sonye Funk, Avroheml (Abraham'l) Kleinbard, Zeydl Yakobinski, Dora Kirpitch and her brother, Zundl Kirpitch.

However, the wagon was now strictly guarded so it was no longer possible to jump. In Warsaw our thirst worsened even more, because there was no more frost on the walls.

[Page 154]

We therefore asked the guards to bring us some water, but had to hand over either a watch or a finger ring for a small pot of water.

In the evening, the train started again. When we asked the guards where we were being taken, they answered that they didn't know themselves. The older Jews with Zeydl Filipski at the head, did not take off the tehilim[5] any more. So, we left the second night, and no one knew where to.

On the third day, we passed a railroad station where Jews and Christians were clearing away the snow. When we came close to them, they made a gesture with their hands under their throats and shouted, "Flee, you are being led to the slaughter!"

Immediately, a weeping began among the women, and the psalm prayers became very loud. An exclamation was heard that we were being taken to Auschwitz. But no one knew where it was, we had never heard that name before. Only two hells had appeared to us so far: Maidanek and Treblinka.

Night fell. Yakob ordered us to burn everything we still owned. Aizik Brustin was the first to take a bundle of banknotes and set it on fire. His example was followed by almost everyone who still had some money. A little fire was burning in the middle of the wagon. We all had tears in our eyes, and a darkness settled heavily on our hearts. A complete gloom surrounded us. The next morning, Tuesday, January 21, 1943, we arrived at Auschwitz station.

Translator's footnotes:

1. I have combined several sentences here, because there was a duplication. Yakov (Yankl) Kozaltshik was called "The Pig", because he was so tall and bulky.
2. Shishkes= in general, a shishke is a pine cone. Given the grammatical form, Shishke could be a derivative of the masculine given name Chizkiyahu, so the expression could mean something like Shishke's son or of Shishke's family.
3. Malkin= Małkinia Górna. The station of this village was at that time a stopover on the Warsaw-Białystok railroad line for those trains that transported, i.e., residents of the Warsaw Ghetto to the Treblinka II extermination camp
4. (1) tfilen, tefilin = the Jewish phylactery, capsules of black leather, from which hang black leather straps (retsues), and in which lie pieces of parchment with prayers or verses. The tefilin are worn by adult

men (sometimes women, as well) on the head and on the left arm, most commonly early in the morning on weekdays when praying.

    5.   the tehilem or tilim = Book with the 150 biblical psalm hymns attributed to King David

---

[Page 155]

Chapter Thirteen

Death—Life

We had been standing at the station for an hour, and no one came to see us. Only the guards marched around outside with their shoes clacking. But suddenly, trucks and cabs appeared, from which tall, murderous figures with skulls on their hats got out. With each passing moment, more and more of these people are arriving. Just now, a group of SS[1] soldiers is already standing there, armed from head to toe. They spread out around our train so that there is one of them every five meters. And there, we also see people in striped clothing and with numbers on their chests and pants. They run back and forth. A tall man with a hoarse voice runs after them, yelling, "Quick, forward!" He holds a rough oak stick in his hand. The people in the striped clothes look well; each wears polished shoes. Who might they be? What kind of people are they, we ask each other.

The trucks gather and park next to each other. On the sides there are big wooden stairs. Every moment, more and more murderous faces can be seen. Everyone in the train car pushes to the window to see what is going on. The women are packing up their things and crying desperately. The elderly Jews have their eyes rolled upward, shouting, "Ya'anha Adonai Beyom tzara!..."[2]

Zeidl Filipski is standing there, dressed in his talis (tallit) and tefilin. His two-year-old child is next to him, holding a tsitse[3] in his trembling little hand. Next to me is one of my young cousins, the other is with his mother. Suddenly, there is a rumbling at the door, which falls wide open, and a wild shouting pierces through the carriage: "Everybody out! Leave the packages! Women here, men there!"

[Page 156]

At the door stood several young bandits, beating people's heads with rough sticks in their hands. When Zeidl Filipski appeared in the doorway, all the sticks hit his head and he immediately fell into a pool of blood. Yakob, dressed in his one shirt, stood in the first row of men; I in the second. "Line up five to a row!" the SS-men shouted, banging people's heads. The women stood to the side of us.

A tall, older officer with a cigarette in his mouth, positioned himself in front of us, holding one hand behind his coat. His murderous eyes gleamed like those of a wild tiger. His gaze immediately fell on Yakob. After a few minutes, we were all standing one behind the other in rows of five. Opposite, five trucks stood waiting for people. The old officer approached us, separated the first two rows of five and led them to the heavy wooden staircase. We moved the stairs next to the open truck and climbed up on them.

"Downwards, you cursed swine, dogs!", we heard the cursing of the officer, who was a little shaky on his feet.

We quickly descended and got back in line. First, they picked out quite a few girls up to 20 years old and put them to the side. Then the killer went to us and pointed with his index finger whether we should go to the right or to the left, asking everyone about his profession. Together with Yakob and several other young people, I stood on the right side. Immediately, they counted and checked us a few times. When they reported that we were already 150 people, they stopped sorting. The elders stood on the left side. Blood was running from some of their heads. Opposite the wagon, stood a group of young girls, and in the very back — women with their children. Among us was *Pinye Klas*, but his father was in the second group. Pinye gestured to him with his hand that he, his father, should leave his row and stand with us.

[Page 157]

When the murderous officer turned his back on us, the father quickly ran over and stood in line with us. After him, another one wanted to run over, but one of the SS-men noticed this, came running and hit him on his head with a stick. The man fell into a pool of blood. When they ordered us to march off, the trucks were already on standby, packed with women, men and children. My last glance was at the little children who were waving to us, and at the women who, with tears in their eyes, were shouting and waving their hands to their husbands who were among us.

We marched off, guarded on both sides by SS-men who gestured pointing their guns at us to walk close together. One last time, we looked around and saw the trucks from which scrabbling hands were reaching out to us. We march. We feel dizzy. No one knows where we are going. Just now, we see in the distance high barbed wire fences and small stone houses where many people are standing like shadows, dressed in gray striped clothes. The closer we get to the wire, the more clearly we see their emaciated, helpless faces. Finally, we stop next to a wooden barrack with dyed windows, where several SS-men are standing. One of them holds a paper in his hand and counts us off several times. The SS-men who accompanied us come to a halt. We march into the camp.

Translator's footnotes:

1.   Hitler's SS ("Schutzstaffel", "Protection Squadron") was divided in several groups with special responsibilities. The "SS-Totenkopfverbände" (&$147;Death Head's Units"), ran the concentration and extermination camps.
2.   Psalm 20:1: "May the Lord answer you in the day of trouble ", transcription according to Ivrit
3.   tsitse (s)/tzitzit: the silk ornamental fringes on ritual garments of pious Jews

[Page 157]

Chapter Fourteen

Birkenau

We were led to block 22. In the middle, there was a long brick oven that stretched from door to door. Close by stood a small, fat man with a yellow tape on his sleeve[1], on which was written: "Block-Ältester" ("block elder"). Next to him stood several young boys, beautifully dressed with red, chubby faces.

[Page 158]

Two SS-men remained in the barracks. They had us line up on either side of the stove, and the block elder gave a speech: "You are now in a concentration camp, and you must know that one does not live long here. And therefore, even if you live longer, hand over everything you still have hidden. Because, you will not benefit from it in any way. We will take away your clothes. If we find the smallest thing of value on someone, he will be shot on the spot!"

No one moved to shake out their clothes, because we had already done that in Krynki. However, everyone emptied his pockets of everything he still had left there. We had to put everything in a small box that was on the stove. Then, the block elder acquainted us with the "laws" of the camp. And he informed us about where all the trucks had been taken. In case that one of us cried, he immediately got several strokes with the cane by the beautifully dressed, brazen youngsters and the block elder. A young SS-man invited Yakob to box with him, and Yakob did not dare to refuse. Two hours later, SS-men came and took Yakob to another camp towards Auschwitz, which was three kilometers away from Birkenau. After the control, the registration began. Several clerks sat on the stove at long, narrow tables on which piles of papers were lying. Everyone had to give their name and data about their family, the year of their birth, what disease they were suffering or had suffered from. Everyone had to sign, and then, one by one, we had to go in a line to a table, where two people stood with needles in their hands, tattooing a "run number" on everyone's left arm. My number was: 93886. During the tattooing, tears welled up in our eyes and we saw black dots.

Now that all of us already received a "stamp" and the clerks also finished writing everything down about us, an order is given: "Line everyone up five to a row!" Next, we will be led to the bathroom, where they will shave off our hair and take away our civilian clothes. Before we made it to the bathroom, it had already become quite dark. There was no living person to be seen in the camp. The frost crunched underfoot. Outside, a blizzard is raging. We march to the bathroom, and when we enter, we are immediately welcomed with a rain of beating and shouting. A Pole stood by the entrance and hit us over our heads with the buckle of his military belt.

[Page 159]

In a few minutes, everyone was already standing naked on the cold, wet cement floor. We threw our clothes on top of each other. Only our shoes with the buckles we wanted to take with us. However, we still had to pass a shoe inspection, and those, who had new shoes or boots, had to give them away and receive wooden slippers in return.

We were then led into a large room, where people stood with razors in hand and shaved everyone from head to toe, after which we were rubbed with a green, burning liquid. This was called "delousing." Now we were driven "with the help of" cane blows under cold showers, and whoever was not under the cold water, received quite a few blows with the cane. The windows were broken out, and snow and wind chased in from the street, seizing the naked, shivering people. Each of us looked strange. We all chattered our teeth – and no longer recognized each other.

"This is the real hell here!", some said. For ten minutes, we stood under the cold water, then we were herded into a big cold room, where the window frames were missing, and the wind and snow were hunting us [again]. Every step we took was like being on ice. In addition, the "accompaniment" was made by blows with sticks and leather belts.

In one corner of the large room, there was lying a large pile of clothes, with quite a few people standing and sorting. After a few minutes, they began to pick out shirts. Each of us got a wet, torn shirt and then got in line for underpants.

[Page 160]

Even the underpants were wet. The laundry had been specially dipped beforehand in that green liquid for delousing. The underpants were short and mostly torn. In a second corner, we were issued jackets and pants. The tall or fat people were given short jackets, the short people were given large, long pants with long jackets. We exchanged everything among ourselves. Everyone quickly put on the wet, cold clothes, and immediately the sticks flew again over our heads and backs with the order that we had to line up on the street. They did not give us hats and socks because they were not allowed for recruits. We were told, "Now you will be taken to the quarantine block where you will get used to the camp, only after that we will treat you like all other citizens of the camp and give you hats and socks too!"

Then, while working on the road, we really felt the cold. Our wet underpants and shirts were frozen and it looked like we were wearing clothes made of tin. It didn't help to jump or to snuggle up to anyone. The heavy frost and the wind exerted their power. I was one of the first to run into the street, and the cold was already penetrating all my limbs.

As we stood on the street next to the baths, waiting to be led away to our block, we noticed in the distance, above the little wood, a high fire, from which the surrounding sky turned red; and the air was enriched with a smell as of roasting meat. At first, no one could explain what kind of fire it was. We thought that there was a fire in a village. But when our escorts, those thugs who were also arrested – most of them Poles, but also Jews among them – noticed that we had our eyes turned to that fire, one of them said: "You don't know what this is? That's where your families are being burned who were taken away with the trucks today." Tears welled up in the eyes of all of us. The wintry full moon shone over our despairing faces. Everyone cried in silence, because it was forbidden to cry in the camp. Many wept because they had not been taken away together with their wives, so they would already be among those who no longer suffered grief and torment. So we stood there, our eyes fixed on the red horizon, and no longer felt the cold, until several SS-men came running to us with their sticks.

[Page 161]

There are five of us in line again. Again we are counted several times. Each SS-man and assistant then counts again once more. When they are finally done counting, we hear a yelling in the surrounding silence: "Forward march!"

We stopped in front of block number 19. Immediately, several sleepy faces with rough sticks came out and looked at us coldly. They must have been angry with us for disturbing their sweet sleep or something else, anyway their looks were angry and piercing.

The block elder, a short, stocky person with small eyes and a shaved head and neck, speaks Polish-German and waves his rough stick which he calls "interpreter". At the side stands a tall, sleepy clerk holding a pack of papers. He is discussing something with the SS-man who led us here. An order is given that we are to line up ten at a time: The small ones in the front, the big ones in the back. Along with the command, the "interpreter" comes into action, and the blows are echoing in the silent environment. Behind the block is the high wire fence, which is illuminated by large lamps. Every 5 meters there is a watchtower from which the barrels of machine guns protrude. A silent groan emanates from the broken windows. The yelling of a night watchman and cane strokes can be heard. The counting and overcounting is progressing very slowly. First, we are taught how to stand in line. Just now, in front of two drunken SS-men, the Jewish and Polish "natshalstve"[2] points out with great assiduity how loyal they are towards the camp and how well they teach us the "first parshe breyshes"[3] [4].

[Page 162]

Near the barracks, there are lying old, thrown clothes, torn slippers and several tin cans.

Finally, we are lined up correctly and counted over, and now we are called out one by one by the number on our arms. Everyone holds up their sleeves looking at their number several times to keep it in mind and to call out "hier"[5] at the right moment after the call. If someone does not answer "here" in time, he immediately gets the bill: blows on his head. Each of us received blows while we stood outside the barracks for an hour; some on their heads, others on their backs, and a lot even five, six blows in a row. Finally my number was called and I quickly answered "here", but still I got a firm punch in the side from the "shtubaves"[6], which stood in two rows by the door {of the barracks}.

We looked at the occupants and did not understand if these were humans or bipedal animals. When I entered, the stench of the toilet bowls in the middle of the room rose to my nose. On the sides, walled in bricks, there were a kind of "beds" that looked like pig cages, one above the other. Several frightened eyes peeked out of the cages, only to immediately hide their heads under black blankets again. In the roof, there were windows that were open all the time, so that the "bed places" were covered with snow. The walls were wet and white frost had formed in some places. Attached to the side of the door was a small room where the block elder lived. Inside, there was a small stove that heated day and night. For the block itself there was no single [heated] stove. The people lay here crammed together in groups of 12-15 on a "bed place", covered with a single blanket, which was pulled back and forth until it tore. For this, everyone then had to pay with 25 lashes, or do squats for 10 minutes – with a heavy chair in their hands.

We were divided into 12 people per "bed place" and were told to wait for the order to crawl into the cage. At all the three-story bed places, they positioned 36 people each and then instructed them where each 12 of them would have to sleep. Our "twelfth" had to sleep on the wet cement.

[Page 163]

Our heads had to be stuck out in front, so that we could be counted. It was forbidden to lie with the arm above the head [or any other position where the head was not visible].

Then the block elder's yelling rang out, "Everyone to your beds!" We had to take off our shoes and put them next to our heads, one next to the other. Then we heard another shout, "Block, rest!" Anyone who spoke a word was threatened with a cane blow into his face so that his teeth would fall out.

We all lay on a side and shook when we just exhaled. Both the block elder and the night watchman walked around, passing each "bed" and gawking at us.

"Sleep now, because soon you will have to get up again!" we heard the voice of the block elder.

However, no one could sleep a wink. For now, lying on the cold, wet cement, we only felt the cold more strongly. From above, where the other 12 lay, sand trickled into our eyes.

Everyone pondered: what kind of hell is this? What have we fallen into? Better to be dead than to torture ourselves like this… The night watchman walked around, back and forth, with his crude stick in his hand. As soon as he heard a murmur from a "sleeping place", his rough oak stick struck immediately – on all 12 persons. So, lying on one side, we spent the first dark night of hell in the terrible death camp Birkenau near Auschwitz.

Three o'clock at dawn we heard a whistle from the block elder, and immediately the sticks began to fly over our heads. After a few minutes, everyone was already standing on the "Appelplatz" [roll call place] in the surrounding dark, cold night. Everyone ran to the wall. We obstructed each other. One ran out without shoes, the other without his jacket or shirt. After a few minutes, the block elder showed up with the "Stubendienste" [room servants], each of them with a rough oak stick in his hand. And a smashing on the heads of the black crowd of running people began.

[Page 164]

"Ten to a row," we heard wild yelling, accompanied by hard blows on our backs and heads. We ran from one end of the wall to the second, not knowing where to line up. In the middle, we all bumped into each other. So it took more than an hour before we finally all confused and tired, stood in a row of ten, the smaller ones in front, the bigger ones in the back. One row stood at the distance of an outstretched arm behind the second. The block elder walked between the rows, elbowing the chests and backs of the trembling people.

So we stood outside, in the winter cold, until half past five. Then a sleepy SS-man came and counted us several times. Upon his arrival, the Blockälteste had given the order, "Attention! Caps down!"

This order was given to us even though we didn't have any caps yet. The only thing that mattered was the movement with the hand, so that the impact was heard. After counting off, we started with "exercises", "caps off" and "caps on", and the one who took his hand down too early or too late got blows with the oak stick over his shoulder or head.

These exercises lasted 2 hours. After that we were ordered to disperse, just across the square in front of the block, which was fenced with barbed wire. The neighboring blocks grouped into commandos and marched off to work. We will not go to work yet, because we are still in the "Schonungs-Block" (mercy block).

At 12 o'clock everyone got a potato with some green grass, the portions were for 4 men on one single plate. This was our breakfast and lunch in one. We had to eat with our hands and were not given a drop of water. Although the snow was dirty, everyone took a pile of it and quenched their thirst with it, which was tormenting us more and more every moment.

Most of us got diarrhea right away, but it was strictly forbidden to go to the toilet. Only once a day, in groups, were we allowed to relieve ourselves.

[Page 165]

Therefore, people made in their pants and fell down on the muddy place. At two o'clock in the afternoon, they let everyone back into the blocks. Upon entering, everyone had to take off their shoes and immediately climb up to the "buks"[7] (bed place). So we lay there, not speaking a word to each other. For that was strictly forbidden, and everyone was beware of the stick. For the smallest peep in the "buks" all got cane strokes over the whole body.

At six o'clock in the evening a whistle sounded again, and again everyone had to go to the "Appellplatz" (roll call place), the lineup had to be completed in a few minutes.

At 6:30 a.m. the same SS-man came again, with a badge hanging on his chest, which read: "Lager-Polizei" (Camp Police). Again, we were counted several times; the roll call lasted two hours. Then we were allowed to disperse in the square. The majority already had blackened and swollen eyes and some had split heads. I got two strokes of the cane on my shoulder and could not move one of my arms. On the very first day, the faces of each of us changed. Everyone had gotten blue, dried up lips. The diarrhea had increased and the air was enriched with the smell of death.

The mound with the dead from the neighboring blocks had increased in size; they lay one on top of the other. One was still moving his foot, the other his hand. No one went to them. In our block there were no dead yet, all of them were newcomers. However, everyone knew that tomorrow he could be on the mound, among the half-dead and dead, and everyone felt desperate; many were already talking about suicide. It would have been a very easy death: One could walk to the electric wire, get within a meter of the wire, and in one single second you would have been attracted and burned.

At 7:30 they started to let us back into the block. Again the same. Everyone has to take off their shoes and stand barefoot in the snow. At the door, two "shtubave" stood next to a box and distributed pieces of bread. Another stood a little further away and smeared a little jam on everyone's face instead of on the bread. A little further away stood the block elder with his deputy, and both of them beat the people's hands with sticks so that their bread fell to the ground. If someone bent down to pick it up again, he immediately received a second blow on the head and remained down on the ground. People with pieces of bread lay around on the ground like stones or rags.

[Page 166]

In the corner next to my "buks" were the toilet bowls, where many people stood, holding their pants in their hands, but it ran down their pant legs… For this, everyone got a cane blow on the rear and ran back to their "buks", not knowing where they had lain before.

A shout from the block elder could be heard: "Block, silence!" and a dead silence hung in the air. On my "buks" everyone lay confused and moaned quietly.

Each of us changed on the very first day, both externally and internally. Previous people were transformed into wounded, helpless animals in one day. After two nights of lying in the "buksn", everyone felt small animals running all over our bodies, but we could not drive them away. They increased more and more and already crawled over our faces. Our blankets were besieged by lice. Everyone scratched himself bloody on his body.

Now we were in the so-called "quarantine block" for 6 days, where we were to be adapted to camp life. For the whole six days we stood more in rows on the roll call square than we were in the block. On the sixth day each of us was given a hat (and those who had no shoes were given heavy, wooden slippers) and torn civilian coats with a red stripe down the back. In the front, on the civilian pants, they marked everyone with red paint. On our right trouser legs, the numbers we had on our arms were sewn in. These numbers were also sewn on the left side of our coats. In addition, on one side there was a yellow Star of David, the sign that we were Jews. We were made to suffer twice: as a Jew (yellow Star of David) and as a political arrestee [red mark][8]. Jews were called upon to do the hardest, most unbearable work.

[Page 167]

On the seventh day, a Sunday, we were lined up in "Arbeitskommandos" (work crews), and immediately, people appeared with sticks in their hands and a yellow patch on their sleeves with the inscription "Kapo"[9]. Twice we were instructed how to pass the room of the "Blockführer"[10], where the murderous figures [lit. "faces"] of the SS were standing. We all had to march with our left foot (first), and whoever could not change his step sequence [fast enough] received a firm blow with the oak stick.

That same day, during morning roll call, one of our block, Yashe Zelikovitch from my shtetl, was caught while trying to exchange bread for water with a Russian prisoner of war. At roll call his number was called out, and, together with the "block elder", the SS-man gave him 25 strokes of the cane. Yashe's father stood in the same line at the roll call and had to watch and listen to the death cries of his son, who, finally, was killed for his screaming and thrown against the wall, where quite a few already were lying having perished on the [electric] wire. This was the first victim from our transport.

At eight in the morning, we marched out to work. In the first line of five, the "Kapo" walked and yelled, "Left, left, left!" Now, we arrived at the high, iron camp gate. On the left, there was a small, wooden barrack, by which 10 murderous Germans stood, peering wildly at the marching, pale human shadows. We hold our hats in our hands, heads held high. An old, gray, bandit "yeke"[111] stands there smiling cynically, muttering something to his "comrade." The "Kapo " reports how many people have arrived and gives the name of the work crew. We hear the word "krematorium" and "with 300 prisoners" while marching out. Two young SS-men stand on either side of us and count us as if we were the most precious things in the world.

We turn left and march along the muddy path towards the grove.

[Page 168]

Finally, we stop at an empty place, where "bages" [sacks? panniers?] are deposited, in addition bricks, mounds of sand, stones, barrels, pitch and boxes with spades, heavy hammers and so on. At the side is a tractor loaded with heavy, large stones, and near it are quite a few civilian people. All of them hold sticks in their hands, and, having their eyes turned toward us, they smile cynically. The "Kapo " and several Polish foremen count us again and additionally, assign 2 men to each group. For every 20 men, a "foreman" is assigned who wears a narrow yellow ribbon with the [German] inscription: "Vorarbeiter".

The foreman of our group leads us, cohesively, to a box. Everyone takes a spade or a log and goes towards the civilians. But one of them comes up to us, positioning us to dig a narrow pit two meters deep.

After we worked on it for a few hours, I asked the master what they were actually going to build there where we were digging?

"A crematorium will be built there to burn all the Jews", the master replied with a smile.

At first, we did not understand these words at all, but later, we already saw with our own eyes how quickly a high, thirty meter thick chimney had risen there, from which red tongues of fire blazed up to the sky.

The first day, we worked until 5 o'clock in the early evening. Then we walked again, cohesively, to the camp gate. Now an orchestra was playing and it was easier to march to the beat.

"Left, two, three, four," the "Kapo" yelled before we approached the camp. And when we were already very close to the room of the block leader, we heard, "Caps off!", and a shout of the "Kapo": "300 prisoners – Crematorium 1 – back in camp!"

Again, they counted us and wrote down the number before crossing everything out again [and recounting]. The orchestra is playing to the beat. We are marching on the "camp street" to the block.

The "camp street" is black with marching groups. From some groups, dead and half-dead are carried.

A stroke of the gong sounds, and everyone quickly runs to their blocks.

[Page 169]

On the camp road, quite a few people are left dragging on all fours in the mud.

As we line up for roll call, we all get the reward for a day's work in the form of blows over our heads with the oak cane.

We are already lined up in rows of ten. The block elder does exercises: "Caps off". "Caps on", and whoever takes his hand down too late or too early receives a firm blow so that everything spins in his head and black stripes dance in front of his eyes.

After the roll call, we are led to the latrine in groups, cohesively, five in a row.

Exterior appearance of the crematorium in Dachau, mountains of dead lie next to it and (North) American soldiers look at it with bewilderment on the first day of liberation.

[Page 170]

It is already 8 o'clock in the evening, and meanwhile, we have not yet had breakfast before our eyes.

Each of us had had to deal with a fainting spell ten times[12]. But it was not hunger that tormented everyone so much, but thirst. It burned like fire in our bodies, and our lips were covered with cracked, sticky skin. There was no more snow either. Everything was turned into sticky, black mud. The whole camp had become one big swamp and people could not pull their feet out even after a hard struggle. Those who sunk in, had to leave their wooden slippers there, and those who even fell down, no longer had the strength to stand up again and remained stuck there until it was over for them.

*Klausen – observing the Jews
marching into the camp*

*Kaduk – in the camp by the electric
fence, shooting at a refugee from the
Gypsy camp behind the fence*

[Page 171]

No one paid attention to the other. Everyone knew that the same fate was waiting for him as well.

Water became the main problem for us newcomers. Our meal consisted of half a liter of grass soup and a rotten potato and was taken standing over one bowl for 5 people. We were called the worst and dirtiest words. The most terror was spread by the block elder and the camp policeman, an SS-man. When he was tired of beating us, he used to write down the number of a person's arm, and at the roll call, he would get his punishment. The punishment consisted of 25 lashes or 10 minutes of so-called "sport", after which the person lay half-dead in the mud.

After two weeks, 20 men were missing from our transport, which consisted of 150 men when it arrived at the camp. Half of them had gone themselves to the wire, in groups of three or four, holding each other arm in arm. The next early morning after the death of *Yashe Zelikovitsh*, when it was still pitch dark, it was his father, *Milke Zelikovitsh*, who was the first to go to the wire, taking with him a young person, *Katriel Engenradt*. They fell by a shot in the chest, five meters from the electric wire.

When roll call began, the two people were missing, but were immediately found next to the wire. Each detainee bore the number of his block, and when someone was missing during roll call and was found by the wire, one could immediately determine from which block he was.

Almost all of our transport suffered from a general diarrheal disease which prevailed in the camp. Dozens of prisoners died of it every day.

After two weeks, we were transferred to another block, number 13, where about a thousand prisoners were tormented. The conditions in this block were much worse than in the previous "quarantine". The block elder and the block clerk embodied bandits in every respect. The *block elder, Rozen*, was a Slovak Jew and the *clerk, Adek*[13], a Polish Jew.

[Page 172]

The block elder was one of the oldest Jewish arrestees, with the number 27,000. The only "names" he titled us with were: "You dirty scumbags, you pig dogs", and simultaneously, he would "honor" us with cane blows over our heads. The clerk Adek, a small, powerfully built "man", had a brusque, hoarse voice. He was constantly seen without a hat, with a clean-shaven head and a rough, oaken stick in his hand. Whoever fell into his hands did not survive.

His way of killing was to deliver a firm blow on the prisoner's head, and when he fell into the mud, he used to place the stick on the victim's neck and stepped on the ends of the stick with both feet, until the victim's tongue came out and a white foam wetted his lips. Only then, the "Stuben-Dienste" ("room services") used to grab the victim by his feet and throw him to the wall, where other dead and half-dead people were already lying on top of each other.

[Page 173]

Immediately, when we arrived at his house, Adek gave us a speech with the words:

> "You dogs, you will not live with me for more than one week. I want you to know that you
> are now in block number 13 with Adek, and I want you to know what awaits you there!"

Block 13 housed the worst work crews, such as "Crematorium number 1 and number 2" and "Excavation works in the Vistula". In these 3 work crews, a Jew would not endure more than two weeks. At the crematoria, one had to work 24 hours in a row at a stormy pace.

In a pit next to the crematorium are lying mounds of human skeletons, which could not be burned because of the great shortage of coals

From (such a) work crew, they used to bring in 20-30 dead every day, half of them half-dead, who left the next morning for block number 7 – the block of death.

I worked in the "Crematorium Number 1" crew, and had to haul bricks. The amount of work grew before our eyes. Dozens of civilian Germans were employed here and every day, a tall officer came from Berlin, inspected the work and intervened.

Our "Kapo" was a German, an imprisoned criminal with a green triangle [on his clothes]. There were various identification badges in the camp; political Aryans wore a triangle [or "angle"] with the point down [on their jackets or shirts. Jews wore a red angle with the point upwards and a yellow angle with the point downwards, which altogether made a Star of David. Additionally, every Jew had to wear the first letter of his country of origin: for Poland a "P", for France an "F", for Romania an "R" and so on. Thieves wore green angles with the point down, and sabotagers wore black angles with the point up. The majority of the "Kapos" were imprisoned criminals who were rewarded with cigarettes for each murdered prisoner.

[Page 174]

When we got to work, the "Kapo" used to order that we should open our mouths. And whoever had a gold tooth was placed aside. Later, these people were assigned the hardest work, they had to drag 25 bricks over the scaffolding up to the chimney. Anyone who could not do this job at a run was thrown from the highest scaffolding down to the earth.

At the very top, there were standing a number of young SS-men ready to do this inhuman "work" with diligence. For one day, I worked carrying bricks, and if I hadn't been able to get another job the next day, I would have also been lying murdered in a puddle of blood below. But I then worked for several days making clay and unloading bricks from the trucks.

The dead people's gold teeth were usually torn out, for which the young SS-men could drink schnapps. In addition, they received a present from camp commandant Schwartz: a packet of cigarettes for each dead person.

The orchestra played to the beat, and the dead were carried four at a time, on the shoulders, to the camp command ("Lagerkommandatur"), whose members stood at the gate and gloated over our unbearable suffering.

In the first week, 40 of our 140 men were murdered. The remaining ones were all in very bad condition, so that every day whole groups had to move to block number 7 – to the "precinct". Block number 7 represented a transit center to death, of which 1500-2000 people of all nationalities were taken out[14]every second or third day, but the majority were Jews. Russians and Poles were already taken out when they were only half dead.

People of all nationalities were in the camp: Jews, Russians, Poles, Czechs, Yugoslavs, Greeks, Spaniards, Germans and so on. Also, a "Strafkommando" (penal-command), abbreviated "S.K.", was there, where the strongest Jew had a life expectancy of 5-6 days. The "S.K." was separated from the general camp by a high, brick wall, covered with barbed wire fence at the top. The "sin", for which someone was put in here, was talking to a civilian worker or women. The latter was exceptionally strictly forbidden.

[Page 175]

For this, one was punished with six months of S.K., which meant to live only for 6 more days. The work in the S.K. consisted of digging in the Vistula while standing up to the middle of the body in water. Every five prisoners had an SS-man next to them as a supervisor, who used to beat them with a stick from morning until evening. In its block, the S.K. exacted a special strict discipline: One had to stand barefoot at roll call for several hours, and there had to be strict silence all the time until after work.

Any communication with the camp was denied, and when quite a few detainees went to the kitchen after dinner or to the bread store, they were led under gun-point by the murderous commando leader. There [in the S.K.] were also those, on whom a faint suspicion had fallen that they might have wanted to escape. The only way to save his life, definitely was to escape. Although it was impossible to implement this. Because of the electric wire at the height of two and a half meters, it was impossible to get out of the camp. From the work crew, it was also difficult to escape, because ten people each were guarded by one SS-man. Even if someone managed to escape sideways, he was usually searched for by thousands of SS-men with sniffer dogs. That same day, the fugitive used to be brought back to the camp alive or dead. A victim, who was still alive was then hanged the next day in the middle of the camp, and everyone had to be present at this ceremony. The dead body used to hang for several days, with an inscription above him in German and in Polish: "This is what awaits everyone who escapes!"

After eight days of work in the squad "Crematorium Number 1", I decided to go to a different crew, at "Barackenbau" ("Barracks Construction"), which was one of the better squads.

The next morning, I positioned myself in the new work crew "Baracken-Bau", which included a hundred workers with two "Kapos": namely, a "Head Kapo" and an ordinary "Kapo". The "Head-Kapo" was a German of 60 years. Always with a smiling face, and always without a stick. Everyone considered him a "father" of the squad.

[Page 176]

He is a political prisoner, and the workers of his crew have a very good opinion of him. I stand among the people of his crew. Fortunately for me, one worker was missing that day, because he had fallen ill. So now, together with me, there were exactly one hundred of us. But the change was not as easy as I thought. In the camp and in each block, there was a regulation that everyone had to stay continuously in a single work crew.

Here we see a gassed Jew being thrown into the oven of the crematorium, which was carried out by the "Sonderkommando", whose members were also killed later

When the murderous "Kapo" saw that I was missing that morning, he ran through the camp looking for me. He then found me in the work-crew "Barracks Construction". At first, I was hit hard on my back with his stick. But the old "Head Kapo" immediately stood in front of me and refused to let me out of line.

[Page 177]

One Kapo pulled me towards him, and the other pulled me into his crew. The two ambitiously got into a dispute about who would win the victim for himself. And the old "head kapo" won! I left, to work in a new squad. That's when I realized what a difference the Kapo made in terms of the work situation. Here too, the SS was present, also with sticks in their hands, but we were already working in such a way that we were not immediately seized, if we stood there just for a moment without working.

Our Kapo had built a hut in the field, where he sat for hours with the SS-men, and we used to stay between the boards, or on the roof of the barracks. When the old Kapo was in a good mood, he, together with some of the arrested, used to go to the women's camp and bring a kettle of soup. Very few Jews worked in our squad, the majority were Poles with old numbers; they had come in 1942. They had already been through measles and chicken pox and gave me lessons on how to fight the difficult daily battle for survival.

My job was to haul up boards to cover the roof.

One day, when I returned to the camp from block number 1, where also the murderous Kapo from the work crew " Crematorium Number 1 " was staying, he examined me from head to toe and made a gesture with his hand, gnashing his yellow, protruding teeth.

The old Kapo had told me to report to him if the other kapo would hit me. But the murderous Kapo did not beat me anymore, and from that day on, I worked in the squad "Barracks Construction".

Every day, the ranks of our transport group became emptier. When I used to come back from work, I did not recognize my comrades, because everyone changed in appearance from day to day. The mounds with the dead on the wall grew, among them lay acquaintances from my shtetl. Five people were already missing from my "buks" [box, the sleeping place made of cement]. Now I slept in the middle box, where you could not sit up and it was dark during day and night like in a tomb.

[Page 178]

Sleeping together with me were Yudl Kaplan, Isaiah (Shiye) Glezer, Motl Kirzner, Pinye Klas, Shiye (Shia) Shapiro and two people from Grodno. So far, all of them had "held up" well. Everyone was fighting for their lives every day. Once, when I came home from work, I did not recognize my friend Yudl. His whole face was swollen and tinged with all colors: blue, yellow and red. At roll call, standing next to me, he told me, what he had been through during the day. After the roll call, he ate nothing, because when he received his portion of bread, he received cane blows over his hand and fell into the mud. I carried him to the block and put him in our "box". After two hours, he rose with wide, staring eyes and asked me for some water. I jumped down from the "box" to ask for a drop of water from someone. But when I returned to the "bed", I found my comrade Yudl Kaplan dead. All night, I lay in the box with him, and after three days, the same happened with Shiye Glezer.

On Sundays, our squad did not work. Therefore, all of us used to retire back to our blocks and sit down against the wall. Opposite us, the first rays of spring were already roaming around. All the other work crews used to work until 12 o'clock in the day. After that, all except the "crematorium commando" used to march into the camp and get shaved and have their hair cut. The shaving was done on the roll call square. First, 10 men were soaped up before they were all shaved with one single knife. The shavers received a soup refill for this. The haircutting was done in the same way. Later, the block elder made a check, and those who had not yet been shaven, received a portion of caning.

Sundays, moreover, new stripes were applied to the clothes, and buttons were sewn on with wire. Those who still had a little strength also washed out the mud from the whole week. We were not allowed into the blocks, and standing in the mud for half a day was worse than being on the work detail. It pulled the marrow out of our bones.

The Sunday afternoon was also used for selections.

[Page 179]

This brought death to hundreds of people. When we heard a signal and the shouting: "Blocksperre!"[15], then we already knew that the "Galgen-Mengelyer"[16] was about to come to carry out a selection.

Everyone had to strip naked in the block and then to go completely naked to the roll call area, where we had to stand in line, looking and waiting, until the executioner would come.

When Mengele appeared with the other officers, we all trembled all over. Everyone knew exactly that death was going there, from which one could not buy oneself free.

Mengele, an elderly, tall, slim person with a long face and large, shining eyes like those of a tiger, used to walk serenely with long strides, one hand buried in his coat, a cigarette in his mouth. In the same pose, he stood at the railroad station, where the human transports arrived, and all had to pass under his murderous gaze: With a single movement of his left index finger, either to the right or to the left, he sent tens of thousands of people to the gas chambers, and with the same composure, he carried out the selections on the men and women.

His name alone spread terror throughout the camp. But now, there was a second executioner, a sadist, the "Rapport-Führer" [report leader], who received the report, whether everything was properly in order, and forwarded it every day to Berlin, to the "Judenvernichtungs-Amt" [Jewish Extermination Office], to [Heinrich] Himmler and [Ernst] Kaltenbrunner.

In addition, there was (Josef) Schillinger[17], a small, powerfully built man who constantly kept his head tilted a little to one side, with dark brown, piercing eyes. He was frequently present in all the barracks. If someone fell into his hands, he did not survive. His method of beating consisted of grabbing his victim by the lapels, shaking him violently, then gnashing his teeth so that his jaws would go up and down. Finally, he would push his elbow hard against his victim's temple so that even the strongest would immediately fall over unconscious. But he never was satisfied with that but would take a stick, put it to the unfortunate's neck and squeezed, until death freed the victim from the savage sadist. His chastisements usually lasted a minute. He had a particularly large hatred on Russian and German political prisoners.

[Page 180]

This beast did not live long. At the end of 1943, he was shot in the crematorium by a Jewish artist. She had come from an internment camp from Berlin, where 1600 Jewish American citizens were staying.

I worked for two weeks in the "Barracks Construction" crew. One Sunday, early in the morning, our block had to perform squats next to the wall as a punishment. There, at our feet, lay a mountain of corpses that had been dragged out of the "boxes" today.

Most of us were already unable to stay on our feet, and many were left stretched out in the mud after doing the squats. They no longer felt the cane blows of the clerk, Adek. Suddenly, the "Arbeitsdienst-Führer" [fatigue duty leader] appeared, together with several detainees in the function of clerks.

He ran to the block elder and talked to him, while his gaze fell on the seated people, who now looked like frogs in the mud, with their heads held high.

The "Arbeits(dienst)-Führer" pointed to us, the sitting ones, and the block leader called one to stand up. The fourth one he pointed to was me, and I had to get in line. In this way, he called up 50 detainees, the majority of whom still looked "good", although this "goodness" consisted only in the fact that they were wearing more or less clean clothes.

We were led to the bathroom, where we threw off our lice-ridden clothes and got under the cold shower. No one knew for what purpose we had been chosen, everyone believed something different. The majority thought that we would be sent or transported to another camp.

[Page 181]

After washing, we all got clean shirts and new striped clothes: Pants, a jacket and a coat. After that, we were told that we would be working in the "Aufräumungs-Kommando" [clean-up squad], which was called "Canada"[18]. It was known as Canada, because in this squad, everyone had enough to eat and could live "like in Canada".

Before I came to this warehouse, I had heard already about this squad and seen people who worked there. Most of them were old detainees, who had come at the beginning of 1942 and first stayed in the Auschwitz camp. After that, they were transferred to the subcamp, Birkenau, which continued to grow every day with new barracks and additionally, with new plans for new large camps. The environment was swampy, the earth was one big mud, but thousands of detainees worked hard, digging channels into which stones were thrown, to dry out the earth. All the surrounding villages had been destroyed and their houses expropriated; the empty area, where people used to work, was littered with small camps like Bana, Yanozhne, and even smaller camps with up to two to three thousand detainees. The camp was 40 square kilometers in size and was guarded by five chains of posts. To its one side flowed the Vistula, to the other were the Beskid Mountains, which were well visible from the camp.

From the bathroom we were led to a wooden barrack, number 17, where also the work crew "Barracks construction" was located; and next to it, in barrack number 16, was "Canada". The block elder, a German with a "green angle", valued discipline and cleanliness as much as circumstances allowed.

Life was very different in the barracks than in the stone block. Now, there were three bedsteads, where no more than 6 people slept, that is, two in a bed, with a straw sack on the side. Like in a casern, the bed had to be well made every day. Compared to the previous hell, this was paradise. It is more light and airy here. The toilet device is next to the door, and good care is taken that it does not overflow. The toilet is brought out [and emptied] according to a certain order. In this respect, there is no difference between old and new detainees.

[Page 182]

The same law applies to all of them. Anti-Semitism is significantly less pronounced here, because the Poles of the barracks like to approach the Jews who work in "Canada". The clerk is a Slovak Jew, he too has a hoarse voice. He is a restless person and does not spare with sticks. However, he only beats Jews. He is a little afraid of the Poles, since they are old detainees who "have already been under the horse and on the horse"[19]. The strokes of the cane intended for them are usually given to us – but with soup it is the other way around.

Among us fifty people, two of our transport were included: Me and Ayzik Tzigel.

I slept together with Ayzik in one bed, the others were locked away from us. No one from the camp dared to enter our barracks. The next morning, we were led to work, three kilometers from Birkenau, where there were five barracks, next to which lay piles of suitcases, packs and bedding, covered with blankets.

The work crew "Canada" numbered 300 people with two Kapos, one a German, and the other a German Jew.

When we got to the workplace, the Kapo gave a speech in front of us, in which he said that we all had to work like machines and were not allowed to eat while working. Moreover, it was forbidden to take food into the camp.

There were also quite a few SS present. One, an "Oberscharführer", was called "The Grandpa", the other "Oberscharführer" was called "The Dad". Both were tall and fat, with red, murderous faces. They constantly had rough sticks or leather whips in their hands. At the tip of the whip was a piece of lead, weighing 200 grams.

We were assigned to different jobs, I was to load heavy sacks of rags onto the wagons. All at a run, driven by young SS-men. And if someone got out of breath, he was beaten with sticks or had to do the so-called "sport": "Lie down! Get up! Lie down! Get up!", and so it went, countless times….

[Page 183]

We worked 12 to 14 hours a day with one hour rest for lunch. The transport groups were already all beaten bloody. The Kapo, Serele, boasted of his beatings, and was virtually idolized by the SS.

Several hundred Jewish women also worked here with an overseer, an SS woman, who carried a wolfhound that helped her torment the debilitated women.

In this regard, a special chapter consisted of a single lavatory, where no more than one person was allowed to go. Almost all of them, however, suffered from diarrhea and could no longer control themselves.

When three or four women gathered next to the toilet, the SS woman noticed this immediately and rushed her loyal companion, the dog, to them. And he understood quite well what he was needed for ... The dog used to grab one of the women by her dress and drag her across the yard. And when the dress was torn so that the dog could no longer pull it, he bit the body until the blood ran over the yard. The SS used to delight in it and toss and roll on the floor, laughing, while encouraging the dog: "Tighter, tighter, grab, grab!"

Such scenes occurred every day for both women and men. Every day, two or three such victims were usually brought into the camp on a cart. Shootings were also common. It was strictly forbidden to deliver [to others] a piece of bread, even if it had been lying in the mud already.

There was a carpentry squad working in the vicinity of our workplace, and they usually asked us to pass a piece of bread through the wire fence. But the SS used to be careful watching the wire fence through a crack in the barracks, and just in the moment, when someone would bravely threw bread across it, a revolver shot would be fired and hit his head, so that the offender [lit. captive] fell into a pool of blood.

Such incidents were very common. Despite the danger of death, bread and canned food were still thrown over for the hungry comrades.

[Page 184]

While marching to and from work, we were forced to sing German songs, and if someone did not sing, the Kapo or the "Postenführer" [guard of the camp] would hit them with a stick.

The work in "Canada" consisted in taking over the things of an arrived transport. When a transport arrived at the station, everyone left their luggage in the wagons. Then about 50 "Canadians" came to load all their luggage onto trucks and take everything to the so-called "Effektenlager" [stock store], where 300 men and 400 women were working; everything was sorted and well searched here. When something sewn in was found, they usually tore the concerned garment and throw it to the rags. The very good and new items of clothing used to be collected in a magazine [military storehouse] and sent to Germany on a weekly basis.

There [also] lay piles of luggage and suitcases thrown on top of each other, which one brought from the transports day and night. Shoes were also transported to Germany. The women worked sorting the laundry and sealing it: Everything was packed in dozens of parcels and tied with ropes before being sent to Germany.

The same was done with bed linen. The old ones were torn up and thrown to the rags, the new ones were sent to Germany. Every day 10-15 wagons were fully loaded. Valuables, such as gold, money, watches, silver and gold glasses, as well as everything that was counted as valuables, were collected in large, locked boxes with a hole into which the objects could be thrown. Such a box was usually transported to Berlin every day.

The clothes of the gassed people were also sorted in this way. All paper passports and photos were burned so that no traces of them would remain.

After work, a strict check was carried out. Everyone was forced to strip naked and their clothes were thoroughly searched. Woe to him with whom they found something.

[Page 185]

The punishments were different, depending on what was found in the detainee. For a box of canned food, you got 25 lashes, from which you used to fall down unconscious. The "Grandpa" beat with his leather strap until blood flowed. While he was beating, the unfortunate victim had to count himself, and if he miscounted and said, for example, "5" instead of "6," he had to start again from the beginning. For beatings, there was a special bench on which the victim's feet and hands were clamped in holders.

Sometimes, when many were to be beaten and the "Grandpa" was already tired, the "Dad" was called to help; then both were beating and having a lot of pleasure.

I got five lashes on the very first day for picking up a piece of sugar from the ground and putting it in my mouth. This was noticed by the "Dad" and he, immediately, paid me my "wages" for it. These were my first "counted" lashes of my camp life. In the meantime, I was already registered as a "camp resident" and at the same time, as a "Canadian". In "Canada" it often happened that all for one took blows. If one of a group of 20 people committed even the smallest "sin," all 20 would get the punishment. Most of the time, we were given collective punishments. However many advantages this crew had, there were also many disadvantages.

No day went by without a cart, carrying a number of beaten people. Those who had received 25 lashes, could not go to work the next morning, so the majority of them had to transfer to Block 7, where they met their death.

A human being was transformed into a running machine in this squad. Everything had to be done at a run, accompanied by caning. The SS were constantly drunk, and they satisfied their animal instincts by tormenting us.

A number of other punitive measures were also implemented.

It was very strictly forbidden to speak a word with a woman, who worked on the same yard.

[Page 186]

For this, you got 25 lashes or a "report"; and that meant: 3 months "S.K." ("Strafkommando").

Various women worked here, most of them Jewish. They represented only one percent of former thousands of living women. Most were from Slovakia. The same discipline applied to the women as to us. They also used to get the same caning. All too well known was the warden with her dog, who was a sadist in every way, both outwardly and inwardly. Even when a smile appeared on her face, it seemed cruel and cynical. The SS boasted [of special cruelties] in front of her, and she in front of them. Man has been turned into a toy here. The men also had to take off their caps in front of the SS woman, which gave her pleasure.

Very frequently, there were inspections of high officers and generals. The "high lords" always used to come to inspect the looted goods.

When such a commission arrived, they used to intensify the beating and tormenting. In this respect, every SS-man wanted to surpass the others, to receive an award for it. Often, the camp commanders "Schwartz" and "Hess" used to come. On such days, not two or three, but 10 or 15 people tortured to death were brought to the camp.

All food found in the luggage had to be delivered to the camp kitchen. The SS people kept the canned food for themselves. After a few days, we were allowed to carry bread into the camp. After work, each of us got a loaf of bread, which was strictly controlled. Usually, I also poured a little tobacco into my pocket, mixed it with bread crumbs, and brought that to the camp. I distributed the tobacco and bread to the still living Krinkers, who kept already waiting for me with impatience, because it was very strictly forbidden (for them) to come to us in the barracks. The strong smokers, like *Yashe Margolyes*(*Margolies*) and others, felt happy when I gave them some tobacco. Every day, I also provided another comrade with my shirts and sweaters.

[Page 187]

I used to put on torn clothes and, with great difficulty, would [change my clothes and] dress in new clothes at work. We were strictly forbidden to carry pocket knives. We could only smuggle them [to the camp], when we went to the train station in the middle of the night for a transport was arriving.

As I mentioned earlier, I remained together with *Ayzik Tzigel*; we shared a "bed" for sleeping and worked together. After five days of working, he received 25 lashes for trying to carry five pieces of sugar into the camp. He was taken back to the camp on a wagon. The next morning, he was sent to another block, from which everyone was usually taken away in unknown directions.

Now I was left alone. I was assigned a Jew from Grodno, to share my bed with. We became good comrades, but unfortunately the situation did not last long. Once, I decided to smuggle a box of sardines into the camp for the "blokovn" [person in authority?] in order to persuade him to take two people, *Yashke Margolyes and Yehoshua Shapiro*, out of the "Crematorium Number 1" work crew and put them in another squad. Thus, on the walk from the train station back to the camp, I took a box of sardines with me. But when we had to pass the block leader's house at the gate, we were searched, and the box of sardines was found on me. My number was noted, and for the moment, I was released. The next morning, I went to work as I did every day. But at lunchtime, the "Zeyde" ("grandpa") called my number and I had to go to him, knowing what to expect.

"Bend down, blighter!" he yelled wildly at me, pointing his finger at the "bench". No reason for the punishment followed, the order had to be carried out immediately.

So I lay down on the "bench", the Kapo clamped my hands and feet, and the "Zeyde" yelled, "Count!" "One!"

[Page 188]

A blow with the braided strap. The piece of lead [at the tip] slashed into my belly. After the first blow, I felt a sharp pain under my heart and felt dizzy. Cries and tears escaped from me, and immediately, a second and third blow fell. Each blow tore a piece of flesh from my body. I counted to "five", but then the Kapo already began to count, because I could not even scream anymore. When they untied my hands and feet, I fell unconscious to the ground.

So I was lying there under the "shap"[20] until the evening. Then, I was put on a cart and taken to the camp. It was only on the way there that I felt the pain. My bedmate put a compress on me with a wet towel[21]. The whole night, I lay on my belly and moaned. The next morning, I barely managed to go out to the roll-call. Two comrades supported me under my arms. But I could no longer go to work. That was, how my three weeks in "Canada " ended.

* * *

That same day, towards evening, the block clerk called my number, and I was led away to block number 3, where those were standing, who had returned from the precinct or those, who had been beaten and could not go back to work. Block "three" was one of the worst and dirtiest blocks. A brick block with 700 prisoners, 600 of whom were only shadows of human beings. They were no longer fit for work, and therefore they were facing the threat of block number 7. The block elder is a Jew from France. A very strict man, but even he cannot fight the dirt in his block. The block number 3 is the way to death. Every day, 30-40 victims are carried out to the wall. The whole day, we had to be on the street. The camp elder drove us from one place to the next, and in this process, quite a few fell down under the canes and died. The healthier inmates were selected to do camp work. They had to carry stones so that the only camp road could be paved. One day I was still lying on the road, and the next morning they had already assigned me to carry heavy stones. I shared the sleeping place with a former Kapo, an Austrian, who had received 25 lashes from the "Rapportführer" Schillinger.

[Page 189]

Being in the camp, we usually saw the trucks, which were fully loaded with people, being transported to the grove. There was a small, brick hut with two wooden barracks. After half an hour, a fire used to flicker out of the pits, and black clouds of smoke darkened the blue sky. Two crematoriums were already complete. Their chimneys were covered with iron, so that they would not burst from the great fire. The height of the chimneys is thirty meters. They are separated from each other by a wide road, and each crematorium is fenced with an electric wire, which is already surrounded by high, wooden watchtowers.

Opposite our camp was the women's camp. We used to watch from a distance, as shadows of women moved over there, without hair, without shoes, in a single blouse or in torn shirts. We were very strictly forbidden to stand near the wire and talk to the women. This was well supervised by the camp Kapo. At the slightest suspicion that one had raised his hand to make a gesture in the direction of the women's camp, there were ten lashes on the spot or a report that meant three months "S.K." [Strafkommando]; this punishment also applied to the women. The women were completely isolated from the men; and no one knew who was still alive, and who from the transports was still in the camp.

From our transport, a group of 17-to 20-year-old girls had come to the camp, but none of us knew if any of them were still alive. The hundreds of women, who worked opposite us in the camp, were very closely guarded. Whenever the women marched to or from work, we were driven off with sticks to the sides of the road. However, if someone managed to get closer, he still did not recognize a familiar face, because both the women and the men had changed very much in appearance. Often I stood at the side, focusing my gaze on the women, who dragged themselves along like shadows, searching for an acquaintance, for someone close to me…

[Page 190]

From our transport, only a few dozen had remained. Every day, their number decreased even more. A few were transported away to a subcamp, to Bana[22]. One transport was assigned to work in a "Sonderkommando" (special command), which was completely separated from the surrounding camps. We were strictly forbidden, to exchange a word with its inmates. However, we knew very well what kind of work they were doing.

The majority of the people in the Sonderkommando looked fine. Whenever they entered the camp, they carried in sacks of food. Often, they would throw bread over for their acquaintances. The only one of them, who came from our shtetl, also used to throw a piece of bread to one of us, which we would share.

Once, I managed to talk to him through a hole in the wall, which they had hacked out. That's how I learned that another one from our shtetl, *Shloime Avnet* (*"the Blond One"*), also worked in the crematorium. He had come there three months before us from another shtetl, and they had assigned him to this work right away.

Through the hole, I was often given a little water and a piece of bread. At the time, while I worked in the camp, both [above mentioned] used to be in the block, because they worked in night shifts. I usually waited a moment when no one noticed, and then we talked. Through them, I learned exactly, what happened during the gassing and burning of people, and about the fate of our relatives. For two weeks, I worked in the camp, building the road. Later, they set up a new work crew from block three. The Kapo, who was my bedmate, became the Kapo of the new squad, which was called "Abort-Baracken" [toilet barracks]. There were 40 people working there, all from block three. Our work consisted of building foundations for the construction of ovens and water pipes for the new camps. Seven camps were under construction, each with 32 [residential] barracks. The work progressed at a rapid pace.

[Page 191]

There were several civilian Poles working with us, with whom we were forbidden to speak. We were only allowed to work and to obey all the orders.

The Kapo treated us well. He did not beat us and did not urge us to work. With me together in the squad, also one of my shtetl worked with me, *Pinye Klas*. He quickly became acquainted with the civilian Poles and began to trade with them secretly. The trade consisted of selling a shirt or a pair of civilian pants without stock stripes, plus, among other things, shoes. These clothes would be obtained from those who worked in "Canada" and in the "Sonderkommando". Pinye had a cousin in the "Sonderkommando", Othniel Leibovitch. He used to "support" him with the things he needed. I established a "partnership" with

Pinyen, and what the civilians brought in return, we divided among ourselves. The Kapo deliberately looked away. We usually also received a few eggs from the civilians. We carried them into the camp and then exchanged them in the canteen, which was only for the Poles and Germans. We illegally traded for cigarettes. And these, we then exchanged for bread. This is how we conducted our illegal trade. At night, just as we were about to leave for the camp, an SS-man came to me who had been standing in the next barrack, keeping a close watch on me. He instructed me to raise my hands and examined me. I had 5 eggs in my pocket at that time. The SS-man took the 5 eggs and wrote down my number. I already knew what was waiting for me.

Three days later, after the second roll call, my number was called. The block elder led me to the "Rapportführer" Schillinger. Usually, every day such "sinners" came to the "rapport" (situation report), and now, when I was standing there, about ten people had already gathered, among them a few Kapos, who had not given enough beatings. Individually, the "crimes committed" were read out. Only one answer we were allowed to give: " Yessir!".

[Page 192]

After the individual reading [of the accusation], the judgement followed:

"Number 93886 was punished with five nights of standing cell!"

"Yessir!" was the answer.

That same night I was led into a narrow "chimney" of 80 square meters, where it was pitch black, with very little air. 20 centimeters of water, in which they had poured some "flarik".[23]

Of our transport, only 10 people had remained in Birkenau. Our work crew increased from 40 to 50 people. The master sent 20 of them to work in the women's camp, digging foundations for ovens and pouring clay for the new barracks.

Among these 20 people, whom the master had designated to work in the women's camp, were myself and Pinye. We were instructed that it was forbidden to talk to the women, even if one recognized his sister there. When entering the women's camp, it was noted how many were going in, and when going out, we were recounted. In addition, there was always a strict check when going in and out; especially letters were searched for. The women's camp had the same number of barracks and stone blocks as our camp. There was the "Toten-Block" (block of dead), number 25, from which some naked, tormented skeletons were taken away each day by trucks. When we first marched to work in the women's camp, skeletons of women cast vacant glances at us, searching for familiar faces. The women looked terrible: In long, gray dresses, without hair, with bloody feet. There was an empty place there, which was called "the plyazhe" [the Beach]. There were usually hundreds of women, lying semi-conscious under the hot sun. They were forbidden to leave the assigned place. The women's camp was overcrowded with inmates, and every day, hundreds of them remained lying on the "plyazhe", and the sun would burn them until eternity.

[Page 193]

Those who could not go to work were given less to eat, that is half a liter of water with pieces of red beet. Also the women suffered from the typical camp disease: diarrhea. They too, were subjected to selections several times a week, carried out by the same cold murderer, Mengele.

In the women's camp there was a leader named "Drekslerke"[24]. Her mere appearance in the camp caused terror among the women. She usually came with her dog, and just in the same way as in our camp, there were also the roll calls with the selections. Moreover, there were SS-men there all the time, who had the task of making sure that the men did not talk to the women. At the slightest suspicion, 25 lashes were threatened.

On the third day of my work in the women's camp, while I was shoveling sand, an SS-man came up to me, with a large dog at his side, and asked me what I had been talking about with the woman. He pointed his finger at a girl standing in the distance. Taking off my cap, I answered that I didn't know anything, that I hadn't spoken to the woman.

"You were very well talking to her, cursed dog!" and he poked me in the chest with his hand.

I continued to say no, only the SS-man insisted.

"Yes, you did speak to her! Come with me to the camp leader!"

So we went to the camp leader. We stopped at his house, the SS-man ran in and made a report about me. He then came back with the well-known murderer, Oberscharführer Moll[25], a short, sturdy man with a round, fat face. He measured me from head to toe and then went back to his office.

The SS-man stopped and smiled under his black whiskers.

[Page 194]

"In just a moment, you will tell what you said!"…

I didn't answer a word but waited for my punishment: Either 25 lashes or a note of my number and then "S.K.".

Soon, the murderer Moll came out with a rough stick in his hand: "Now, will you testify what you said, you dirty dog?"

"I didn't say anything, Herr Oberscharführer", I replied, and still stood there with my hands hanging down as if frozen.

"You'll talk soon!" He shows me his cane and laughs coldly. I do not answer but wait for further orders.

"Bend down, you pig!"

The SS-man standing to the side grabbed my head, and I felt a hard blow. After the sixth blow, which I got on my back, I passed out.

When I opened my eyes again, I was soaked from head to toe. There was an empty bucket on the side. Around me stood: the bandit Moll, the SS-man and several SS women. Everyone laughed and poked me in my sides with their boots.

"Get up, you dog!", I heard the screams of the sadist Moll, and another blow hit my body.

I got up and the SS-man grabbed my head again, and the beatings began again. I no longer felt any pain, only heard the counting and laughter of the sadists standing around, who were enjoying themselves in this bestial "sport".

For the second time, I counted 20 lashes until the murderer Moll stopped, turned to me and laughed. Sweat ran from his face.

"So, now you won't talk anymore! March to the camp, to work!"

[Page 195]

He instructed the SS-man to take good care of me, that I was working hard.

This had been my first punishment, which I had received simply because of a false accusation by the SS-man, who wanted to prove to the camp leader that he was loyal and paying good attention. Until evening, the SS-man stood next to me and drove me to work. I only felt the pain when I returned to the camp, after roll call. Again I put cold compresses on and next morning, I didn't go to work.

On the third day I went back to work, because there had been seizures in the camp, as I learned from a room service. The seizures went as follows:

All block leaders, together with the elders and block elders, had gone to the camp to find those who were hiding and not going to work. Most of them could no longer work, but they did not want to go to Block 7 either. Now that all ("refuseniks") had been herded into one place, a truck arrived, onto which all were herded with sticks and transported to the crematorium.

This day, one of our shtetl was also taken away, Yehoshua Shapiro, who had already been lying next to the wall and could no longer go to work. All my efforts to take him to our work crew had been in vain. He was already unable to stand on his feet.

Our small group was getting even smaller with each passing day. During the time I worked with Pinye in the women's camp, we looked for a familiar woman's face, but we found none. Whenever we asked the women who worked in the same barracks and carried the excavated earth out, we got the same answer: There is no one left from our transport, everyone is already in the crematorium.

Every day, Schillinger came to us on a bicycle to check our work. In the process, he constantly administered slaps to our Kapo for not speeding up the work.

[Page 196]

Thus, the Kapo decided to watch out if Schillinger came. Then everyone should work harder. In fact, he often gave out slaps then, when some of us sat idle.

The Kapo ordered me to stand all the time at the door of the barracks and watch, whether Schillinger or another SS-man would show himself. In that case, I was to give a sign that one should work. Every minute that we gained by idleness meant for us to live a whole hour longer.

So I stood at the door and paid close attention. When the Kapo went around the camp, we usually all lay in the pit, holding our work utensils in our hands, so that we would be ready to work immediately.

I watched the women who passed by incessantly. Maybe I would meet someone from our shtetl after all! I just didn't want to believe that none of them should be there anymore. Usually, together with Pinye, I went around the "plyazhe" with a cartload of bricks and searched, but I found no one.

I meet the only girl from Krynki

So another two weeks of hard work went by. Two weeks of tormenting body and soul, with no hope that tomorrow would provide something better for me. But anyhow, time still fulfilled its mission to bring me something new. And something unexpected happened, something new, which illuminated my further hard life in the concentration camp and awakened courage in me to endure.

I'm standing at my post as I do every day. Before my eyes, pale, mournful women are moving around and carrying earth – for whom and for what, who knows?…

Suddenly, I see something incredible, something that can only be some sick perception: There's a girl in a torn shirt, from which parts of her body look out on the corrupted world. Her feet are bound with paper, and blood is trickling out from underneath. Her head is shaved, her face small and pale. She drags

[Page 197]

a large bucket to pour it out. Her eyes are so familiar to me. But I am afraid of my own imagination – maybe it is only me who thinks it is my classmate Rochele Zakheim!

I'm exchanging ideas with my friend Pinye about my assumption. We decide to call her by name when she gets back from work. A few minutes pass. Standing there, we are already very impatient. At that moment, the little creature, like a pitiable ten-year-old child, shows up. The bucket she is carrying is already empty. She walks with slow steps; we can see that she is at the end of her strength. And yet! The face is similar to that of Rochele at former times. I had stopped at the open door at my post. Pinye was going off sideways, and when he saw her approaching the barrack, he called softly, "Rochele!"

"Avroheml!", we heard her answer, and then she immediately fell down to the earth.

SS-men walking past us turned around. I did not dare to move from my place, because I knew all too well that it would cost us both our lives if I walked toward her.

I remained in my spot and watched Rochele pass out on the floor, so close to me!

"Heart, can you really bear so much?", I think today, remembering that shuddering moment. There, I am standing at the door, seeing the only girl from Krynki, my comrade of my sweet school years! Later, both of us were active together in the children and youth organization "SKIF" ['Socialist Children's Union']. Together we attended lectures on the struggle for a finer, fair life. We spent the summer in the camp, went on trips together, and our songs used to echo in the wide surroundings. Now, there lies a shadow of the always laughing Rochele.

Now she is weak and helpless, and I do not even have the human right to help her up from the blood-soaked ground. A couple of girls pick them up and bring them to the barracks. In front of me reveals a great sacred goal: to help the only surviving girl of my native town Krynki.

[Page 198]

Pinye decides the same. I bribe my capo. He gives me the number on her arm and informs me that she is in block number 9, that is, that her days of life are numbered. The Kapo became my liaison between me and Rochele. He delivered my first few words to her, "Hang in there, we will help you as long as we live."

When he returned, he brought me a piece of paper on which she had written, "I remained the only one of the whole transport."

Now we had to give her concrete help: First of all, to dress her so that she got a better appearance. Because in the condition she was currently in, she was one of the first candidates for going into the crematorium. To get clothes for her, we had to hire the Kapo and pay him well, to provide her with them. In particular, we had to pay him for causing the German women who held a leading position in the camp to take Rochele out of the block. We bribed those "women" especially with good cigarettes, silk stockings and other luxury items, for which we risked our lives each time we smuggled them in.

A few days later we manage to have her taken out of Block 9, and Rochele gets work in "Canada". There, she no longer needs clothing (by us)[26]. She receives food through me and Pinye, how much we can only bring over. Her situation is improving every day. We often see each other from afar and write letters to each other. She washes my shirts for me so that I look clean and "mannered". A good appearance prolongs the life of the detainees. I also feel more courageous, and the painful days seem to pass more quickly. I don't know if I was in love then with her, my current wife, and if there could even be love in such a terrible, hellish situation. But I know very well that she had given me a lot of strength to be able to endure the most terrible period of my life.

However, the happiness of being in the same camp with Rochele did not last long. Lined up in "rows of five," the Kapo led us out of the women's camp. Rochele accompanied me silently from the side. I took my last glances at her – and saw that she had big tears in her eyes.

[Page 199]

In our camp, I told everyone from our shtetl that Rochele Zakheim was here. And that we all, as long as we lived, had to see to do our utmost to keep her alive. I and Pinye pledged to spare no effort to get her out of the present situation. I also told the Kapo that I had found a sister in the camp who was in a very bad situation, as a result of which she could be "taken out" at a selection every day. The Kapo agreed to be helpful, that is, to effect patronage by the German women who kept a head position in the camp. We made an effort [in return?] to procure a dress and shoes. Every day we "brought" cigarettes; we received "onions" organized by the Poles, who received a "parcel from freedom" in return. We procured and brought everything we could to the women's camp, giving courage and hope to the only girl, who now no longer felt so miserable and was gaining more courage with each passing day.

The First Passover in the Camp

Life in all concentration camps transformed man into a bipedal animal with all its base instincts. Man has quickly lost his human dignity, his inner balance, his former human feelings.

The only ideal and effort was to figure out how to get another piece of bread or a few spoonfuls of watery soup to satisfy the beastly hunger. Death, which lurked at every turn, did not affect us as much as the terror of hunger.

The camp man imagined that after a few pieces of bread and a few spoonfuls of soup he would gain the strength to control death. And one must add that an inner, incomprehensible urge and will to live, and to survive the bestial Hitlerism, was deeply rooted in the hearts of each of us, although death accompanied us like a shadow all around.

[Page 200]

In our camp, I told It was characteristic that every person who was so close to death developed a particularly strong will to live.

The old concentration campers, who had been imprisoned for several years, forgot bit by bit that outside the electric wire there was another world where free people lived in dignity. They also forgot their former nearest and dearest, and in general everything that had been before. It seemed to them as if dozens of years had already passed, and that what was happening there on that piece of earth was a normal occurrence and would remain forever. Very seldom did we hear from an old concentration camper, such as a block elder, a clerk or a Kapo, a reminder of his past in the free world.

The camp man simply erased the memory of his past and lived only in an uncertain "today". Whether we would experience the next day was not certain, and with the red sky, the black smoke and the selections that spared no one, the " tomorrow " was no longer in our thoughts. We only lived in the present[27]. Every time the cold murderer Mengele showed himself in the camp, he already knew exactly how many people, whether healthy or sick, he would send to their deaths today.

So it is quite understandable that in such gruesome conditions no one knew the exact date or even a holiday. A holiday was whenever someone got hold of a piece of bread or a little watery soup. In the camp, there were also very religious Jews and Christians, who silently and secretly said a prayer, so that the block elder could not notice it. My bedmate was an elderly Jew who prayed silently every day, both at work and at camp and roll call, while looking around intently on all sides. From this Jew I learned that tonight was Passover.

Previously, we were only aware of one day of the week when we only worked until 12 noon, and that was Sunday.

[Page 201]

The names of the other days and months became quite foreign to us. Thus our enslaved life flowed away.

When I learned that today was Passover, my heart throbbed violently. I remembered my former home in the free world, when we had lived together with my family in the happy, laughing shtetl. When we went to the forest to pick nuts, played with dyed eggs and drank the sweet Passover wine.

Near Passover, the Nazi beasts began transporting tens of thousands of Slovak, Czech and Hungarian Jews from Carpathian Russia. They had been told that they would be taken to the Garden of Eden, where they would live like "God in Odessa."[28]

Just before Passover, the first two crematoriums began to burn, incinerating ten to fifteen thousand healthy people in 24 hours. Incessantly, day and night, the chimneys spewed out thousands of innocent human souls.

Here, in the gruesome, cruel death camp, where human life had not the slightest value, there were still people who could love each other, and on whom the camp climate and living conditions had not had such an effect.

When the pious Jews from Carpathian Russia came to the camp and saw the "Garden of Eden" to which they had been brought, they walked around on the first day of Passover with their heads hanging down, and some of them kept their bread in their pockets, not wanting to eat leaven. A few of these Jews worked with me, and when I told them about the fate of the families who had been taken away from the railroad station on trucks, they did not want to believe it and even said that we only wanted to frighten them.

The only place where people could talk freely to each other was the toilet. There, in the silence, one carried a little bit of conversation concerning the sad situation and all our fates, which had already been sealed before.

[Page 202]

Only a few of the transports were allowed to pass through to the camp, but they too, like the greater part of the transports, would be sent to their deaths in a few weeks, one a day earlier, the other a day later.

The Gypsy Camp

The new camps were quickly completed, and right after Passover, transports of Gypsies began arriving in camp "e", which had 32 barracks. Most of the Gypsies, whole families, came from Germany. Therefore, the "e" camp was called "Gypsy camp".[29] Our old camp was transferred to a new one, called "d" camp, which consisted of 32 wooden barracks, two kitchens, a housing unit for the block leader, plus two latrines, which already had a more modern status than the old ones. There was also a bathroom, where one could have a wash every day. In the new camp, I was taken to Block 20, where the block elder was a French Jew, named "Zhulte".

It was very strictly forbidden to talk to the Gypsies. In the first period, the Gypsies were in a privileged situation. Their clothes were not taken away, nor was their hair shorn. They all spoke German. Among them, there were many former soldiers and officers of the German Wehrmacht, who had been withdrawn from the front because of their Gypsy origins.

The Gypsies also had to undergo a roll call, but it did not last as long as ours. Among them, there were many pregnant women and small children, who also had to stand during a roll call.

The Gypsies were not conscripted to work, but therefore they were given less to eat, not 200 grams of bread, but only 100. Every day, their mortality rate increased, and for the sick there was already no place to lie down. The number of Gypsies was 12,000.

[Page 203]

For a while, our squad worked in the Gypsy camp, and I managed to talk to many of them. Some of them showed me military awards from their army days in the Battle of Stalingrad. With each passing day, the Gypsies lost more and more of their belief that they could once again return to freedom. Thus, in a short time, their number decreased from 12,000 to 7,000 people. One Sabbath evening, a commission with several generals arrived from Berlin. They drew a sign on each barrack with a red pen. This meant that all living people from this barrack would have to be gassed. The next afternoon, the chief of all crematoria, Oberscharführer Moll, arrived on a motorcycle and issued a decree: "Blocksperre!"[30] This regulation also applied to our camp. Immediately the gongs sounded in both camps, and our hearts pounded. We already had enough experience and knew what that meant: namely, that the next candidates [for the gas chamber] were either us or the Gypsies.

We saw through the cracks of the barracks, how trucks flew into the Gypsy camp, and soon after, the loud screaming of women and crying of children could be heard. I climbed onto the top bunk, which was close to the skylight. In front of my eyes, there were

Gypsy Camp in Auschwitz

[Page 204]

SS-men in two rows with canes in their hands, yelling, "go, quick, tempo!"

The cries for help reached the sky. Several women were rolling in the street. Revolver shots and shouts of "oh God!" could be heard, along with the cries of young men, "I was a German soldier after all, I was in the war for our Fatherland!"

It took two hours before the camp with its 7000 inhabitants was emptied. In the crematorium, some resisted. Thus, the Gypsy transport ended its life. The next morning, the SS-men found four children hiding in the latrine. They were led to the crematorium the same day. Absolutely nothing remained of the fact that just one day before 7,000 human had been there suffering, but alive.

Greek Jews arrive

All four crematoria are already in operation. The "Sonderkommando" (special command) has increased in size. Now, a railroad line has already been laid directly to the crematorium. Summer has arrived and one can feel the fragrant air of the surroundings. A little wind tries to soothe the unfortunates, but immediately, the summer air turns into the air of death. The smell of roasted flesh escapes from the crematoria, and when the air pressure drops and the smoke descends to earth, the whole area is filled with the smell of death. In the hot summer days, both "Canada" as well as the "Sonderkommando" were enlarged. Therefore, everyone knew that the arrival of new transports to a greater extent was expected, but no one knew from which country. Anyway, immediately when the first transport arrived, the whole camp knew that they were Jews from Greece. Each transport numbered 1500 people, 200 of whom were allowed into the camp. Between 4-6 transports arrived every day. After a few days, the camp was overcrowded with men and women. Selections happened more regularly now. The arriving people did not know where they were and where they were being led. They all had to go their last way under the hot sun, accompanied by the orchestra.

[Page 205]

All crematoria were spilling smoke during day and night, and when they became overcrowded, they began to burn the bodies in large pits. The whole horizon was one red flame.

The newly arrived Jews in the camp knew immediately about the grim fate of their families.

Most of the Greek Jews did not know a word of Yiddish. Some of them could speak Hebrew. Their usual language was Spanish or Greek. Immediately they felt the full force of camp life.

Boger-the "human sadist" leads a Jew to be shot, with his hands tied behind his back

A Jew hangs on the wall in the bunker

[Page 206]

They were beaten more than others, because they did not understand what the sadistic murderers were saying to them.

After a very short time, most of them became "Muselmänner"[31]…During each selection, the Greek Jews were singled out first and foremost. Despite the large outflow of arrested Jews, the camp was constantly overcrowded. The number of "Laufnummern"[32] grew up to 134,000, of which 10,000 were still alive.

In the yard of crematorium number 1, a barrack had been built, and in the days when the Greek Jews arrived, our squad was detached to work there. We saw healthy men and women enter the crematorium, all dark-skinned, with their children in their arms, driven by the murderers with canes in their hands. Every day I met with Otniel Leibovitsh and Shloime the blond. They informed me about the incidents that occurred during the gassing of the Jews in the crematorium.

Today when I met them, they told me what had happened to a little boy. It was already the third transport. Whole mounds of gassed people lay next to the ovens.

The people who arrived with the trucks, had to undress and were driven into the gas bunkers by the Nazis with canes. Then the murderous sadist, Moll, poured in a green powder from a can, and after ten minutes, everyone was already lying there dead. After that, the workers of the "Sonderkommando" opened the doors and fans drove out the gas. After entering the bunker, when the corpses were loaded onto elevators, they noticed that a little boy was lying at the wall, still moving his eyes and his tongue. They carried the child out of the bunker to a second room, where they laid him on a sheet and waved to him several times. After a few minutes, the child revived and regained consciousness. The murderer Moll immediately called the camp doctor Mengele and told him, that this child had survived, although all the others had already died. The cold sadist Mengele took the child to his laboratory, where various experiments were carried out on living, healthy people. Next day, Mengele returned, bringing the child with him. He was dead, with cuts all over, and was wrapped in a blanket. The child's heart and lungs had been removed and the top of its skull sawed off. Later, the murderer Moll told the Kapo of the "Sonderkammando", what the professors of the laboratory had found out concerning the child: The child would have lived to be 132 years old and become the strongest person in the world. The gas had not been able to penetrate his heart. All the child's strength was in his long black hair.[33]

[Page 207]

For two months, there was no end to the Greek transports. 50,000 Jews arrived, of whom only 10,000 were admitted to the camp. After several months, only a few dozen of the 10,000 were left. Immediately after the Greek transports were stopped, prisoners from our camp were started to be transported to other camps, such as Avizhne [Jaworzno?], Buna[34] and Blechhammer, to work in the coal mines.

Also the ten people from our transport, who had remained in Birkenau, were sent to the other camps, so I was left alone with Otniel, whom I now saw less often.

It became very difficult to talk to those who worked in the crematorium. I also couldn't meet Rochele as often now. Our squad fell further apart. I could no longer get into the women's camp. My situation worsened and I now had to go hungry more often. All my comrades had left with the transport (to the other camps). Our work crew was reduced to 20 people. We no longer worked together with civilians. Now, we were transferred to barrack number 18, where I got a very bad place to sleep, that is, next to the "barrel".[35]

The block elder, a "Volksdeutscher" (ethnic German), used to strike right and left, especially at us Jews. I began to feel that the day was approaching to be taken out on the occasion of a selection. Especially with regard to Rosh Hashanah and Yom Kippur, I was particularly fearful.

[Page 208]

On those two days, the cold killer committed a massacre of both us men and the women. On the first Yom Kippur, they took out from our camp 3000 people, the majority of them Greek Jews. In the women's camp, too, it was mainly the Greek women who met the same fate as the men; since they did not know German, they suffered even more than the others. In our camp, the workers usually got an "allowance" twice a week, which consisted of 300 grams of bread and a piece of sausage made from horse meat. The Greek Jews used to exchange their sausage for cigarettes and their margarine too, for something else. The camp elder then issued a decree that the Greek Jews would no longer receive an "allowance". This was the punishment for exchanging their portions.

In the middle of 1943, a transport of non-Polish Jews was sent to Warsaw to clean the bombed ghetto. Very many Jews were brought back after a short time in a half-dead state. They were all immediately taken to the crematorium. Also from the other camps like Jaworzno, Dora, Blechhammer and Buna, transports were brought very often with completely exhausted people, who were no longer able to work. Not far from the camp, downed German and enemy planes were brought to be worked on by thousands of people, mostly Russian prisoners. From this squad, people used to flee more often. Every week, usually two or three Russians escaped and remained, as if disappeared into thin air. No matter how much effort and energy they expended to find them, the Nazis never succeeded. If one was missing, the news spread everywhere. Both in the police commissariats and in the camp, the siren used to give a sign, screaming, as if a thousand enemy planes were approaching to bomb. If one was missing, all the SS-men were ready with their wolfhounds. The squad, from which there were often escapes, was called "Zerlege-Betrieb" ["dismantling plant"]. There, the planes were chopped into pieces and loaded onto rail cars. The aluminum sheet was taken to Germany to be used to build new airplanes.

[Page 209]

It was characteristic that Poles or Jews who fled, were caught immediately, but when Russians used to escape, they were impossible to find.

I began to work out a plan to successfully escape. My only goal was to get to freedom in order to make known to the public what happened in Auschwitz.

Together with another Jew who worked in "Canada", *Ravuke Garbatke*, we began to concretize the plan. We decided to escape from "Canada", starting from the railroad station. With great difficulty, I managed to get back to "Canada".

Our plan was to hold on to a passing train and then jump off 50 kilometers past Auschwitz, to flee to the Beskid Mountains. We reported for work at the railroad station and waited for a favorable opportunity. But everything turned out differently. During the time we were at the station, no trains used to pass. So, we waited completely in vain. Every day was even longer and harder for us to bear, and I didn't meet with Rochele anymore. I really wanted to get her inside to work in the "Women's Canada".

After strong efforts at the women's Kapo, I managed to get her work in "Canada" [again?], where she was considered my sister. However, the same severe punishment was threatened here, if one spoke to a woman. The women worked in special barracks and were closely guarded; but despite the many precautions I [usually] managed to talk to her briefly. Rochele then told me about the painful sufferings she had endured before meeting us, and about the fate of the other girls, who had all perished. The last to perish was *Mertshe Yaglam*, who had been with Rochele in death block number 25, from where she was led to the gas chamber.

[Page 210]

When the trucks drove up to pick up the women, the cold murderer Mengele performed the selections together with Dr. Hessler [Hössler?], who was only acting in the women's camp. The bandits decreed that those women, who still have the strength to get out of the "box", should go out to the roll call square. Out of a thousand women, a few dozen then came out and were ordered to walk there and back. Of them, seven were set aside. Among them was Rochele! All the others were taken to the gas chamber. Mertshe Yaglam also died at that time; even before she was taken to the crematorium.

After two months of work in "Canada" I fell ill with epidemic typhus. I was taken to the "precinct" into a block where 300 typhoid patients were lying. The doctor, who cured the sick, was Dr Schorr from Warsaw. Among the sick were Jews, Poles, Russians, Germans and French. Selections were made only among the Jews. All those, who had a fever above 38 degrees, were taken away to the gas chamber. After I had lain for ten days, a selection was made. Doctor Schorr instructed me to get dressed and take a broom in my hand. At present, I had a fever of 39 degrees.

At ten o'clock in the morning, the cold murderer Mengele appeared, accompanied by quite a few SS officers, and soon we heard: "Jews have to line up in rows of five!"

I stood to the side with the broom in my hand and swept out. There were 76 Jews in the block, of whom the murderer Mengele put 70 at the side. Then he turned his stern gaze on me, asking, what I was doing there. Dr Schorr answered him that I was working as a "Stubendienst" (room service).

In the evening at 5 o'clock, a truck arrived with six SS-men, each holding a cane in his hand. The block clerk read out the numbers. Everyone walked quietly to the door, glancing back once more. Dr. Schorr stood to the side with a pale face and big tears in his eyes. There was a dead silence in the block. Everyone felt enwrapped by death. Immediately, after the murderer Mengele left, I lay back in bed. My thoughts flew far into the distance. I would have liked to go back to the camp as quickly as possible, in order to continue our plan to escape.

[Page 211]

After 6 weeks of bed rest, I recovered, but remained very weak. My body was only skin and bones, my eyes were deep in their sockets. I knew that I would not last much longer in such a condition. When I came back to the camp, I was no longer accepted to work into "Canada." I now had to work in the squad "Zimmerei" ("Carpentry"), where the same Kapo was as then in the "Barracks Construction". I worked only a little. Every day, I visited the "Sonderkommando", where I got a piece of bread from Othniel and Shloime. After three days of work in the "carpentry ", I felt very bad and could no longer march out to work. *Shloime* then took me and hid me in his bed, where I used to lie from early morning until the evening roll call. I also got food from him.

So I lay there for two weeks without marching out from the camp. On the 1st of May, we worked only until noon. After that, everyone stayed in the camp and "celebrated" May Day; in the afternoon, we gathered with *Shloime* at his "box" and sang workers' songs. Meanwhile, a guard stood at the gate to signal us in case SS-men came. *Othniel* often sang Russian songs. He was always cheerful, although he knew that he might not live to see the next day.

Shloime was the exact opposite. He, a constant dreamer with a silent, melancholy look, used to say to me, "Avroheml, we must free ourselves, or at least fall like heroes in battle!" *Shloime's* thoughts were always busy making plans how to blow up the crematoria so that no one could be gassed anymore.

[Page 212]

As I wrote before, I was in block number 18, where 95 percent were Russians. I slept together with four Russians, all of whom worked in the "dismantling plant." One of my bedfellows once confided a secret to me. He asked me to bring him two large knives and a battery. I immediately understood for what purpose this should be.

Russians Escape

I left for the "Sonderkommando" [special squad] and asked Shloime for the things. He, immediately, gave me two "Holy Sabbath Knives" and two batteries. Shloime promised to bring me as many knives as I wanted. I brought the knives to the Russian, who took them and thanked me, saying that the things would be very useful, but I should not tell anyone about them. The Russian, a former major in the Red Army, became my best friend. We used to share our food. When I brought a piece of bread from an acquaintance from "Canada" or from the "Sonderkommando", I shared it with him. When he got a few potatoes from his comrades, he brought them to me already boiled from the squad. This is how we settled in, hoping we could keep it that way as long as possible. Often, we lay on the beds for hours, and he [the Russian] used to tell me about his battles and how he, being in an unconscious state, had been taken in captivity from which, however, he had escaped twice. As a punishment, he had been taken to Birkenau concentration camp, where – he whispered in my ear – the same plan had to be worked on. That was the only way out, he said. The Russian was called Fedyor Tichi (the quiet one) because although there were so many "Fedyors" in the block, there were no "Tichis" (quiet ones) except my friend.

Fedyor advised me to try to get back to work in "Canada" so that I could bring what I was told to get from there. I followed him and went back to work in "Canada". Rochele was also working there. She knew that I had been ill with typhoid fever. We were in letter contact through my comrade *Zeidl Epstein*, who often visited me when I was sick in bed, bringing along a letter from Rochele. When I came back to work [in Canada], I did not tell anyone about my plans and for what purpose I was now working. Every day, I met with Fedyor, who told me what I should bring.

[Page 213]

He mainly asked for knives, maps, passports, batteries and watches. I usually brought all this when I marched to the train station at night. I knew that I was threatened with the gallows if I was caught with any of these things. Therefore, I was very careful. Often, there were strict searches at the gate – while a map was under a bandage wrapped around my arm, or a compass or a watch was hidden in my shoe. But knowing what purpose it was for, nothing has been too difficult for me. I knew that my knife would be used to fight the murderous Nazis, and that with the help of the map they would try to find their way out of the camp without getting into another one. I also brought shoes and civilian clothes. Only my friend Fedyor and I knew about it. In case there was a strict control, but I had to deliver the requested things on the same day, I usually got them with the help of a girl from "Canada". She used to hand over the things to my comrade who worked in the women's camp. Otherwise, I only used to get wristwatches through the girl. However, she did not know for what purpose. Usually three people escaped in a week, and only very rarely one got caught. The camp command put all its efforts into catching the fugitives and finding out where the "maline" [hiding place] was from which they used to escape. Once, when they caught three fugitives, they could not get out of them where they had been hiding. All three were kept in the bunker[36] and tortured. They cut pieces of flesh from the body of one of them and poured pepper into his wounds. But everything was to no avail. The next morning they were sentenced to death by hanging. One of them was put on the gallows as a dead man. The other two made a heroic resistance, fighting with their feet. Before they were hanged, the whole camp was summoned. SS-men were placed around it in case of a riot.

[Page 214]

When the death sentence was read, one of the condemned cried out, "Comrades, I die for the Fatherland, take revenge for my blood, I die for Stalin!"

As soon as he had mentioned the word "Stalin," the camp commander, Kramer, ran to him with a knife and cut out his tongue. A torrent of blood poured out onto the ground. Choking screams could still be heard. The camp elder pulled the chairs away from under the condemned. A gasp was heard, and then all three hung in the air.

After that, we all had to march past, each with his head pointed at the dead. The deceased remained hanging like this for two days. But despite all this, the escapes did not stop. Every third to fourth day, the siren wailed that another one had escaped. And again, as usual late at night, the SS-men ran out with their dogs like poisoned mice but came back without success. Finally, the camp command understood that it was an organized escape movement. They immediately transferred a Russian colonel into the S.K. ["Strafkompanie"], with the inscription "i.l." [inside the camp][37]. The colonel was not allowed to march out to work. He only worked in the camp as a street sweeper. That's what they did with everyone who was suspected of escaping.

This colonel was the main organizer of the escape movement. He determined who and when to flee.

Fedyor promised me that the day would come for me, too, to be destined to escape. In the meantime, however, I should continue to work actively to enable others to escape. At the same time, 5 people escaped on their own: The clerk of Block 26, two Kapos, a Dutchman and a German Jew. They bribed an SS-man who led them out of the chain of guard posts. But then, this SS-man shot them all and, back in the camp, reported that five people had escaped and that he had shot them all. He received an award for it. All five were taken to the camp. They were laid down by the camp gate so that everyone would see them. A similar case occurred with the person in charge of block number 3. The SS-man, whom he had bribed, also brought him back dead. Several Russian women also escaped from the women's camp, but they were caught.

[Page 215]

Later, the clerk of the women's camp, a Czech girl, Malye, escaped together with a Pole. After four days of searching, they were both caught in Katowice. Malye was stuck in the bunker. During her interrogation, she took a bottle that had been on the table and split the head of "Oberscharführer" Boger[38]. For this she was sentenced to be burned alive. The Pole was hanged in our camp, in the presence of all the detainees.

I have mentioned before the heroic Jewish girl who shot with her own hand the notorious sadistic murderer Schillinger. However, this circumstance is worth describing in more detail. It was the end of 1943, and at two o'clock in the night a transport was brought with American citizens who had been interned in Berlin. The SS were sure that these people would not resist, so they were led to special crematoria. There was no selection at all, but all were led to death right away. The fourth truck with people drove up to Crematorium 1; on it was a young girl, an artist.[39] The people brought by the truck before were already in the bunker; their clothes were hanging in the "undressing room". At that time, the murderer Schillinger was on duty and walking around, prodding people with his cane to undress faster and tie their shoes together.

The young girl, wearing her coat and holding her reticule, walked around the crematorium, reading the inscriptions on the walls.

[Page 216]

The murderer Schillinger ran to her with the words, "Miss, why don't you undress to take a shower?"

"I don't want a bandit like you to see my naked body," the girl replied.[40]

This made the killer's blood boil, and he struck her on the shoulder with his cane.

The girl jumped up to the killer, grabbed his hands and gave him with her head a sharp blow into his face. He dropped the cane and reached for his revolver. When he had already stripped off the holster and was holding the revolver, the heroic girl dug her teeth into the flesh of his hand with the last of her strength and bit down hard. The pain was so intense that the killer dropped the revolver from his hand. The girl grabbed the revolver and immediately shot the killer in his chest. He, immediately, fell dead in a pool of blood on the cement. A second SS-man then rushed in to seize the revolver. But the girl shot a bullet at him, too. After that she shot into the electric lamps, so that it became dark in the whole crematorium. When the other SS-men heard the shooting, they ran out of the crematorium. They set up machine guns in the windows and shot at the girl, who defended herself to the last bullet and died a heroic martyr. The crematorium had been destroyed by the bullets. The remaining people who were in the bunker had heard the shooting and had run out naked. The next day, they were all lying shot in the yard of the crematorium. Many found death on the electric wire.

As I have already written, I was the only one of our transport who remained in Birkenau, after the second remaining one, Otniel, who had worked in the crematorium, was sent away on a transport together with another 200 workers of the "Sonderkommando" in May 1944. They were taken to Lublin, under the pretext that there they would work there. But right after they left the train, they were taken to the bathroom. From there, they were led to another room, 5 at a time, and shot.

[Page 217]

The "Luner"[?] Kapo *Leyzer Harontchik* (now staying in the state of Israel) had, during a selection, sent Otniel Leibovitch to the Lublin camp, i.e., to his certain death, because the latter had refused to shave him at the same time as an SS-man.

Still remaining in the "Sonderkommando" was Shloime the Blond, who now began to work out a plan to blow up the crematorium, to put an end to the burning of people.

In the "Sonderkommando" were brought 20 Russians from [the KZ] Majdanek, who did the same work there as before in Majdanek. Among the Russians, there was a former major who, together with Shloime, worked out a plan to put an end to it all. When I came in to Shloime to get some knives or a pair of civilian pants from him, I usually found him lying with the major in a corner of the bed, quietly whispering to each other.

"Avroheml, we will shortly put an end to our criminal work! We will fall, but as heroes!" These were the words that Shloime spoke to me.

The work had to be done extremely secretly, because there were many traitors in the camp who would send their own comrades to their doom just for a piece of bread, or even for some watery soup. When we found such a traitor, we used to throw a blanket over his head and punch him properly in his sides.

Shloime confided in me that they were working on building a bomb. The [gun] powder for this was brought by the women who worked in the [gun] powder factory. Since the women were very strictly controlled, all this happened only with the greatest difficulties. But despite all these troubles, individual women used to bring a bit of powder every day in their shoes, handing it over to the designated man, who would deliver it to Shloime.

[Page 218]

The plan called for four crematoria to be blown up at the same time. Then, the barbed wires of the women's camp were to be torn open so that everyone could escape. Opening the barbed wires of the men's camp was too difficult because the men' camp was far away from the crematorium, whereas the women's camp was only separated from the crematorium by a barbed wire.

The work to enable escapes also continued. Every week, three to four people escaped. They disappeared off the face of the earth. The preparation of the uprising developed at a rapid pace. We in the camp knew, where the front was and that the Russians were approaching our place. We also knew that we would all be killed at the last minute before the Nazis were defeated. This is what happened in Lublin: 70,000 people were shot there in several hours.

In the first row, there had been the Jewish prisoners. A few days before the uprising, the murderer Moll learned of the plans. That very evening, he summoned the Jewish Kapo Kaminski and demanded to hand over to him the people who were at the head of the organization. After torturing the Kapo for two hours, he shot him and threw him alone into the oven.

After two days, something went wrong again in crematorium number 1. It happened in the morning at 10 o'clock. One escaped from crematorium number 1 to crematorium number 3, where Shloime was working, and reported that the operation had failed. Thereupon, those from crematorium number 3 detonated their bomb and threw the German Kapo and the "Oberscharführer" alive into the fire. The crematorium was destroyed! Everyone then rushed out to the courtyard and ran to the guard towers. With bare hands, they heroically defeated quite a few guards' posts. They took their rifles and ran to the crematoria 1 and 2. There, they tore the barbed wire from the women's camp and the majority fled.

[Page 219]

The SS immediately understood what was going on. First, they ordered all the squads to lie face down on the floor and not to raise their heads.

The siren began to whistle and the SS ran to the crematoria. The heroic fighters defended themselves in the yard of the crematorium. The majority fled, taking with them other prisoners who were working near the crematorium.

The whole courtyard was laid out with red bodies, among which was Shloime, with his belly shot through. The SS issued a call for help and then circled an area of 50 kilometers. So they then managed to bring back those who had escaped. Most of them defended themselves with their bare hands and fell as heroes in battle.

Crematorium "three" had been completely destroyed and no longer could anyone be gassed there. Shloime fell like a martyr in the fight for the honor of the Jewish people. Glory be to his memory!

Work crew "Canada"

I worked in "Canada". We, who were called by the Nazis "the Litvishe" or "the Grodner", or "Bessarabia Dogs", were beaten the most, whether by the Kapo or by the SS. And we were driven to do the worst work.

The work in "Canada" went its course. Every day the same. In good order, the wagons were loaded with clothes, shoes, bedding and rag sacks.

The work was already so well established that we thought it had been going on all our lives and would stay that way forever. Forever, we will be hunted down and tormented with the stick. Eternally, we will be led to and from work under duress. We had already completely renounced freedom. If we ever wanted to remember the past, the beautiful world where people could go and do whatever they wanted, we would paint inner pictures of freedom, each on our own[41]. But when we raised our heads and saw the black smoke with the red flame, then the sweet dreams disappeared and the vision of death took their place.

[Page 220]

When I used to meet Rochele for two minutes, behind the wall of the barracks and hidden from the murderous SS eyes, we would talk about freedom. What would it be like if by chance we again became free people? I usually did not believe that this could ever happen because I knew only one thing: we would have to free ourselves alone! I did not deviate from my plan to escape for a single minute. Usually, when I was lying on the bed with Fedyor and we were talking about our plans, I asked him if we would be able to get Rochele, too, out of the camp and lead her to the Beskids Mountains. The meeting point of all the refugees was located there.

It was our plan to first escape, and when we were already a larger, armed group, to raid the camp and free all the prisoners; this was the only way to freedom. In the "B" camp, there were Czech families, women, men and small children. They usually received parcels and letters. It was called "Czech Family Camp". It was the same with them as with the Gypsies: At first they still wore their civilian clothes, but a little later their civilian clothes were dyed with red stripes. Their treatment became stricter every day; the rations became less. With each day the mortality increased, until a "commission of the dead" of some generals arrived from Berlin, who pronounced the death sentence on the whole Czech camp. Before the execution of the mass murder, each prisoner had to write a card with the words:

"We are alive and well. We are well. We work and earn."

[Page 221]

Sunday evening there was a block lockdown in our camp. We knew that the entire Czech camp was being led out to the crematorium. The people put up a heroic resistance, when they were driven into the bunker.

Into their camp, fresh transports were brought from other camps, such as Blizhin [Blochin?] and Hungary.

Now, a new, large camp was created, which was called "Mexico". Nobody knew, for whom this camp was and who would live there. Later, we learned that women from Lodz were to come to the camp; the crematoria were preparing to receive 70,000 Jews from the Lodz ghetto.

"Canada" prepared to take their packs and clothes, and I prepared to leave the camp. After the first transport of Jews from Lodz, my friend Fedyor told me to bring a map, a compass, three batteries and three watches. This would be for myself. After I had brought that, I should leave "Canada" and go to work in the "dismantling plant", from where I would escape together with two other people, among whom he, my friend Fedyor, also would be.

I quickly brought three large knives and three watches; a compass was given to me by a girl from Sokolka, Rochel Malski. I also brought the compass to the camp, and Fedyor carried it all away to the place from where we would escape.

Now, all I needed was the map – one of the most important things we had to have. But annoyingly, I did not find such a map, showing Auschwitz and all surrounding villages and shtetls – which were now camps, and therefore had to be avoided.

Fedyor spurred me on, shouting that it was our turn now and we had to escape as quickly as possible to allow a free space for others.

During this time, 50 women and 50 men were selected to go to another camp in Birkenau, into the "Effektenlager"[42]. Also Rochele was among the 50 women, so I was left alone. Every day seemed pointless now. I was only occupied with the thought of how I could procure a map to leave "Canada" and put an end to camp life as quickly as possible.

[Page 222]

I also knew that I would have great difficulty in leaving the work squad, since they wanted to enlarge it in view of the expected arrival of 70,000 Jews from Lodz. But this problem, however, I would solve later. The main thing was that I got a good idea of how to "organize" a map at the SS:

An SS-man was coming with a cart to clean the bathrooms. Around the wagon worked 5 people, to whom the SS-man paid attention. It was in the morning. I went by with a pack of clothes, from one barrack to another, and saw the SS-man's coat hanging on the fence. A portfolio was sticking out of the breast pocket. The SS-man to whom the coat belonged went into the bathroom and the cart obstructed the door. I decided to pull out the portfolio; only, how was I to do this without anyone noticing? Back in the barrack, I took a pack of clothes and went to the second barrack, stopping next to the coat and pretending that the pack was heavy for me to carry. To adjust the package, I leaned against the fence, next to the coat. Then I pulled out the portfolio, put it between my clothes and ran into the women's barracks. There, I took out the portfolio and hid it well until evening.

The SS-man ran across the yard, shouting that he had lost his portfolio, which contained important papers….

In the evening, when the cart had already left, I went to the bathroom with the portfolio. I found a map with the whole plan of the camp and where the guards were. I tore up the other papers, such as a book about the "Hitler Youth" and various documents about awards, and threw them into the toilet.

[Page 223]

I wrapped the map around my foot, tied a bandage around it and entered the camp (with it).

When Fedyor saw the map, he was very excited. I told him, how I had "organized" the map, and he gave me a friendly pat on the back. On the same day, I told the "Kapo" that I no longer wanted to work in "Canada". After the "Kapo" reported this item to the "Schreibstube" [the clerk's office], I was confirmed that I should no longer work there. Instead, they assigned me to work in the worst crew, the "dismantling operation" – exactly the squad from which I was supposed to go to escape. Also, my friend Fedyor was working there. I signed up for the new squad as a locksmith and went to work there the very next morning.

It was Sabbath, and on this day three people escaped, two Russians and a Pole. The SS searched for them with their sniffer dogs, but without success.

We did not march back to the camp. All thousand prisoners stood silently in a row of five. Later, the camp commander, Kramer, arrived and reported that he would shoot every tenth one unless we testified where the three were.

But neither beating nor "making sport" helped; everyone was silent. In any case, no one knew where the refugees were hiding. Sweat ran down from everyone like water. Others already had split heads. The murderer Kramer took out all his rage on us. Immediately, the square was surrounded, where we had been working together with the SS: every five meters, there was standing now an SS-man with a machine gun. We were taken to the camp and positioned separately next to the kitchen. Then Kramer, together with several SS, took out 50 people to shoot them, if we did not say where the three were. The 50 stood to the side, all pale as lime, and waited.

[Page 224]

We stood until ten o'clock at night, everyone petrified, forbidden to stir. The fifty were led out of the camp under heavy guard, and we were ordered to go to the block. We received our punishment: no bread for three days and every day, standing an hour longer on roll call.

The fifty were not shot. At 12 o'clock at night, they were brought back to the camp. They had only wanted to scare us.

Monday, we went back to work. Now, the guard was very reinforced. Each group of 20 people was assigned a soldier from the Air Force who was responsible for the 20 people.

No one was allowed to move even one step away without reporting it to the soldier. Every hour, there was a presence check.

The escape was done in the following way:

> The fugitives had to lie down for three days and nights, and on the third day, when they did not longer hear the siren whistle, they came out of their hiding place at night and slowly crept towards the Vistula. They then had to swim across the Vistula and make their way to the fields.

Me and Fed(y)or[43] worked together in a group. I still didn't know, where we would hide. Fed(y)or was stalling me from day to day, telling me that the time had not yet come. We had to wait, until the guard would weaken.

It became very strict now. We were not allowed to take a single step to the side without a report. We postponed our escape for a week. During this week, I was to become more familiar with my work and workplace.

There, where we were working, was a large field covered with broken parts of airplanes. Every day, they brought new wagons with shot down airplanes.

The work was very hard and dirty. The soldiers of the air force were driving us with sticks to make us work faster.

[Page 225]

There were lying mountains of sheet metal from gasoline cans, engines, wheels, and mountains of aluminum that, each day, were loaded onto rail cars and sent to Germany.

As for the location of the hiding place – I still didn't know, where it was. It would be revealed to me on the last day before our escape. Only one of the three of us knew about it. Also, I did not even know, who the third of us was.

After three weeks of working on the squad, F(y)edor told me Monday morning that we would escape today. I immediately, wrote a farewell letter to Rochele and passed it on to my friend to give it to her when I was no longer there. She was the only one to whom I confided the secret of our escape.

Monday morning, we march out to work as we do every day. We are divided into groups; me and Fed(y)or are together in one group. The third, a Russian, went into another group, working next to us. I am introduced to him. A very courageous person, a former lieutenant.

We decide to go to the hideout ten minutes before 5 p.m. . At ten o'clock in the morning, Fed(y)or showed me the place, where our hideout was to be. It was a wheel of an American airplane. There was room for two men there, and in a second wheel-for the third.

The entrance was through a cut-out door, which was difficult to notice. There, where the two wheels were lying, there were also hundreds of other wheels, so they did not stand out. In the wheel you had to lie three days and nights and then leave it. The plan is brilliant. From these two wheels, 50 people had already escaped. The sniffer dogs could not run over the gasoline that had poured all over the place. The fugitives usually poured some snuff on a second place, just not near where they were hiding. The dogs then started sneezing and couldn't get anything done. Every minute dragged on as if made of pitch. I already wanted to lie in the wheel so much! At twelve o'clock at dinner, we met all three and agreed on the order, in which we should go.

[Page 226]

Fed(y)or was designated to go first. I, second into the same wheel, and the third was to go last into the second wheel.

The control was the same as every day. Every hour, we had to line up in rows. At 4 p.m. we lined up for the control. The soldier counted us off and then told us to go to work. We usually worked until 5. Every passing minute seemed like a year. Me and Fed(y)or are standing not far from the place where the wheels are lying. We work chopping up wings. Every minute, the soldier makes his rounds past us, shouting:

"Quick, quick, this must be finished!"

We work with our heads down, as if he doesn't mean us.

I catch a glimpse of the clock: it's half past four. Fed(y)or puts aside his hoe, looking around in all directions. I stand at my work. The soldier is just away at a second group and is talking to another soldier there. Fed(y)or runs with tiny steps to the wheels. I see him bend down and open a little door on the wheel. Now, he is already stretched out on the ground and after two seconds he is already inside. The door closes again.

I am still in the same place, my heart is beating even harder. Now, I will soon put an end to my camp life! Either I am free or I end up on the gallows. I turn around. The third friend waves to me.

I cast a glance at the mountain of wheels and at the wheel, where Fed(y)or is lying. We have agreed on a sign that I have to give Fed(y)or, before I go to the wheel.

The two soldiers stand and talk to each other with their backs to me. I decide to put down the hoe and go to the wheel. Suddenly, I hear a shout: "Hey you dog, come here real quick!"

I turn my head and see how the soldier waves his hand to me to come to him. My heart is pounding, but I am not embarrassed. The third comrade looks at me to see what happens next. When I am with the soldier, he leads me to a mountain of aluminum and instructs me to make room, so that a tractor can drive in there. He has brought a few more people here, and is now standing alone with his stick in his hand, screaming: "Faster, faster, this has to be done today!"[44] It will soon be "closing time". Every piece of tin fell from my hand.

[Page 227]

The soldier simply did not step away from us for a single moment, and then a whistle was heard and the order: "Line up!"

We've lined up in 4 rows of 5. There are four in the last row. The soldier shouts: "Where is the fifth?" His lips are trembling. He runs around like a madman, yelling at the "foreman." All groups march to the large field, where everyone forms up to march back to camp. But our group remains standing on the spot. The command leader[45] comes to ask, what is going on. The soldier stammers in a trembling voice: "One is missing!"

The command leader shouts, gestures with his hands, curses, runs around back and forth. We are asked, if we don't know where the person has gone? Maybe he is asleep? The numbers are called out.

Immediately, it is known which number is missing. We all answer synchronously that we do not know where he is. We know that something will happen to us; we will be tortured. We are ready to endure whatever may come. After five minutes, we hear the choppy whistle of the siren. In a moment, SS-men with their dogs start running. We are led away to one side of the field.

"Knee bends!", the commando leader orders. Immediately, several SS-men position themselves around us with rough oak sticks. The commando leader shouts at us to tell where the Russian is, where he is hiding. We remain silent, because in such a case it is better to only listen and not say a word. Or just to drone out: "Yessir! Yessir!"

Every minute, more SS arrive.

The camp commander, Kramer, is coming on. His eyes gleam wildly, as if he wanted to devour us with them. He walks past us, gives one of us a hard shove in his stomach with his boot, yells at the commando leader and the soldier from our group.

[Page 228]

The soldier, looking pale, is standing there and stating, that at four o'clock, everyone was still at work, and that he stood next to us from half past four until five o'clock.

Kramer yells wildly, "Well, then where is he?"[46] The soldier remains standing without answer, arms drooping and also shouting after each word, "Yessir!"

Kramer curses and shouts to the right and to the left: "Golly, golly!" He yells at the commando leader, who stands bolt upright like a pole, arms stretched down, "Every day we're missing prisoners!"

Kramer goes back to us, yelling: "I will shoot you all like dogs if you do not testify, where the Russian is!" We sit there with trembling knees. The one, who got the blow with the boot in the stomach, is lying there in an unconscious state. He is a Greek Jew. Kramer goes to the victim, gives him another firm blow and quickly runs away to the SS, who are standing in rows, holding the leashes of the dogs in their hands.

Kramer speaks to them, and they all swarm out like a cloud of locusts over the work area. A blind shootout into the mountains of tin can be heard. We stand up. Soon the order comes, "Lie down!" Then again, "Get up!" Half of our group is already lying beaten up on the lawn. I fall down with my last strength but can hardly get up. My tongue hangs outstretched from my mouth; I lack air. My body is wet. The Greek Jew lies and struggles with death. His eyes stare at the sky. The other prisoners, who until now have been in the "standstill" position, have also been ordered to do "knee bends".

The killers leave us for a few minutes to consult among themselves. Now, their canes "work" to the right and left. The Russians are swearing wild curses. The caning is given to those, who are already half-dead, shaking with their arms and legs and not being able, to stand for a minute with bent knees. Dozens are lying beaten up. Soon, the murderers are coming to us, shouting, "You cursed, dirty dogs!" – and even more "beautiful" names.

[Page 229]

Everyone in our group is lying stretched out and completely broken on the grass. The SS laugh and rejoice that they have won a "victory" over us.

In this way, we remained lying there until sunset. The SS came back with their dogs – sweaty and unsuccessful. The workplace was surrounded with SS. Kramer gave the order that we should return to the camp. Those who could not get up were put on a truck and taken to the camp. The rest marched in rows on foot to the camp. There, they positioned us all separately next to the kitchen. We had to stay like that until three o'clock in the morning, without food. At three o'clock, each of us was taken individually to our barracks, and at 4 o'clock, we had to go out again to the roll call square. After the morning roll call, at 6 o'clock, we were led back to work.

We were all dead tired and additionally, got more beatings that day than the other days. There was no lunch for us. People were dropping like flies from hunger. This day was the worst day of camp life for us. In the evening we were taken to the camp and each of us was given half a liter of watery soup. We did not get any bread with it. The guards increased, they counted every five minutes, and we were held responsible for each other.

The three days were now over, and the guards were withdrawn. My friend Fed(y)or had successfully escaped alone. However, the colonel decided to suspend the next escapes for a few weeks.

But after a few days, three runaway Russians were brought back, enchained. They had been captured not far from Auschwitz. All the anger was vented on these three people. The camp commander, Kramer, wanted to find out at all costs, where the hiding place was; and he succeeded. The three were tortured until they revealed, where they had been hiding. When they first pointed to another place, they were not believed, and they were tortured further, until they showed the right place. After two weeks of torment, they showed the two wheels, then they were believed. After six days, they were shot in the crematorium. The escape movement stopped. All my plans fell apart.

[Page 230]

Beginning of the Nazi collapse

In the camp, people knew that the Germans were suffering great defeats on all fronts. The front at Vitebsk was broken. The Russian armies went ahead with giant strides. The Western Front was broken. The Germans were leaving France, Holland and Belgium. We in the camp knew that our lives were now even more in danger. Any minute, there could be an order to make the camp "cleansed", which meant killing all the prisoners.

Meanwhile, an order came to evacuate the camp towards Germany. The Nazis needed manpower and therefore began to transfer thousands of prisoners to other camps.

Every day, they sent out transports, liquidating many squads. There was also an evacuation in the women's camp. The transports from Lodz were the last to arrive in Auschwitz. With the last transport, they brought the "King of the Ghetto", Chaim Rumkowski[47], and threw him together with all the others into the gas chamber. The first to be evacuated were the Jews of Lodz, later the Hungarian ones. In October, the order came to evacuate the old prisoners. On October 17, no one marched out to work. Transports of 2000 people each were assembled. On October 15, I went to the "Effektenlager" in order to say goodbye to Rochele, who was doing the same work there as in "Canada".

[Page 231]

On the 17th, our whole barracks was sent to another camp in Germany. When we left Birkenau, they dressed us in civilian clothes. Everyone was given a long coat, large wooden shoes and new, round hats. We did not recognize each other. First we were led to the train. There, everyone went through the same check as if they had arrived at the camp only yesterday. It was forbidden, to take more than one spoon. We were led to the train, strictly closed and guarded. There, everyone was given half a loaf of bread, a portion of margarine of 100 grams, a cane blow as a surcharge, and then we were packed sixty people into a wagon. The wagons were very tightly closed, without any gap. Next to each wagon remained three SS. We took the last look at the camp and the electric wire. From the grove, the tall chimneys, which were wrapped with iron to not fall apart, peeked out. A bright smoke curled up to the sky. Still, the remaining Lodz Jews were burning, together with the "King of the Ghetto", Chaim Rumkowski, who, with his good speeches, had enticed the 70,000 Jews to work in Auschwitz.[48]

Standing on the train station, everything seems like a dream. Something like foggy sadness lingers in the silence. Trucks, loaded with clothes, are passing by, leaving behind them dense white dust. A wind is blowing over the warm clothes that, just a few minutes ago, had been on human bodies. The other prisoners who remained in the camp stand at the fence and say goodbye to us, waving their hands.

We hear the wild, animalistic yell of the camp commander, Kramer, "All aboard!"

A scramble begins. Rifle butts fall over our heads. After several minutes, we are all in the train car. All my comrades, with whom I have led the day-to-day struggle for "tomorrow", are riding together with me. My "bed-fellows", *Arke Krantzman* and *Itshe Suroski*, are calling me over, to stand together in a corner. The wagon is small and there is little space. The SS-men take up the whole center by the door. Litter (straw) is carried in for them. There's no place for us to stand. Three pairs of large, murderous eyes are looking at us, piercing us with their gazes. One of them shouts, "Golly, what's that air! You stink, you curs!" And with his mouth full, he spits on one of us. We hear a choppy whistle, along with a shout: "All aboard!"

[Page 232]

The wagons give a start; one is bumping into the other. The crowd is shaken up, falling against each other with their whole bodies. The wagons start moving. The door is open. The camp flies by. There, we can still see the chimneys; black smoke is billowing from two of them. From the other two, a thin smoke is curling, quickly dissipating in the air, leaving no traces…

The double-row electric fence runs by quickly. Every stone that lies there screams out a dirge; every grain of sand is steeped in the mystery of a human life.

The wheels are pounding in time, ever stronger by the minute. A transport is being transferred, but not wood and coals, but a transport of living people who want to live and experience the hour of reckoning with the enemy. A cool autumn wind blows in through the open door, which is blocked by three green cloaks. A belt is dangling on them, with the inscription "God with us". On the left side, a revolver, in the hands, next to the legs, a rifle. In addition, large, stuffed backpacks, from which the tip of a white bread peeks out. All our eyes fall straight on the bread. Everyone's thoughts are occupied with the bread: What would happen if someone had the bread in his hand now? In which side would he take his first bite?

The wheels are pounding. We are riding between green fields. Auschwitz is left behind us. Nobody knows where the train will take us. We in our corner decide, to resist in case they take us to another crematorium. I have smuggled through a "holy Sabbath knife" which I keep ready. The others are willing to defend themselves with their spoons; their handles are sharply ground, also serving as a knife.

Night has fallen. We cannot keep our eyes open anymore. Our legs buckle. There is no place to sit down. We are leaning against the other, slumbering. The SS are smoking one cigarette after another, spitting and cursing. But we do not respond to a single word and pretend that we are not meant at all. We fly past villages and towns. There is no end to the night. Everyone falls into a light sleep, only to wake up again.

[Page 233]

Our knees give a jerk and the slumber cuts off. One is pushing the other with his feet. When one of us sits down, there is a shout: "Ow, my foot!" Meanwhile, the SS-men are taking advantage of this situation, attacking us with rifle butts and hitting over our heads.

In this way, we were standing all night. A cold morning wind has brought us a little freshness. The train has stopped. We are reading an inscription with big black letters: "Gleiwitz" [Gliwice]. Now, we already know that we are going to Germany. The SS-men jump down, tapping their feet together and rubbing their eyes. One wipes the second. All three march next to the door. The transport leader walks from wagon to wagon with a note in his hand. Each SS-man stands upright in front of him, hands stretched tightly down, shouting out: "Everything all right!" In this way, the transport leader runs from wagon to wagon, until the last one.

We look out through the open door. Preoccupied railroad workers run back and forth. Everyone glances at the door and keeps walking. The only thing we ask for is bread. A piece of bread – that's what we require. But no one throws bread to us. Everyone passes by, pretending that it is not him, who is meant.

In Gliwice, we have stood until 12 noon. Then, the train is starting, again with the SS-men together with us in the wagon. Now, they are having lunch. Everyone unpacks a long, dry, firm sausage and white bread, and their chins move up and down. Once they cut off the sausage, once the bread, then they bite into it. Slowly, one after the other. We are standing there, silently. All our eyes are now on the knife that cuts the sausage and bread, shining like those of a cat, standing there tied up while a fat mouse jumps around in the distance. All of us had immediately eaten our bread that we received yesterday before leaving Auschwitz, being afraid that one might steal it from the other. We do not know when we will get bread. We are locked in the wagon between four walls without a view, and do not know at all what is planned for us. It's just as if we weren't even there.

[Page 234]

Night falls again. With every minute, the hunger grows even more. We shout at each other, so that the SS should hear, "Bread, why don't they give us bread?"

The SS shout, "Quiet, you pigs! You will get bread tomorrow".

"Why tomorrow? We are hungry today!" the whole wagon shouts in unison. But shouting didn't help; we didn't get any bread.

So, we drove through the second night. The majority in the wagon had no strength to stand any longer; others not even to talk. Hunger dominated everyone. If someone had still thought of escape – now it was nonsensical, because no one had any strength left.

On the third day, we stopped at a small railroad station near Gdansk. The SS told us that we would not go on, but would be dumped in a camp. Nobody knows the name of the camp. We lay there, leaning against each other, waiting for our fate. Two Greek Jews died this morning. They are lying with us. The air in the wagon is suffocating. The SS-men are spitting and cursing with the worst and dirtiest words; it would be us, who are guilty of everything. They were innocent, free from suspicion. (1). Until now, a faint voice could be heard, "Hunger, bread," but henceforth, everyone is silent, because the slightest shout is stifled with the rifle butts of the SS. Everyone is afraid of the last blow with a butt.

After several hours, a few officers came to our transport. They looked at the "goods" that were brought to them. In our wagon, there were already two dead, and the rest were half dead.

Stutthof

We were herded out of the wagons and lined up five to a row. Now, a counting began to control, if no one had escaped on the way.

[Page 235]

The dead were dragged out of the wagon and laid down below to be also counted. From each wagon, they hauled out 2 or 3 dead. Others simply no longer had the strength to stay on their feet. The only thing everyone wanted now was a piece of bread, and later, come what may. Hunger plagues us all and pulls us down to earth. Everyone has withered, blue lips.

The murderous officers take their time. They stand comfortably in the distance, sneering at us, pointing their fingers at the victims, who have gone down on their knees, with their heads lowered to the earth.

The air is fragrant; we are in a forest among tall conifers. The sky above us is saturated with moisture. The night has fallen. We are still standing in the side yard. The SS officers burst into loud laughter, hearing the reports of those who came with us.

Suddenly we hear a wild, drunken shouting: "Ahead, march!"

One is linking arm with the other, and the dead are placed on a cart. We march over yellow needles in the deep forest-not even knowing where to. Marching with me in line are my "bedfellows." Each of us is determined to defend ourselves if we are lined up to be shot. Meanwhile, we march with short steps in the darkness. Each of us is sure that this is our end and we will be shot here. We decide that as soon as we see the SS moving away from us, we will throw ourselves at them and tear their necks open with our teeth.

The majority of the whole transport is no longer capable of resistance. Only a tiny percentage is still able to do so, if the bullet does not come even earlier.

Escaping is impossible. After each meter, SS-men are walking on both sides with guns held out, ready to shoot.

[Page 236]

Behind us, we hear a gunshot and a groan. They have shot someone who could not go any further. If we keep going like this, everyone will fall down. No one knows, where we will march and how long we will have to walk like this. Everyone is sure that this is our last march; may what has to happen anyway, just go faster. This is the wish of all of us. Again a shot is fired, accompanied by a long "oi!". Once again, they shot someone. The wagon is already overflowing with the dead. Wild screams can be heard: "Ahead! Quick, you dirty dogs!"

Around us it is dark; the path is swampy. Suddenly, we see small fires approaching us from afar. Now, we are already next to a narrow field; and we stop. The fires come close to us. We can clearly see a locomotive with dense black smoke coming out of it. To the locomotive are attached small open wagons. We stop next to these wagons and are counted again. The dead on the wagon are also counted.

Fifty people stand next to each wagon. An order comes: "Board!"

None of us has any strength left. Immediately, the wild SS-men come running with the butts in their hands, bumping and hitting from all sides. There is a scramble, a rush from one wagon to the next. One wants to hide behind the other. The SS-men take advantage of the situation, beating everyone over their heads and backs. There is a groaning of people, who have fallen down to the earth. The others are stepping on them. Those, who have already managed to hastily get into the wagons have not received any blows. The ground is covered with people. Each of them croaks and shouts with his last strength: "Shoot me, shoot me, you murderers!"

I am in the wagon. My hand is swollen from a blow. Now, what can come will. None of us is capable of resistance anymore. The broken and the dead have been placed together in the last wagon. Now we are believing that we are being led to the crematorium.

[Page 237]

Only one thing we wanted – might it already be over! The hunger and the beatings have broken in all of us the strength to resist.

The locomotive starts moving. In each wagon, four SS-men are sitting, with rifles at the ready. We drive into the forest's darkness. From the last wagons, we hear a moaning and wailing.

The wheels are pounding, the locomotive is whistling. So, we were driving for more than one hour.

The locomotive has stopped next to a large warehouse, the lighting of which could be seen from afar.

We have left the wagons again, lining up in rows of five. Some of us were lying unconscious in the wagons. The living, half-dead and dead have been counted. The transport is in order: all 1200 people are present. We marched to the gate of the camp. Above the gate is hanging an inscription, illuminated by electric lamps: "Wald-Lager Stutthof".[49] At the gate, SS-men line up on both sides, counting us again as we march in. The dead and half-dead are brought into the camp and left on the street, next to the wall of a barrack. We are taken to an empty barrack with no beds and no floor. All of us have fallen to the bare, wet ground, being dead tired. So we have been lying there until dawn, with everyone groaning and gasping.

At four o'clock, two SS-men came in with sticks in their hands and shouted: "Roll call! Roll call! Everybody out, out, you cursed dogs!"

Soon, we were standing one behind the other, ten to a row.

At six o'clock, a block leader came and counted us twice. After roll call, we were led to the bathroom. There, everything started all over again. Once again, we had to strip naked. The clothes were put into the delousing chamber. All this took place with the accompaniment of caning.

[Page 238]

The cold showers were the worst. Outside, a cold, wet autumn wind whistled. The windows in the bathroom were broken, and the draft chased over our emaciated bodies. All of us shivered and snuggled up to one another.

After we took our bath, we were herded into another large hall, where everyone was given their clothes. Now, after the bath procedure, we were led to blocks "two" and "three" in the camp. These were two blocks for Jews only, with special discipline and special leaders. We had to wait out the roll call longer than anyone else. Sleeping was even worse than in Auschwitz, on a narrow military bed, where four of us had to sleep: Two at the foot side and two at the head side. Immediately, when we tried to stretch out on the beds, most of them broke apart and one fell on top of the other. The beds were three-tiered. When the top tier broke, all four fell down to the middle tier. However, from the impact, the middle tier also bent, and so all eight people fell onto the bottom bed, which of course as a result also collapsed.

No one had known or heard anything about the "Stutthof" camp before. But now, we felt the rigor of the camp, which could well be called "camp of the dead" on our backs. Here, too, there were women who worked at cleaning the clothes of the captured soldiers. The women's camp was separated from the men's camp by a high electric fence. It was very strictly forbidden for women to stand next to the fence and talk to men. There was a crematorium here as well, just not on such a huge format as in Auschwitz. Rather, it was an ordinary stone house with a tall chimney, wrapped with iron hoops, to keep it from falling apart from the heat. The crematorium was enclosed by a high, opaque fence. A brick-paved path led to the door. There were not as many people working here as in Auschwitz, just twenty, but all with different nationalities. Only the Jews were gassed; people of other nationalities were burned, when they were already dead. The majority in the camp were Poles, from the Bialystok area. I even… met a Pole from my shtetl Krinik [Krynki], a former assistant policeman of the Germans. When we met and I asked him, "Edzhik Tsarnyetski [Czarnietzki], you are also here in the camp?" he lowered his head and asked: "Jeszcze żyjesz? – you are still alive?"

[Page 239]

The Pole furnished me with greetings from my shtetl Krinik. He told me, what had happened to those, who had fled into the forest, and about the surrounding peasants.

Those, who had hidden in the boiler of the bath at that time, he said, had been caught and shot in the middle of the market. Several peasants were also shot.

About himself, he told me the following:

After our shtetl had already become "judenrein"[50], the former ghetto commissar collected everything that the Jews had left behind in the last "two camps". He collected the clothes and linen in the large "Bes-Medresh"[51]. The Polish assistant policemen had to take care of it. But once, when he had been standing guard alone, he went inside and took out various clothes. During this "work", however, he was caught by the ghetto commissar, and, as a punishment, he was taken to the forest camp at Stutthof.

* * *

The work of the prisoners in the forest camp took place in several military factories, such as shoes and weapons factories. Several hundred people worked there. The camp numbered 6000 men and 4000 women. Other prisoners worked unloading ships coming from the port of Gdansk. The forest camp was located 30 km from Gdynia, and those, who worked in the harbor, usually left every day at 5 o'clock in the morning and returned at 8 o'clock in the evening. Every day, they brought back dead and wounded from the hard work, which consisted of unloading stones and cement.

The Jews in our camp were mostly from Vilnius and Kaunas. We were the first to arrive from the Auschwitz death camp. Most people of our transport had already been in Auschwitz for up to two years. Therefore, we already knew better how to wriggle out of both blows and hard work.

[Page 240]

In particular, two camp policemen distinguished themselves by walking through the camp with large wolf dogs. And the person on whom they set the dogs, knew only too well that he would not survive. Those who still managed to survive the bite wounds in their arms or legs, among others, were taken to the crematorium, where they were gassed and burned. Every day, victims were usually brought to the crematorium. For this purpose, a special cart with four large wheels had been constructed. This cart was pulled by ten people, driven by the sticks of the kapos, who walked alongside. Every day, hundreds of sick people were taken from the women's precinct and led to the crematorium. Burns were performed even when there were no sick people. Because according to the order of the camp commander, 100 women and all sick people had to be burned every day.

Of our transport, which numbered 1,200 people, dozens were missing every day. The cold, the wet, cutting winds from the sea, the hunger – all that was breaking the remaining bit of our health every day. All of us had only one hope: The liberation was already knocking at the door!

Knowing that the Nazis were already perishing now, each of us wanted to live all the more. For so long, we had endured all the heavy, terrible torment, and now that we were already on the threshold of liberation, we did not want to die, after all!

Each of us had only one desire: To experience the day of liberation – and then it should be what it will.

But it was very difficult for us to fight against nature, against the biting winds and rains that tormented us 18 hours a day. In the camp, we became recruits again. There, too, we were quarantined for a week, which was much worse than going to work.

[Page 241]

Then, everyone was assigned to specific work. It goes without saying that Jews were called in to do the heaviest work, but especially ourselves, who had just joined the group. I had to go to the harbor and unload sand from the ship. This work – under sticks – was very hard. We were driven to and from work. But they didn't do that for our relief, but to make us work more hours.

I decided to leave, on a transport to another camp. Maybe it would be better there. Transports were frequent, because any small labor camp that lacked workers, could buy them at the Stutthof forest camp for very cheap money.

Civilian companies, such as Krupp, Müller and Kaiser[52] can also buy people at low prices. If a leader of such a company comes to the camp to buy 100 or 200 slaves, then things can get better-or worse. But we'll worry about that later. For now, the main thing is to get away from the wind and rain. And I, too, am determined to leave for another camp. Maybe I can even escape from there, because here, it is absolutely not possible, and after a few weeks, I will have no more strength to do so. Every day that passes in the camp, is like a whole year. Each of us, standing tired and broken by the hard work, knows what awaits him after work, when returning with his last strength to the camp. Then, everything starts all over again. The SS, the block leaders – they don't care whether we worked all day or not, since it would be us who had to pay for our "debt".[53] In the evening, at roll call, after returning to the camp, we usually stand from 7-9 o'clock. The count dragged on for a very long time. At 9 o'clock we were then lined up in a "goose line". There were shoving matches and the murderers usually took advantage of this. After all, everyone wanted to be the first to return to the block in order to get their portion of bread with jam spread at the entrance, whereby the latter was usually smeared on the nose. When distributing bread, the same tactics were used as in Auschwitz: The victims were the sick and the weak, who could no longer stand on their feet. They were not given any more portions of bread.

[Page 242]

After a three weeks' stay at Stutthof, a civilian master came to demand 1200 Jews to work. I was one of them. Almost all of those, who had come from Auschwitz, were selected for this transport that no one knew where it would take us. The 1200 people were divided into two groups, 600 each. Again, we were led to the bathroom. Everyone was given new clothes: black coats with red stripes on the shoulder.

On October 15, 1944, we left the Stutthof forest camp.

Tai(l)fingen Airfield

There are sixty of us in the wagon, guarded by two SS-men. Everyone gets a piece of bread with sausage, and we are leaving snowy, white fields behind us. We set off in the evening, and the longer we drive, the more we feel the frost. Everyone huddled together. On the first night, four people in our wagon froze their feet off. One of them was my comrade, a Bialystok lad, *Itshe Suraski*, who was crying in pain. On the second day, there were already twenty people who had frozen feet. So we drove for four days. Every day, we got 200 grams of bread and one liter of water. On the fourth day, we arrived at a small train station with the signage "Tailfingen".[54]

There, we stayed for the whole night. The next morning, the "buyers" came to look at their "purchased goods". New murderer faces surrounded the train. Then, we were ordered to leave the wagons and line up in fives. Those people with frozen feet could not move from the place.

[Page 243]

I also had a toe frozen off my left foot, but I was able to walk. Again, we were counted. A tall, skinny SS officer showed us his long "nageike" [whip] and waved it in the air. We were still standing in the row, when he, in front of us, gave a speech. He introduced himself as the camp leader, and made ten of us responsible for one, meaning that for one escapee, ten would be shot. Among other things, he also spoke about the discipline that would prevail in the camp. Finally he asked, if we had understood everything.

Those whose feet were frozen off were loaded onto a truck. The rest of us walked to the camp, which was located three kilometers from the railroad line on an airfield. No people were housed there yet; we were the first to live there in the new camp. The camp consisted of a large hall (hangar), where broken aircraft were repaired. When we entered the empty, large hall, we were all shocked: only an earthen floor and no beds; the roof and walls were riddled with machine-gun bullets, being fired every day by the Americans and the English.

Without beds, without water – this is how the new camp presented itself to us. The commander, who looked like the "wild Tarzan"[55], with big, shining eyes, gave us a speech again. He informed us that what we could see was all they had prepared for us. If we wanted to have beds, we should build some by ourselves. And if we wanted water, we should build a well ourselves.

Around the hangar, there was a wire fence with several high towers for the guards, who were already standing there with rifles pointed at the hangar. A small hut was standing at the side, called the kitchen. All around, there was mud up to the knee. From among us were selected a camp elder and several Kapos, plus four people for the kitchen and a cleaning person. On the same day, the work squads of 30 to 40 people each were formed, and each squad was given a name.

[Page 244]

The carpenters got to work right away. Boards and nails were available. The camp leader, to whom we gave the name "Tarzan" right at the beginning, left the leadership of the camp to several people, and thus something like a "Jewish government" came into being. In the evening, the first roll call took place on the street. Everyone was up to their knees in mud. The camp commander counted us off, and whoever moved his head, received a blow with the nageike ([whip]. Standing at roll call for two hours, some of us fell over in the mud.

Among us were Jews from Poland, Greece, Holland, France, Belgium and Germany. The leadership of the camp fell into Polish [Jewish] hands. Now, we were deep in Germany, between Stuttgart and Tübingen.

The first night in the new camp, we slept on bare, wet earth. Everyone covered himself with his own coat. The snow stormed inside, but we all slept well, because we were all dead tired from the exhausting four-day[56] journey.

At four o'clock in the morning, we already heard the whistle of the camp leader. After five minutes, all of us were standing in rows of ten on the street. The sky was black. The full moon laughed down at us as if to tell us: "Children, your plagues are all in vain, you will not live to see freedom anyway!" A shining star beckoned us down from the sky: "Hold on, kids! Your freedom is dawning already!"

Again, they counted us. Everyone stood there frozen, not moving his head, because we already knew what else awaited us. Of the 600 people, 70 already did not come out of the "block" today. Most of them had frozen feet. The sick were all lying in a row, so that they could be counted (as) well.

At 5 o'clock, the camp leader's shout went up, "Work squad, form up!"

SS-men had already been standing at the gate – with their hats pulled down over their ears and knocking one boot against the other.

[Page 245]

They are waiting for us. Among those, standing there with their guns, are Russians, Ukrainians and Poles. The Ukrainians are wearing uniforms of the organization "Todt"[57] with a red ribbon on the right arm, on which a swastika is shining.

Camp leader Tarzan is standing with a paper in his hand, calling out the names of the squads. The work crew I am standing in is called "Rasten [Reusten] Number 2"[58], which is the name of the quarry, where we have to work. Our crew consists of twenty people. When we are already standing on the other side of the gate, six guards grouped around us with rifles at the ready.

"Ahead, march!" one of the guards yells wildly, and the others are prodding us with their rifles. We are marching on a snowy white path, between two forests. Nobody knows, where we are going. Around us is deep darkness. Every crunch of a step is echoing. We walk cuddled up, the heads lowered between our shoulders, our eyes fixed on the night.

So we have been marching for two hours, until it has become light already. Now, we see high, rocky hills in front of us. We pass small villages. The farmers are casting cold glances at us and quickly get out of the way, making room for us. Behind some windows, a curtain rises, revealing a glimpse of us. Quickly, the curtain falls back down again.

Before marching into the village, the guard elder has announced that whoever left the line to pick something up would be shot immediately. On the side of the road are lying frozen turnips and potatoes. Fixing this [food] with his eyes, everyone wants to gulp it down. Thus, we have passed three villages; and in each one the same is repeated. Behind the third village, there is a small wall with a tall, white, wooden building, around which are heaped mountains of small and large stones. There we stop.

[Page 246]

Two civilian masters are looking at us, smiling at each other. The guard lines up around the building. Two civilians assign us to work, which consists of drilling deep holes in the rock of the hill, into which dynamite is then poured to cause a blast, which would create larger and smaller stones. And these stones we have to work with. The large stones are pounded with heavy hammers and loaded into small wagons, which we take away to the "stone machine" to prepare small rock for the building of highways and airfields. Work is proceeding at a rapid pace. The master is not interested in whether we are hungry or full. He demands what is due to him. None of us has drunk a single drop of water today. We will get lunch at the workplace. Everyone is already waiting with great impatience for the truck to bring us a little watery soup.

I am working with the heavy hammer, which is almost as heavy as I am. I no longer have the strength to pick it up, but the fear of blows from the guards helps me to lift the hammer. All of us can barely keep on our feet. But that is none of the civilian master's business; he cares little. For him, the only thing that matters, is that we work and still get more done. As soon as he realizes that one of us is lagging behind, he reports it to the guard, who then "pays" us for it immediately with butt blows over the back.

We have worked thus until one o'clock; then we had lunch. For 20 people, there were 15 liters of watery soup, consisting of beets with water and bitter grasses. The lunch break has lasted an hour; then – back to work. Now, the civilian master himself takes a stick in his hand, driving the work to a faster pace and yelling that we had eaten, so now we would have to earn our food with work!

"You dirty, lazy Jews", that has been the only shouting of the master. But his yelling did not annoy us as much as his rough stick, which he has used to accompany every word.

"Ah, may the time of reckoning come! But how are we to experience it? Even if it is only for a minute! Then we, the slaves, who now walk with heads bowed to the earth, will, with revolvers in our hands, speak to the old 'Jekke', who now feels himself a hero over 20 human shadows".

[Page 247]

Gassed Czech Jews in the death wagon of Munich –
40 wagons with people arrived on the day of liberation

[Page 248]

And the longed-for minute will come! But none of us knows whether at least one of us will live to see it. All of us are between the teeth of the wild tiger, and, close to the moment of being gobbled down, each of us is fighting with his last strength for every day, for every hour. Maybe today, maybe tomorrow, the longed-for freedom will come!

To others of us, this just seems like an empty dream. We don't even know, if there is a world at all beyond the fence, on the other side of the guns. We don't know what's happening in the world – as if we were living somewhere on a discarded, wild island, among savage people. Only one thing gladdens our tortured hearts: the silver airplanes flying in large groups over our heads, accompanied by sunrays to the big German cities and factories. When we hear the familiar sound, we bless those, who are gliding across the skies,[59] determined to bring us freedom. We see, how the faces of the great "heroes" are turning pale, as they shout, "Airmen! Airman alert!" And, how their hands are trembling together with their guns!

Only when the sky is covered with airplanes, we pause from work. We worked until 6 o'clock, and it had been really dark, when we lined up five to a row. Four rows of five under rifle. So, we have been starting the march back again. No one of has the strength anymore to endure this life. We are hungry and broken, with heavy wooden shoes, to which the snow is sticking, hindering walking. Our hearts are crying. We do not speak a word to each other, as if we were mute. Our imagination reflects to us only one single thing: a piece of bread! The whole twenty of us think the same. No one thinks about freedom anymore. Everything has died off. Only one thing is still alive in the world. Just one: That is a piece of bread!

So, we march with slow steps. No one is listening to the shouting of the drunken guards, who scold and shout that we should go faster. We no longer hear anyone. Not even when one gets a butt in the side does he feel the pain.

[Page 249]

There is no more spit in our mouths. Our lips and palates are dried up, and our tongues are swollen from the cold. "Oh, a piece of bread! How happy a man is, who has a piece of bread to eat!"…

One of us has fainted; he cannot go on. His eyes are half-open, his head tilted back. Everyone stops. The guard is giving the fainter a kick with his boot: "Get up, damned pig-Jew!" But the fainter no longer hears the wild shouting. Four men take him on their shoulders, and we are marching on. In the evening at half past nine, we arrived next to the gate of the camp. The others, who came earlier, are standing in the street, in rows of ten, at roll call. The whole camp is waiting for us. The camp leader is gnashing his teeth like a wild wolf, shouting and scolding with the dirtiest words. We lay the half-dead on the ground, and all are lining up for roll call.

"Stand still! Caps down!"

We stand transfixed. Recounted. The camp is in order. Now, everyone is lining up for his portion of bread.

Tired, we return to the large, cold hall where there are no stove and no beds. Only wet, black earth, and for covering only one blanket for five people. Through the holes, the snow is falling in. In a corner, there are already several dead bodies, over which white chlorine has been poured. The one of our squad who fell over, is also already lying among the dead. The murderous "Tarzan" had smashed his lungs with the tip of his boot, shouting: "Lazy dog, you're only pretending that you can't get up!"

Comparing this camp with the previous ones, we were very disillusioned. In Auschwitz, each of us thought that things could not get any worse. It was the same at Stutthof. But now, when we came here between fields, into this big hangar, where 600 people were herded to build highways, but were not given any water and no beds to sleep in, with just 200 grams of bread to eat with a little cold watery beet soup… this is really unbearable now. On the very first day, there are already so many dead and half-dead people lying there!

[Page 250]

We worked this way for two weeks, and out of the 600, 400 of us remained. Thus, the camp leader Tarzan somewhat improved our situation. He brought beds and straw, and a blanket for each. The food also improved. But it was already too late; the majority of the camp was dead sick. Every day, the mortality increased. After six weeks, 300 tortured, debilitated prisoners remained.

Both the cold and the snowfalls contributed to the destruction of the camp. After two months, we were no more than 150 people fit for work. Every day, the American and British planes flew and strafed the camp. During a night shelling, when we were not allowed to go out on the street, 60 people fell. The pilots did not know that this was a camp with Jews inside. For them, it was a military point that they used to bombard daily.

When there were no more than a hundred of us left being able to work, ten people were selected, among whom was myself. We were to work in the "bomb crew", digging bombs. The work consisted of driving over the towns and villages and digging out the bombs that had not exploded. We were very content with this work. First, we were given more to eat and second, we were able to "organize" something on our own. The work was very dangerous. Every second, we risked death. Just a small movement with the shovel in the bomb, and it would explode, if it still had a detonator. The Germans usually did not approach the places where we were working. Therefore, we used to work as we liked.

[Page 251]

My work involved unscrewing the igniters. My hand wasn't even shaking, because I had nothing left to lose.

Then the camp in Tailfingen was disbanded. The healthier persons were transferred to another camp, that is, a small labor camp: Steinberg [Schömberg]-Dautmergen.

Steinberg–Dautmergen

Between two dense forests, not far from the large city of Balingen, there is a small town, called Steinberg [Schömberg][60]. Two kilometers through the forest, you would come to the small village Dautmergen. There, in the forest, a camp with 7 barracks and a kitchen had been erected. The majority of its inhabitants were Poles. The camp elder, *Manek*, was also a Pole; he was a sadist and murderer. Every day, he would murder two or three Jews with his own hands. Most of the Jews in the camp were from Lithuania. On January 18, our "bomb squad" was transferred to this camp. As soon as we arrived, we read in the pale, emaciated faces of the Jews what miserable conditions they had to endure.

The work in the camp consisted of building large "oil factories"[61]. The oil was extracted from the rocks of the mountains by means of large pipes. This was hard forced labor. Even the strongest prisoners did not last more than 3 weeks. Very often new transports arrived with people of many nationalities from other camps, including Russians and French. There was no crematorium. The dead were buried not far from the camp on a hill where large pits had already been dug. The dead were taken away on a cart; this work was done by certain people of the so-called "corpse crew".

Once a week, the sick were taken away to unknown places. From the work sites, every day dead and half-dead were brought in.

[Page 252]

I had only one plan: Escaping from the camp. But there was no day for implementing it, because the guard was very vigilant; and if a fugitive was caught, he was tortured to death.

I did not work at the rock [quarry], but in the squad "Lilienfein". Our work consisted of camouflaging the factories as protection against air raids. It was not hard work; we had to weave straw and green leaves. I worked together with my friend, Mr.[62] Zlotogurski, who encouraged us to hold out until liberation. Zlotogurski, a French Jew, was talking every day with French prisoners who were informed about the latest news from the front. Now we knew that the days of our camp life were numbered, "one way or another"… Each time we saw the flocks of planes covering the sky, it was pure joy for us. We also knew that the Allied armies had already marched across the Rhine and were advancing at a rapid pace on German ground. All this gave us courage and strength to fight for our survival. Each day we left behind, brought us one day closer to liberation.

We were all too aware that the tiger could still devour us at the last moment. But after all, we knew one thing for sure now: our killers were already lost, and their days were numbered!

On April 12, twenty-two people were led into the camp in shackles. They all wore full hair and were in civilian clothes. After a few hours, we learned what kind of people they were:

Eleven French partisans, eight Russians and three Poles[63]. After being held in the camp for wo days, they were sentenced to death by shooting. The verdict was carried out just as American planes were flying overhead. It happened after work, at 7 o'clock in the evening. A truck was lighting up the camp street. The whole camp had to stand on the side and watch everything.

[Page 253]

Eleven SS-men with rifles on their shoulders were standing in the middle of the street. Soon we saw two rows, each with eleven men tied together, being brought in. The condemned walked with their heads bowed, wearing only their shirts and no shoes. In the middle of the street they stopped. Two murderous officers looked at their victims. There is a dead silence. In the air, the sound of airplanes is arising. Suddenly, the surrounding silence is shattered with the Russian exclamation of one of the condemned:

"Comrades, we die for freedom! Death to the murderers! You shall take revenge!"

Soon an order is given, "Prepare the gun!"

The eleven SS-men are taking position behind the backs of the bound men.

Another command: "Gun to the neck! One, two, fire!"

Shots rang out from 11 guns, intermixed with a final scream: "We die for freedom! Revenge, revenge!"

The other eleven stood to the side, watching their comrades lying in a pool of blood.

Another command: "Gun to the neck! Fire!"

And so the others are lying on the ground, in a pool of blood. The murderers, rubbing their hands, are satisfied with their "victory".

But shortly after, everything is disrupted by a loud noise from a squadron of airplanes.

"Lie down, lie down!" the "heroes" who just a minute ago have shot 22 young people are yelling. The surroundings are lighting up from a rocket. Each of us is praying silently: "God, may you send down some bombs, mixing up the earth with us and with the murderers!"

The planes turned around three more times, before they flew away, leaving a white spot in the sky. The 22 shot were immediately handed over to the "corpse command"[64]. The earth was soaked with the blood of young lives who had fought for freedom.

[Page 254]

On April 15, an order was given to send away all sick and weak prisoners. No one went to work that day. The camp numbered 12,000 people, from which 9,000 sick and weak were selected. The reason for the selection was that people could just in time be taken by train from the camp to Dachau. The others would have to walk, and those who could not keep up on the way would be shot immediately. Promptly, I decided not to take the train, come what may! I wanted to walk, and maybe would be able to escape on the way.

The next morning, April 16, the people on the list were led to the transport. The camp became empty. We went to work, being aware now, that the days until the decision were numbered. Moreover, we were informed about the American President Roosevelt's death. Every hour that passed now, brought us closer to the decision. Together with some comrades, among them *Abraham Fenigstein* and *Izak Vaserzug*[65], I decided to escape at the slightest opportunity during the march out into the forest and wait there for our liberation. There is nothing to lose now. Anyway, the murderers would not let us fall alive into the hands of our liberators. But meanwhile, we are working as before. Many squads have disbanded due to lack of workers. Already, work was being carried out "with heads bowed ": The civilian engineers waved their hands in resignation, since after all, everything was lost. On April 17 we heard the first echo of cannon shots.

The Liberation

The Schömberg-Dautmergen camp was considered one of the worst camps in southern Germany. On a hill, in a mass grave, were lying 15,000 dead. The SS had another special camp, which adjoined our camp. Most of the SS had left with the sick; only about a hundred SS-men remained.

[Page 255]

Every day, we could expect an order to leave the camp.

The cannon fire was getting closer every day. But we did not know exactly where the front was. Every day, two or three planes flew over our heads, but even during their descent over the barracks, they would not fire a shot, but moved away.

The SS walked around with their heads down. We used to stand for hours at the roll call, without a block leader coming to count us. If he finally did come, he used to count only quickly, just to disappear again. Together with my comrades, I worked out a plan to escape. We absolutely needed civilian clothes for this purpose. All of us wore striped camp clothes after all. During work we were no longer beaten and driven to work faster. Each individual from the SS was only concerned about himself. The civilian masters comforted us with the words that we would not stay in the camp much longer and would soon be liberated. The Allied armies would make good progress and capture new cities every day. We, however, knew all too well that the murderers would never allow us to experience the moment of liberation. We had to take freedom with our own hands.

On April 18, just like every day during our camp life, we got up at 4 am. The roll call lasted until 6. Then we formed up to go to work.

It is a beautiful spring day. The sun is warming our limbs. We are marching out of the camp, everyone to his work. Arriving at the work site, each takes his tools, one a shovel, the other a hammer. Like the other last days, we are working comfortably. The civilian master is walking around as if he were drunk, he is unrested and has a scowl on his face.

At 10 o'clock the camp leader appears on his motorcycle.

[Page 256]

He calls the Kapo and the civilian master to him, and soon an order is given:

"Fall in, five in a line!"

We don't know what suddenly has happened. The camp commander, a tall, middle-aged man with a long face and two gray, murderously piercing eyes, is now looking like a front-line soldier. His eyes are red and sleepy, his clothes are splattered with mud.

"Quick, quick, you filthy rags", he yells, giving one of us a shove with his boot. Standing in line, we are counted. Then the command: "March!"

We march to the camp, the camp leader driving in front. The sides are obstructed by SS guards. We arrive at the camp, which is full of people; everyone is on the street. Coming in, the camp leader commands us, to prepare for the set off. We will leave the camp soon. Everyone is carrying a sack. Shoes are prepared so that they do not rub. Soon, we see two trucks with clothes: New sweaters, new boots from the SS, with nailed soles. The camp elder announces: Whoever wants to, should take a pair of new boots and new underwear. Everyone is running there quickly, it's a stampede, everyone snatches the things out of each other's hands. Soon the order comes to empty the food stores. Indeed, this is already done in an orderly manner. Each is receiving a liter of jam and a kilo of lard, plus a loaf of bread. All of us have filled our sacks now. One takes a blanket, the other two at once. The majority is walking in new SS boots, but I – still in my old, torn leather shoes. I know all too well how obstructive new, heavy boots can be…

Suddenly, we hear the siren whistle: air raid warning!

Everyone is running. The SS-men are yelling, "Lie down, lie down!"

Above our heads, two French planes appear, flying low over the barracks. Everyone lies there with their heads sunk into the ground.

The SS-men quickly run into the air bunker, but the two pilots have noticed them immediately, and one has already dived down. A shooting and a crashing blow can be heard: A bomb has hit the SS camp. Our camp remains untouched. Later we have seen dead and wounded SS-men being carried away; a total of nine dead and four wounded SS people.

[Page 257]

Shortly after, an order, "Line up five!" We are counted. The SS stands ready, loaded with heavy backpacks. Equipped with hand grenades from head to toe. Several times we are counted through, again and again to groups of a hundred men. For every 10 people, two SS-men stand at the side.

Quickly the camp gate is opened: "In step, march!" the camp leader shouts. We march out through the gate. Behind us, the SS camp is smoking. The dead SS-men are left unburied. Each of us is satisfied with the incident. The camp remains empty. Two dead Russians lie in the middle of the street. The camp leader shot them in revenge for laughing when the planes bombed the SS camp.

The two planes have not flown far; they are turning around opposite the second wood, where the tall chimney from the cement factory is standing. We hear two loud impacts: The chimney has collapsed! A black smoke rises up to the sky. The SS-men are shouting: "Lie down, lie down!" We're lying on either side of the road with our heads sunk in the grass.

The planes are making their laps right above our heads. The SS-men are pale, lying there with trembling hands and feet. The planes are descending to us a couple times, just to rise again, as if they were playing with us. We are not far from the camp. The planes return to our camp; now we hear another loud crash, and clouds of black smoke are covering the barracks. The whole camp is on fire. Just 5 minutes ago, we were still staying in the camp. Now, It's on fire!

The planes are moving away in a different direction. We step back in line. The SS-men are screaming and beating us. We march quickly, at a running pace. The camp commander is driving ahead of us. We have to follow him on foot.

Night has fallen. The SS are getting tired from carrying their heavy backpacks; they hand them over to us. With bowed heads, we are marching through the night darkness. Behind us, shots can be heard from time to time. These are shots of the SS on those who step out of line.

[Page 258]

It is now impossible to escape. We decide to wait for an opportune moment.

Thus we march until daylight; no one knows in which direction. All of us are already tired, most of us have chafed feet, for which the new boots are to blame. The morning cold is getting into everyone's bones.

Most of us suffer from diarrhea, which is caused by the jam and lard. Our situation is getting worse with every passing moment. The strong become weak, the weak can't go any further. The roads and highways are taken by running German soldiers, some with and some without rifles. Most of them are black as the earth. With every minute, the confusion is growing. We don't know where the front is and if there is one at all. The minutes of the decision are approaching. All our lives hang in the air, balancing on a scale. Now, we can't think about escaping any more: The side roads and forests are occupied by soldiers. We learn that we are running towards Munich.

And again, as in the night, the same two planes appear, flying over us, high in the sky.

There comes an order, "Lie down, hide!"

We fall into the deep grass, and each of us prays to God that the planes may not fly away. May they be the protectors of our lives! The longer we can lie and rest our swollen feet, the more chances we have to experience the incredible freedom we have been longing for so much! Still, it is only fantasy, an empty dream. The planes slow down their speed, as if they had heard and understood our prayer. They are descending to us, flying over everyone's heads. The SS-men are pale as lime. They have lowered their heads deep into the grass. The pilots can see us clearly because our striped camp clothes are easy to recognize, and they know right away who we are.

[Page 259]

All our hearts are filled with joy and happiness, as we realize how the planes are protecting our lives, and how they are playing with our killers. As a result, each of us is getting more strength now to endure the last hours. These are French planes; we can clearly see the French flag and the white shining star.

We have been lying thus in one spot for two hours.

As soon as the planes have disappeared, another wild command is given: "March on!"

But after we have gone two kilometers, the planes reappear. We lie down again in the green, fragrant grass.

Thus the planes were playing with us until the sunset. The night has fallen. We are marching in the darkness, not knowing where to go.

Suddenly a motorcycle approaches us, with an SS officer on it. He reports that we are not allowed to march any further because the road is cut off by the French. The French are not far from us!

The murderous camp leader is studying the map to find a way out of our fix. Soon, his order comes that we should march in a different direction. The SS-men are getting even wilder than before. We are marching past small villages and towns. Everything is shrouded in darkness. A rain shower falls, soaking us to the shirt.

An order is given that we should go into a barn. No one understands the reason for the sudden kindness of our murderers. We lie down in the dark barn, one next to the other; most of us fall asleep right away.

After two hours of lying there, we get another order to march on. The rain is getting heavier. The SS-men are standing at the exit of the barn, herding us with sticks like sheep. Everyone is shivering from the cold. We notice that the SS-men are even more evil than before.

We are marching thus into the next day, when again our protectors, the two planes, are appearing!

[Page 260]

The day turned out even better than yesterday. The pilots understood that we were more tired than yesterday, realizing our emptier rows.

Today is Sabbath, April 21. During the night, we haven't been able to go any further, because we were told for the second time that the road was cut off.

Sunday, April 22, very early in the morning, our protectors have been appearing. The paths were full of running soldiers, some with shoes on their shoulders, some without shoes.

At 12 noon, we notice barricades on the street. Our mood is getting happier with each of us knowing that now the decision is very close.

The running soldiers are throwing bread to us. Everyone has become a good person now, only the SS are not getting better – but just the opposite – even more beastly than yesterday. They know only too well what is waiting for them. But we can't do anything yet, because each of us is sick and tired.

At five o'clock in the evening, the camp leader gives the order to leave the highway and lie down in the grass, which we quickly carry out.

The transport leader is informing us that he, together with an SS group, is going to a village to get bread and potatoes for us. A group of 30 SS-men have left for the village. The others are standing around us.

Suddenly we notice all the SS-men removing their "skulls" from their uniforms. Around us, it is getting more deserted every minute. The SS-men are moving apart and mingling with the running soldiers.

After half an hour, we no longer see any trace of SS around us. We are no longer guarded! We look at each other, our eyes shining with joy. Cries of joy in all languages are to be heard: "Guys, we are free! We are free!"

Pure joy is written in our half-dead faces! We fall into each other's arms; most of us are crying with joy, others are lying in the grass, unable to move from the spot. "Free! Free! We are free!"

We are lying there until night falls. Nearby, we hear the shot of a tank. An officer of the Wehrmacht approaches, telling us that we should go to the surrounding villages, but not to steal anything or touch any civilians.

[Page 261]

We are making our way to the villages. The shootings are getting closer every minute. Together with two comrades, I am already in a small town, Altshausen. We are lying in a cellar; the town is on fire.

So we have been lying there until the early morning. Then we decided to go out on the road.

The streets are immersed in flames from the burning houses. On the streets, we recognize people from our camp. Everyone is happy. Soon, we learn that the town is in French hands. We walk to the center of the town, where a French tank and three black tank leaders are standing. We fall around the necks of our liberators. Everyone cries with joy.

Our liberators are sharing cigarettes and chocolate with us. After several minutes, more tanks are appearing. Our liberators' faces are beaming with joy at the successful victory.

They fall around our necks screaming: "Friends, you are free!"

It is difficult to describe the extent of joy which is now embracing us. The French soldiers are providing us medical assistance. The sick and weak people are taken to a hospital. I feel very weak, weighing only 40 kilos. My feet are swollen. We move into German apartments and receive support by the army.

After seven days of bed rest, I get up, feeling healthy. I am already able to walk with firmer steps. One aspect has given us all strength: The feeling to be free men!

We have not yet been able to get used to the idea that Nazi socialism was defeated. And that we, actually, have experienced the incredible **freedom**!

Nekome

> *This chapter, written while still under the impression of the unspeakable horrors and trauma to which the author was subjected, is entitled Nekome.*
>
> *Nekome is a Yiddish term that has its roots in the Hebrew "Nakam"; it is commonly translated as "revenge" or "retribution". However, I am convinced that this translation is inadequate in its meaning and scope when it comes to defining such a multi-faceted term.*

However, out of respect for the complexity of the term and since I am aware that the term "Nekome" underwent a shift in meaning in isolated instances in later years, I will refrain from translating it at this point.

(Beate Schützmann-Krebs)

We have one desire now! Nekome!

[Page 262]

Nekome for us and our fathers and mothers; for our brothers and sisters who died with the word "nekome" on their lips! After resting for eight days, we, a group of Jews and Christians, reported to the French officer, who was the commander of the little town, and asked to be allowed to voluntarily join the French police to catch our murderers. The officer immediately agreed. A police force of 30 men was created. Everyone was given weapons, either a rifle or a revolver. The first task was to clear the surrounding forests of Nazis. Every day, captured soldiers were brought. We had the job of handing over all the soldiers to the French. My comrades and I decided to shoot each captive when we had the chance. After a few days, a military Rabbi came, taking care of us. "Take nekome for our brothers and sisters," he said.

The first ones we managed to catch were two SS murderers from the Auschwitz camp. It was at night. We were already marching from the forest into the town, when we suddenly came upon two SS-men lying there, sleeping comfortably. We decided to shoot them without waking them up first. No sooner said than done. A press of the trigger, bang, and they were both already lying in a pool of blood.

We walked on leisurely. That was our first act of nekome. Every day we became bolder and braver. The civilian population lived in mortal fear. The streets and yards were empty both during the day and at night. Every smallest demand on our part was immediately met.

After a few days I recognized the camp leader of Dautmergen on the street, who was walking in civilian clothes. We decided not to shoot him, because this death would have been too easy.

We stripped him naked in front of everyone and locked him in jail. All night long he was beaten by people taking turns.

[Page 263]

Everyone learned to box… At eight o'clock in the morning he breathed his last.

After two weeks, I together with two comrades were sent to a village to take over the rule there.

As soon as we got there, we took the most beautiful house in the village. We were given two motorcycles for our "cleaning work" that we were to do in the surrounding villages.

The first thing we did was to arrest all the former soldiers who had put on civilian clothes. They were usually sent to work in France. There was one incident during the night. The three of us were bringing five soldiers to the little town. They were tied together, walking on foot. We were driving. When we reached the forest, all five fled in the darkness among the dense branches. We quickly drew our weapons and shot all the bullets into the darkness. Near us we heard a whimpering croak and went there. All five were lying there, entangled with each other. Three were dead and two seriously wounded. We decided to bring the wounded to the town (village) and report the case to the military command. Before we had brought the two to the town, one of them had already died on the way. We reported it, and the next morning all five were buried in the forest.

We received an order from the commandant to drive over the surrounding roads to find all the comrades who had been shot. In accordance with our order, those who could be taken to the Jewish cemetery for burial had to be taken by the peasants to the small town. The others, who could not be moved from the spot, we buried in their place.

After three months of free, tumultuous life, saturated with the feeling of nekome, all three of us were called to the Justice Ministry. There we were proposed to take over the work as secret police officers and to search for all Nazis known to us. With the greatest pleasure we immediately accepted the proposal.

[Page 264]

As a soldier in the French police

[Page 265]

The lieutenant who spoke to us had himself been a prisoner in Buchenwald for five years, and so it was him who gave us deep-felt[66] words that we will never forget: Remember the last words of our brothers and sisters!

We actively set to work. Every police authority had to come to our aid. Each of us had a motorcycle and received a salary. We drove from village to village, arresting every suspicious young person we thought was an SS-man.

Our work was met with success. We found many SS-men in disguise, against whom we filed charges. We also learned from an SS-man that they wanted to blow us up at that time when we went into the barn. There had been a vote, but thanks to five votes against, it was decided not to kill us. The camp leader, however, had at that time very well demanded to blow us up together with the barn.

Also, we grabbed the officer who had given the order to shoot the 22 partisans. This happened on the train. We recognized him and arrested him right away. He was given the death penalty by the military court.

The work was refreshing to us. Never too hard, although we were on our feet day and night.

Once I went to Stuttgart, in the American occupation zone. As soon as I left the train, I recognized a former "Unterscharführer" of the SS in civilian clothes. He was one of the most terrible sadists; a Volga German who lived in the Soviet Union.

I decided to arrest him immediately and turn him over to the hands of the U.S.CAC[67]. I stopped a military vehicle and we went straight to the headquarters. The murderer was immediately detained in the bunker. I went in to the officer, a Jew, and reported to him that I had brought a murderer who had tormented dozens of Jews.

[Page 266]

The officer instructed me to bring in people who could testify to this.

I immediately left for the camp, taking six comrades with me who had been in the Dautmergen camp, knowing the murderer well. At 11 a.m., questioning about the crime began. The officer forbade us to hit the defendant unless he ordered us to…

The murderer was led in. As soon as he saw us, he turned as pale as lime. His hands and feet were trembling.

The officer asked him if he knew what "knee bends" meant.

"Yes, I know", was the answer.

"Well, get started!"

The killer began to do knee bends, but not in the way he had instructed us to do. We showed him how it had to be done...

The officer read him the charges we had brought against him. The murderer denied. He knew nothing about anything, it was all lies. He had never been in the SS and had only been a captured Russian soldier in a prison camp...

Listening to his speech, we were shocked at how confidently he made this statement. As if it were not him who was being talked about.

The hearing dragged on until 12 noon. Several times the officer put his revolver to his temple, but the defendant always answered the same, that he knew nothing.

Each of us gave him a few blows, but that didn't help either.

> "Well, if you don't sign the indictment now, I will give you into the hands of the Jewish camp, and they will do whatever they want to you," the officer shouted at him.

I then added that if we had him in our hands, we would cut out his tongue and pour salt on the wound.

[Page 267]

With tears in his eyes, he stood up and signed the indictment with a trembling hand.

After a few days, together with the indictment, he was handed over to the Russian NKVD [68].

After a few days, we caught another Russian murderer who had served the German power. We ourselves paid him his wages for his murderous deeds.

The call to nekome on the murderers of our eternally persecuted people grew day by day. Deep inside, I was feeling thirst for the blood of the Nazi beasts. With each SS-man killed, I felt a relief on my deeply laden mind.

Oh, if only our six million holy people could see what has become of the "supermen"! How fearfully they turn their eyes on us, begging us, the former prisoners, for mercy for their lives as beasts![69]

But the cruelty of camp life has erased feelings of indulgence from our Jewish hearts.

"Death to the enemy" — this had become the ray of happiness capable of illuminating my lonely life on the blood-soaked German earth.

Fortunately, I later met my friend and life partner, Rochele Zakheim. After many difficulties, we made our way to Uruguay, where we hope to live a normal, free and humane life.

[Page 268]

The exhumation of our 32 holy people in the yard of "Shmerl the Kotlier", carried out by Shmuel Wolf, accompanied by the new commandant in Krynki

[Page 269]

At the Jewish cemetery, before the burial of our holy people from
Krynki

Translator's footnotes:

1.   You can read some more about the system of "Funktionshäftlinge" (functionary prisoners) here: https://en.wikipedia.org/wiki/Kapo
2.   natshalstve = ruling authority. It is meant ironically, because these are functionary prisoners who want to ingratiate themselves with the SS.
3.   parshe (Parasha) = a section of the Pentateuch (the five books of Moses)
4.   breyshes (Bereshit) = "In the beginning", Genesis, the first book of Moses
5.   hier: (German) = "here"
6.   shtubaves: I think these are those juvenile thugs mentioned above. Perhaps this word can be derived from the Russian "shtubov" (= stubs). But I think that it has more to do with the Yiddish "shtub" (house, room), that is, it affects the "staff" who stayed in the barracks.

7. "buks" = "box", the author's nickname for the "bed place", a kind of bunk, plural: "buksn" Return To learn more about the "System of identification in German Camps", see:https://en.wikipedia.org/wiki/Identification_of_inmates_in_German_concentration_camps#/media/File:Wikpedia_system_of_identification_German_camps.png

8. Kapo = Designation for a functionary prisoner who acted as an "employee" of the camp management. For more information, see for example https://en.wikipedia.org/wiki/Kapo

9. "Blockführer" = The "Blockführer" (block leaders) were every day present in the camp, held roll calls and assigned the prisoners of their barracks (block) to "Arbeitskommandos" (work crews) or individual tasks. Read some more here: https://de.wikipedia.org/wiki/Schutzhaftlagerf%C3%BChrung

10. Yeke = German Jew

11. I am not completely sure with this translation.

12. It is more likely that the name was "Arek"; however, I read it as "Adek"

13. "aroysgenumen vern" = they were taken out to be killed

14. German "Blocksperre!" = Block lock!

15. "Galgen-Mengelyer" = "Gallows-Mengele", Josef Mengele, also called the "Angel of Death".

16. Josef Schillinger: A survivor of Auschwitz, Tadeusz Borowski, wrote about him (I translated the original German quote into English): "The blow of his hand was as powerful as a cudgel, he playfully smashed a jaw, and where he struck, blood flowed." His name was often mentioned in the same breath as those Auschwitz murderers, "who boasted of having personally killed tens of thousands of people with their fist, club, or gun." Schillinger was shot in the concentration camp by a Jewish inmate, Franziska Mann, who was incredibly brave. She had previously refused to strip naked because she knew that she and the other women would be gassed afterwards. (Source of quote and information: https://de.wikipedia.org/wiki/Josef_Schillinger)

17. "Canada" was the name given to the "Effektenlager" (effects warehouse), where valuables and personal effects of the admitted prisoners were stored. The looted goods symbolized abundance and wealth, (also) hence the name "Canada". At the latest when a prisoner died, his personal effects were transferred to the "German Reich" for further use. For the workers in the "Aufräumungskommando" (clean-up squad), there were not only better rations, but some of the prisoners also "organized" and smuggled secretly and under enormous risks things not yet registered, partly also under coercion by the Kapo. (source https://de.wikipedia.org/wiki/Kanada_(KZ_Auschwitz)

18. a phrase which, in my opinion, expresses the fact that the old prisoners in question were already well acquainted with the customs in the camp, and possibly also had certain connections.

19. I cannot exclude that the word "shap" in this context is a spelling mistake. In any case, the author was lying unconscious on the floor after the terrible abuse, possibly under the "bench".

20. The translation of this very shortened sentence is not entirely certain. But it arises from the somewhat later context on page 195, when "cold compresses are applied again".

21. The pronunciation of the name is clearly indicated as "Bana" by Yiddish vowel signs. However, I cannot exclude the possibility that "Buna" is meant: https://www.jewishvirtuallibrary.org/buna-subcamp

22. Unfortunately, I cannot interpret this extremely abbreviated sentence. Perhaps it is a bucket of water with a substance, where you could relieve yourself.

23. Margot Drechsler oder Dreschel, find more https://en.wikipedia.org/wiki/Margot_Dreschel

24. Otto Moll, see https://en.wikipedia.org/wiki/Otto_Moll

25. My translation of this very shortened sentence is not quite certain

26. translated a little freely

27. leben vi "Got in Ades"= living grandly, in the lap of luxury

28. From February 1943, Sinti and Roma arrived in Auschwitz and were housed there in camp section BII e. This was a large family camp in which the detainees initially had a special status.

29. Blocksperre: time when leaving barracks by prisoners was prohibited

30. This term originates from the "camp jargon" and refers to those completely debilitated and emaciated inmates of the concentration camps who had already lapsed into total apathy, or, in the course of

their death throes, into agony. They were doomed to certain death. Find more: https://en.wikipedia.org/wiki/Muselmann

31. the tattooed numbers on the arms

32. This sentence makes no sense to me. But maybe there is some reference to the biblical Samson, see: https://en.wikipedia.org/wiki/Samson

33. lit. "Bane" = see also page 191 ("Bana"), I think that he means "Buna" or "Monowitz-Buna", https://www.jewishvirtuallibrary.org/buna-subcamp

34. assume that it was the "barrel" where you could relieve yourself at night, so a kind of toilet bucket.

35. The camp prison was called "bunker" by the prisoners.

36. My understanding is that he was transferred to the punishment wing and was isolated within the camp.

37. He seems to have survived, see https://en.wikipedia.org/wiki/Wilhelm_Boger

38. Performing artist Franceska Mann (Franciszka Mannówna)

39. Schillinger uses the formal form to address the young woman, but she addresses him informally with "du"!

40. In the last sentences, there are again considerably faded words. In order to connect them meaningfully, I had to change them somewhat.

41. Effektenlager = A store like "Canada", where the valuables of the arrivals were collected, sorted and forwarded for reuse.

42. His name is spelled differently, sometimes as "Fedyor", sometimes as "Fedor".

43. He speaks German

44. "komande-firer" = the leader of the command, that is, of the work crew

45. I think it must be "nu, un vu iz er?" and translated it in this way

46. Chaim Rumkowski was the "Judenrat" in the Ghetto Lodz, see also page 231

47. Rumkowski is said to have announced that the Ghetto Lodz was merely being "transferred"; in reality, it was a matter of deportation to Auschwitz. As for his cremation, some sources report that it was the Sonderkommando staff who killed him at the gate of the crematorium, after the arriving Jews from Lodz had told them about the crimes he had committed against the Jews in his capacity as Judenrat. A photograph with Chaim Rumkowski and Hans Biebow in the Litzmannstadt (Lodz) Ghetto can be seen here: https://en.wikipedia.org/wiki/Chaim_Rumkowski

48. "Wood Camp Stutthof"

49. cleansed of Jews

50. Beit Midrash, house of study, explanation see pages 15-21

51. List of companies where forced labor took place during National Socialism, see https://ns-in-ka.de/wp-content/uploads/2017/06/Liste_Unternehmen.pdf

52. free interpretation of a very shortened sentence.

53. KZ-Gedenkstätte (memorial) Hailfingen-Tailfingen, see https://kz-gedenkstaette-hailfingen-tailfingen.de/ see also https://www.youtube.com/watch?v=hw-8 BSIuv mc

54. "The camp leader for the subcamp Hailfingen-Tailfingen was SS-Unterscharführer Eugen Witzig, who had been a member of the commandant's staff of the Natzweiler concentration camp since April 1944." (Quote of an information by Volker Mall)

55. "fartogik"= early morning; I think it must be "firtogik" (four-day)

56. The Nazi Organization Todt (OT), named after its leader Fritz Todt, was a paramilitary construction group for the realization of protection and armament projects. Its workers, often forced laborers or prisoners of war, were uniformed. See https://en.wikipedia.org/wiki/Organisation_Todt

57. Stone pit Reusten, see https://www.youtube.com/watch?v=2bXvHO9SaRk see also, https://www.kz-geden kstaette-hailfingen-tailfingen.de/2010-2020. php and find a film with the eyewitness Israel Arbeiter here https:// www.youtube.com/watch?v=cULivKHypCo&t=136s

58. lit.: "who hover in the air"

59. The Author uses different spellings for this city, which today's name is Schömberg, see https://de.wikipedia.org /wiki/KZ_Dautmergen

60. The Dautmergen concentration camp was one of a total of seven concentration camps that served the murderous Nazi project with the code name "Wüste" ("Desert"): Oil was to be extracted from oil shale for the armaments production of the National Socialist regime, more information here https://www.alemannia-judaica.de/schoemberg_kz_friedhof.htm or http://www.eckerwald.de/dok/Flyer-EN.pdf

61. possibly letters are missing, maybe Her(sh) Zlotogurski

62. As we learn on page 265, they were also partisans.

63. List of those prisoners killed in the Dautmergen and Schömberg concentration camps 1944/45 see http://www.eckerwald.de/dok/liste-1.pdf

64. Both friends survived and emigrated to the USA (information by Volker Mall)

65. lit.: "two words"

66. U.S. CAC = United States Army Combined Arms Center https://en.wikipedia.org/wiki/United_States_Army_Combined_Arms_Center

67. NKVD = The People's Commissariat for Internal Affairs, the interior ministry of the Soviet Union, https://en.wikipedia.org/wiki/NKVD

68. lit. "wolves"

YIZKOR – MEMORIAL NOTICES

[Page 270]

YIZKOR

The "Krinker Verein" in Los Angeles, California, with their respected President Heiman Miller join in the mourning over the extermination of the heroic Jewish people of Krynki which always gave an exemplary of pugnaciousness.

We will honor their memory!

[Page 271]

YIZKOR

The "Krinker Ladies Auxiliary" of Chicago join in the mourning over the extermination of our dear and cherished brothers and sisters who were killed by the barbaric Nazis.

Let us honor their memory!

[Page 272]

> In memory of all our perished and murdered from the Krinker Ghetto.
> We will keep their lightful memory forever.
>
> **"Committee of the Krinker Aid Society in Uruguay"**
> **and its "Women's Committee" (Ladies Auxiliary)**
> Montevideo

[Page 273]

YIZKOR

For eternity the image will be embedded in my heart when my family was snatched away from me for their last walk to Kiełbasin, on November 2, 1942.

Blood flowed from my eyes when the bloodthirsty Nazi murderers took away my father, **Yisroel-Moyshe** (Israel-Moshe), my mother, **Brokhe**(Brocha), my grandmother, **Dvoyre** (Deborah) Pruzhanski, my grandfather Khayim (Chaim)-Osher Pruzhanski, my sisters, **Dorele, Lizele** and **Sonyele**.

My brother **Perets** (Peretz) died as a partisan in the forest like a hero. For your innocent cut off life I have taken nekome in my capacity as a postwar soldier.

We will honor your memory!

The author A. Soyfer (Soifer) and his brother Osher Soifer

[Page 274]

Our beloved, for us immortal parents
Berl and Blumke Zakheym (Zakheim) z"l,

Tormented to death by Nazi fascism in Auschwitz,
on January 18, 1943, at 10 o'clock in the morning.

We, your children, will forever keep you in sacred memory.

Rivl, Heshl and Rokhl (Rachel)

[Page 275]

YIZKOR

Deep is our sorrow and incurable our grief over the tragic death
of our unforgotten mother, mother-in-law and grandma
Hindl Kirzhner, peace be upon her, our brother,
Itshke Kirzhner and sister-in-law
Merkeleye (Merke-Leah) Kirzhner, and their dear children:
Yosele, Khaym'l (Chaim'l) and **Khanele (Chanele) Kirzhner**

Because the barbaric Nazi beasts in the world left no grave for you, these few
sentences shall tell our children and our neighbors that you were killed by the
Nazi beasts in Treblinka (next to Bialystok, Poland) just because you were
Jews!

Your memory is sacred for us!

Sheynke (Sheinke) Kirzhner de Liberman (Montevideo)
Yakev (Jacob) Kirzhner and family (New York)
Moyshe (Moshe) Kirzhner and family (Chicago)

[Page 276]

With painful hearts we remember
the death of our brother and his family,
Shmaye (Shemayahu) Grodzitski
(from the Gabarska Street)

of our uncle and aunt and their families,
Khaym-Mordekhay (Chaim-Mordechai) Lavler
(the carpenter from the Gabarska Street),
Killed by the Nazi beasts,
They died as martyrs, for the glory of G'd - because they were Jews ה״יק

Rokhl-Reyzl Veyner (Rachel-Reisl Weiner) and family
Fayvl (Feivl) Grodzitski and family
Avreml (Abraham) Grodzenski and family
Feygl (Feigl, Feiga) Grodzenski and family

[Page 277]

YIZKOR

With deep pain we memorialize our holy people, peace be upon them:
To our immortal father, **Khayim (Chaim) Lozovski (Lozowski),**
Our brother, **Leybe Lozovski and family,**
and our brother, **Yankl Lozovski.**

We, the surviving brothers:
Eliyahu Lozovski (Lozowski) and family
David Lozovski and family
Shimen Lozovski and family (**Tshako**) (Czakó)
Sheyne Sikorski and family (**Tshako**) (Czakó)
Shepsl Lozovski and family (**Salto**

[Page 278]

YIZKOR
With eternal grief we remember
our holy people who were killed in Treblinka:

Our unforgettable father, who was shot in the ghetto, the day before
Passover, 1942, **Mair Blokh (Bloch)** , brother **Yosl** and
family, **Berl** and family, **Tsipe** and family

The survivors:
Dvoyre (Deborah), Leybe (Leibe) and Meri (Mary) Bloch

With bowed heads, with sorrow and pain in our hearts,
we perpetuate in holiness the names of

Our dear parents,
Our sister **Sheve (Basheva)** and her family,
Our brother **Shepsl** with his family,
Who were killed in a gruesome way by our bloody enemy, Nazism!

Khane (Chane) Kushnier Levin
Artshik Kushnier
Kayle Kushnier-Garfeyn (Garfein)

[Page 279]

In sorrow we remember the passing of the families

Zak and Nayman (Neiman, Neuman), peace be upon them

Sholem (Shalom) Zak and family
Shprintse Zak-Shneyder and family

In mourning for the passing of our sister
Shifra and brother-in-law Shmulke Shinder, and their children
Shimen and **Lilye**,
killed by the Nazis.

Zelde Sokol de Zak,
Esther Sokol de Vitkind (Witkind),
Zalmen Sokol

[Page 280]

YIZKOR

In mourning for the passing of:

My mother **Yokhe (Yocheved?)**, peace be upon her, my sister **Tsivye** and brothers **Nokhem (Nachum)**, **Leybe, Hershl, Tsale (Betsaleyl?)** and sister-in-law and children,

Who were all killed by the Nazi murderers.

Abe Blacher and family,
Shloime Blacher and family,
Gitl Blacher and family,
Esther Blacher-Naliber and family

YIZKOR

May the few sentences be a reflection of our sorrow and pain
for the great loss that the Hitler gangs inflicted on us by murdering:

Our father **Motl Yelinovitsh (Yelinovich)**, mother **Frume**, sister **Krayne (Kreyna) Yelinovich-Kagan**, brother-in-law **Motye** and (their) only child **Yudele**

Sister **Liba Jelinovich-Lev**, brother-in-law **Gedalya** and their only child(ren) **Idele and brother Meni**, who had the opportunity to save himself, but did not want to abandon his parents.

May the innocent spilled blood of the whole family
fall upon the heads of their murderers.

Rachel Jelinovich-Blacher and family,
Leibl Jelinovich and family

[Page 281]

YIZKOR

We are mourning with deep sorrow for our lost parents,
sisters, brothers, brothers-in-law, sisters-in-law and nephews
who were were killed by the Nazi beasts in Treblinka.

In mourning:
Leibl Khashkes (Chashkes) and family,
Lyube (Liobe) Chashkes-Shvarts and family

YIZKOR

We commemorate the bright souls of our dear father, aunt,
sister, brother-in-law and sister-in-law, martyred in Kiełbas in!

Leitshe Kozoltshik (Kozolchik) and family
Mashke Chashkes and family
Esther Feldenbloym (Feldenbloim) and family
Yankl Levin and family, **Itke Gotfrid** and husband

[Page 282]

With deep sorrow in our hearts we remember our children,
murdered by the Nazis in Auschwitz on January 21, 1943, 10 am,
Shi(y)e Furye (Furie), his wife and children.

Our nephews:
Avreml (Abrahaml) Labendik, his wife and child, murdered in Treblinka.

The mourning survivors:
Itshe, Khaya-Sore (Chaya-Sara) Furye and children (NY),
Merke Furye-Vitkind (Witkind) and family (Montevideo)

We mourn the loss of our murdered brothers (and sisters)

Yisroel Manikhes (Israel Maniches) and family
Moyshe (Moshe) Maniches and family
Dvoyre (Deborah) Maniches and family
Zisl Maniches

Peace be upon them.
Yankl Maniches and family

We express our mourning for the loss
of our father at the hands of the Nazis,
Alter Kozaltshik (Kozolchik)
and our sister **Mikhle (Michla) Kozolchik-Starinski** and family
Yisroel (Israel) Kozolchik and family

Peace be upon them!
Frume Kozolchik-Maniches and family

Frume Kozaltshik (Kozolchik) commemorates her father **Alter,** her
sister **Michla** and her family, and her nephew **Israel Kozolchik** and his family

Frume Alter Miller
Kozolchik family

[Page 283]

In deep mourning we remember
our unforgettable family murdered by the Nazi beasts:

My mother **Khaye (Chaya)**, my sister **Yente Khane (Jenta-Chane)** and their families, my brother **Fayvl (Feivl, Fayvush)** and family, peace be upon them!

Glory be upon your holy names!

David Pruzhanski and family

YIZKOR

I mourn the tragic deaths
of my dearly beloved wife **Yente** and my daughter.

Let's honor their memory!

Yisroel Leybovitsh (Israel Leibovich)

May eternal shame be upon the Nazi murderers of my family:

My mother **Elke Furman**, my brothers **Moyshe (Moshe) and Shmuel**,
peace be upon them and the others of the family.

Leybl (Leibl) Furman and family

I am mourning the passing
of my beloved parents and family by Nazi bombs:

Yisroel (Israel), **Shlime**, **Nekhe Khane** (Necha Chana), **Rive** and their children.

Their memory is dear to us!

Heshi Kirzhner

I mourn the death of my beloved parents

Fayvl (Feivl) and Mikhle (Michla), peace be upon them!

They were killed by the Nazis; may these words serve as a tombstone!

Yudl Levin
Zhong

[Page 284]

We mourn the loss of our mother

Itke and our brother **Hishye Levin**, peace be upon them!

David Levin and family

We remember with the greatest reverence the holy people of our families,

Our father **Mikhl (Michal) Levin (Munyes)**,
Our brothers and sisters, brothers and sisters-in-law and nephews, perished by the Nazis

Sholem (Shalom) Levin and family

We mourn the loss of our nearest and dearest

Frume Yeride de Rabinovitsh (Rabinovich)

The Krinker Jews of "Treinta y Tres" join in mourning the perishing of their parents, brothers and sisters by the Nazi-murderers.

May these few sentences serve as a tombstone!

Nisl Kirzhner and family
Borekh (Baruch) Galinski and family
Yosl Galinski and family
Abraham Kirzhner and family
Yankl Stolarski and family
Sime Levin and family
Aharon-Hilel Shafir and family

[Page 285]

In memory of our dear parents

Zalmen and Feygl Losh, our sister **Khane** (Chana) and
Khame (Chama), peace may upon them!

They perished by the bestial Hitlerism

Your sons and brothers,
Sinay and Leybl

In memory of our dear parents

Osher and Dvoyre (Deborah) **Sholokhovitsh (Sholochovich)**
and our sister Esther, peace be upon them,
they perished at the hands of the bestial Hitlerism

Your children: **Bashe, Reyne and Pine**

I join the mourning of our Jews from Krynki and
commemorate the passing of our closest people

Eliyam Soifer and family
(Zhong)

I join the mourning of our Jews from Krynki and
commemorate the passing of our closest people

Fayvl Golts (Feivl Goltz) and family
(Treinta y Tres)

[Page 286]

The Dreyzik Family

The grandchildren of HaRav HaGaon R' Yosef Hatzadik, z"l, the author of the religious
book "אפיקי זהב" (the Golden Channel). — They perished in the gas chambers of
Auschwitz and Treblinka and were not granted a burial place in Israel. After their death, I
am left in loneliness, an eternal mourner. May their light-filled memory be hallowed
among all the holy people of Israel who were murdered by the accursed enemy ימ"ש (may
his name be deleted) of the Jews in the dark years of the Shoa. הי"א

Yishai Dreyzik   - Porto Alegre — Brazil

Mashke Dreyzik and her children **Roze** and **Khane
Dreyzik**, peace be upon them

[Page 287]

Roze Dreyzik Sapozhnik, her husband **Shmuel Sapozhnik** and their little boy **Mair,** peace be upon them!

First row from right to left:
Mariashke Dreyzik (Shayke Dreyzik's wife) and her son, **Roze Dreyzik** (now in a camp in Berlin).
Second row, same direction:
Chaya Glembotzki-Rabinovich (now in Petach Tikva), **Roze Dreyzik, Rishe Dreyzik** and **Lyobe Glembotzki.**
Third row, right to left:
Shloime Zalman Dreyzik, Chane Dreyzik and **Freidl Glembotzki**
At the window, same direction:
Freyde Dreyzik, Chane Dreyzik and **Sime Guzhanski**

[Page 288]

Mournfully, we remember our Krinker martyrs
who were killed by the Nazi murderers.

Let us honor their memory!

*

**The Administration of the "Krinker Aid and Compatriots Society
(Verein)" and its "Women's Committee" (Ladies Auxiliary) in Argentina**

[Page 289]

YIZKOR

In deep sorrow and pain we remember the tragic death of our families.

May these words serve as a headstone on the unknown grave!

**Yisroel (Israel), Hayke and Itsel Veyner (Weiner)
Eliyah Veyner (Weiner) and family**

[Page 290]

We mourn in grief for the perished Jews from Krynki

Khaim Sikorski and family
Meir and **Malkah Sikorski**
Manyeh Sikorski

We join in sorrow for the destruction of our families

Moyshe Lifshitz and family
Shmuel Shmulevich

[Page 291]

We mourn the loss of our loved ones

Breyne Mordkhelevitsh (Mordchelevich) and husband
New York

We join the mourning for the Krinker Jews

Fanni Sikorski and husband

It is with great sorrow that we mourn the cruel loss of our loved ones

Abraham Bloch and family

[page 292]

The Kirpitsh (Kirpich, Kirpitz) Family

In place of a gravestone I commemorate with these words:

My father **Zavl**, peace be upon him!
My sister **Mashke** and her husband,
Sister **Kele-Rachel**,
Mother **Khul (Chaya?)**
Brother **Moshe'l** and sister-in-law

Mere Kirpitsh and family
Buenos Aires

We mourn the loss of our closest people

Moyshe Khayim (Moshe Chaim) Gozhanski and family

[Page 293]

We mourn the passing of our loved ones and families

Motl Maniches and family

We mourn the passing of our loved ones and families

Mates Feinberg and family

We mourn the passing of our loved ones and families

Chaim Feinberg and family

We mourn the passing of our loved ones and families

Itzchak Brustin and family

We mourn the passing of our loved ones and families

Yosl Gel and family

We mourn the passing of our loved ones and families

Dashke Zacharias and family

[Page 294]

In deepest sorrow for the loss of our families

Brothers **Yosl** and **David Yudzik (Judzik)** and families

In deepest sorrow for the loss of our families

Mashke Weyner (Weiner) de Kleinbord

In deepest sorrow for the loss of our families

Moshe Garber and family

In eternal memory of my father
Chaim, Sister Babl and her husband **Hershl**

Velvl Ekshtein (Welvel Ekstein) and family

In deepest sorrow for the loss of our families

Freidl Furye and family

In deepest sorrow for the loss of our families

Rachel Navik and family

In deepest sorrow for the loss of our families

Shimen Sikorski and wife

[Page 295]

We mourn the loss of our hometown relatives and families

Kayle Stolarski and family

We mourn the loss of our hometown relatives and families

Shmulke Volfovitsh (Wolfovich) and family

We mourn the loss of our hometown relatives and families

Asne Kantarovitsh (Kantarovich) and family

In eternal memory of our Shneider family, who tragically perished
far too soon at the hands of the Nazi murderers

Golde and **Sonye Kushnier**
Emanuel and **Broche Terkl**

[Page 296]

Let us honor their memory! With deep sorrow and pain we will always remember the return of the Day of Death (Yortsayt), when our families and loved ones were cruelly killed by the Nazi barbarians!

Esther Levi and family
Memke Kugel
Pinye Grishtshinski and family
David and **Mindl Kuntzevitzki**
Faivl Oygustovski (Augustowski) and family
Itke Levi and family
Leibl Furye
Abraham Fridman and family
Mendl Lavler and wife
Maires Garber and wife
Leibl Losh
Meilech Fridman
Yankl Agunin (Agonin)
Brothers Feldman
Deborah Khosid (Chasid) and family
Berta Tsigl (Tzigel) and family
Chaie Rachel Lev and family
Peshe Gitl Kovalski and husband
Heshl Feinberg
Golde Farber and family
Babl Fridman and family
Israel and **Lifshe Filipski**
Zeidl and Chaie Lev
Chane Zelikovitsh (Zelikovich)
Mair Brustin
Reine Sholokhovitsh (Sholochovich) and family
Simche Gendler and family
Reitze Kaplan and family
Sheine-Chaie Kaplan and family
Rachel Harontshik (Haronchik) and family
Aizik Veyner (Weiner) and family

NAME INDEX

A

Abramovitch, 108, 110
Achon, 9
Adek, 122, 128, 186
Adinok, 13
Agonin, 210
Agunin, 210
Alyan, 32
Anisimovich, 11
Arbultshik, 98
Augustowski, 210
Avnet, 134
Ayon, 13, 32

B

Batyushke, 11
Beck, 34, 35
Blacher, 12, 97, 196
Blak, 98
Bloch, 194, 205
Blok, 98
Blokh, 194
Boger, 144, 150, 187
Borowski, 101, 186
Braverman, 110
Brevde, 18, 19, 94, 99
Brustin, 110, 207, 210
Burtsovski, 21

C

Chaikel, 13
Chashkes, 197
Chasid, 210
Cheikels, 7
Cheikl, 32, 38
Czarnietzki, 165

D

Dande, 11
Dimitrov, 107
Drekslerke, 136

Dreschel, 186
Dreyzik, 22, 202, 203

E

Efraimson, 108
Ekshtein, 13, 208
Ekstein, 208
Engenradt, 122
Epstein, 148
Ettlinger, 1

F

F(P)itshebutzki, 98
Farber, 210
Feinberg, 207, 210
Feldman, 210
Fenigstein, 174
Filippski, 99
Filipski, 103, 105, 109, 110, 111, 210
Fridman, 210
Funk, 110
Furie, 198
Furman, 199
Furye, 198, 208, 210

G

Galinski, 8, 25, 201
Garbatke, 146
Garber, 25, 96, 208, 210
Garfein, 194
Gaver, 106
Gel, 207
Gendler, 99, 105, 106, 210
Gertzke, 18
Glembotzki, 203
Glezer, 24, 99, 126
Goldshmid, 95
Goltz, 88, 95, 103, 105, 106, 202
Gotfrid, 197
Gottlieb, 10, 11
Gozhanski, 206

Grishtshinski, 210
Grishtzinski, 13
Grodzenski, 192
Grodzitski, 192
Grodzki, 13
Grosman, 95, 96, 103
Guzhanski, 203

H

Haronchik, 210
Harontchik, 151
Harontshik, 210
Hatzadik, 202
Hess, 132
Himmler, 127
Hoyroe, 98, 99

I

Itziks, 18

J

Jelinovich, 196
Judzik, 208

K

Kaduk, 121
Kagan, 106, 196
Kaiser, 166
Kalinovitch, 95, 108
Kaltenbrunner, 127
Kaminski, 152
Kananovich, 13
Kantarovich, 209
Kantarovitsh, 209
Kaplan, 95, 99, 104, 106, 108, 126, 210
Kazoltshik, 30
Khashkes, 197
Khazer, 30, 32, 35, 108
Khosid, 210
Kirpich, 206
Kirpitch, 108, 110
Kirpitsh, 206
Kirpitz, 206
Kirzhner, 18, 191, 199, 201
Kirzner, 101, 108, 126

Klas, 112, 126, 134
Klausen, 121
Kleinbard, 110
Kleinbord, 208
Kovalski, 210
Kozalczik, 94
Kozaltchik, 104
Kozaltshik, 30, 35, 90, 94, 95, 107, 108, 110, 198
Kozolchik, 94, 197, 198
Kramer, 149, 155, 158, 159, 160
Kravyetski, 98
Krebs, 1, 180
Kroyman, 40
Krupp, 166
Kugel, 11, 96, 210
Kuntzevitzki, 210
Kushn(y)er, 106, 109, 110
Kushner, 104
Kushnier, 194, 209

L

L(y)evin, 98
Labendik, 198
Lapate, 98
Lasher, 99
Lavler, 192, 210
Leibovich, 199
Leibovitch, 134, 151
Leibovitsh, 145
Lev, 196, 210
Levi, 12, 85, 95, 106, 107, 210
Levin, 194, 197, 200, 201
Levit, 80, 81, 83, 85, 86, 87, 90, 94
Leybovitsh, 199
Liberman, 191
Lievit, 40, 46
Lifshitz, 204
Linski, 25
Lipkes, 32
Listokin, 32
Losh, 201, 210
Lozovski, 193
Lozowski, 193
Lublinski, 13

M

Magid, 1
Mair-Cheikl, 38
Malski, 154
Manek, 172
Maniches, 108, 198, 207
Manikhes, 198
Mann, 186, 187
Margolies, 132
Margolyes, 132
Mastovl(y)anski, 95
Mastovlonski, 7
Mengele, 127, 136, 140, 145, 147, 186
Meyerovich, 11, 22
Miller, 188, 198
Mishkovski, 14
Moll, 136, 137, 142, 145, 152, 186
Molotov, 34, 35, 45
Mordchelevich, 205
Mordkhelevitsh, 205
Mostovlianski, 20
Mostovlyanski, 32
Muglos, 108
Müller, 166

N

Naliber, 110, 196
Natovitsh, 99
Navik, 208
Nayman, 195
Neiman, 195
Neuman, 195
Nievizuski, 25
Nogidman, 98

O

Odinok, 19
Oygustovski, 210

P

Pintl, 13
Pinyen, 135
Pretitzki, 37
Pruzhanski, 12, 106, 107, 189, 199
Pruzshanski, 25

R

Rabinovich, 200, 203
Rabinovitsh, 200
Rabkin, 99
Ribbentrop, 39
Roitbard, 43, 107
Roosevelt, 174
Rozen, 122
Rumkowski, 159, 160, 187

S

Sapozhnik, 203
Schillinger, 127, 133, 135, 137, 138, 150, 186, 187
Schorr, 147
Schützmann, 1, 180
Schwartz, 124, 132
Segal, 98
Serele, 129
Shafir, 13, 201
Shapir, 99
Shapiro, 126, 132, 137
Shimer, 9
Shinder, 102, 195
Shlime, 199
Shneider, 209
Shneyder, 195
Sholochovich, 201, 210
Sholokhovitsh, 201, 210
Shteiner, 96
Shteinsafir, 25, 32, 106
Shushanski, 25
Shvarts, 197
Sikorski, 193, 204, 205, 209
Skavranik, 108
Skovronski, 108
Skvoranik, 108
Śmigły-Rydz, 20, 34, 35
Sofer, 1
Soifer, 189, 202
Sokol, 195
Soyfer, 4, 87, 92, 189
Spodvil(y)er, 98
Stamdler, 38
Starinski, 198
Stolarski, 13, 201, 209

Suraski, 167

T

Tarlavski, 103
Tarlovski, 32
Temkin, 20
Tenor, 11, 25
Terkl, 209
Tevel, 85
Tichi, 148
Tsarnyetski, 165
Tzarevich, 11
Tzigel, 129, 132, 210

V

Vacht, 106
Vaserzug, 174
Veiner, 106
Veyner, 192, 204, 210
Virian, 26, 40, 41, 101
Viriant, 26
Vitkind, 195, 198
Volfovitsh, 209

W

Weiner, 10, 12, 192, 204, 208, 210

Witkind, 195, 198
Wolf, 10, 98, 106, 107, 184
Wolfovich, 209

Y

Yaglam, 147
Yakobinski, 110
Yelenovich, 41
Yelinovich, 196
Yelinovitsh, 196
Yudzik, 208

Z

Zacharias, 207
Zak, 8, 25, 101, 195
Zakheim, 13, 108, 138, 140, 183, 190
Zalkind, 32, 106
Zditkowski, 13
Zelikovitch, 118
Zelikovitsh, 122, 210
Zhuchowski, 101
Zlotogurski, 173, 188
Zuts, 12
Zutz, 106

www.ingramcontent.com/pod-product-compliance
Lightning Source LLC
Chambersburg PA
CBHW050411110426
42812CB00006BA/1865